ADAPTABLE CITIES AND TEMPORARY URBANISMS

ADAPTABLE CITIES AND TEMPORARY URBANISMS

LAUREN ANDRES

Columbia University Press   *New York*

Columbia University Press
Publishers Since 1893
New York   Chichester, West Sussex

Copyright © 2025 Lauren Andres
All rights reserved

Library of Congress Cataloging-in-Publication Data
Names: Andres, Lauren, author.
Title: Adaptable cities and temporary urbanisms / Lauren Andres.
Description: New York : Columbia University Press, [2025] |
Includes bibliographical references and index.
Identifiers: LCCN 2024031707 | ISBN 9780231208062 (hardback) |
ISBN 9780231208079 (trade paperback) |
ISBN 9780231557252 (ebook)
Subjects: LCSH: City planning. | Cities and towns. |
Building, Temporary.
Classification: LCC HT166 .A7229 2025 | DDC 307.1/216—
dc23/eng/20240913

Cover design: Noah Arlow
Cover image: Shutterstock

To everything,
To waiting and in-betweenness,
To creativity and experimentation,
To every step forward and liminal forces allowing the shaping
of better futures.

CONTENTS

Preface   ix

1 What Is the Adaptable and Temporary City?   1

2 The Flexible and Inflexible City   21

3 Adaptability, Activation, and Weak Planning   52

4 Everyday Adaptability, Coping, and Resilience   88

5 Adaptability and the "Cool" Artificial City   120

6 The Pandemic and Postpandemic Adaptable City   152

7 Knowledge, Skills, and the Delivery of the Adaptable City   200

8 The Future of Adaptable Cities and Temporary Urbanisms   223

Notes   *241*
Bibliography   *283*
Index   *305*

PREFACE

All books have a story and can be forged on anecdotes, encounters, and research enquiries. This book occupies a special place in my intellectual and academic journey because it brings together two decades of work conducted in various cities in Europe, North and South America, and Africa. Although my research investigations have evolved through the years, they all shared the commonalities of exploring processes of transformations and adaptations, with particular attention given to nonpermanence in urban making.

Several projects and funders need to be acknowledged here. First, the French Ministry of Research (Ministère de l'Enseignement Supérieur et de la Recherche) funded my doctoral research (2004–2007). Second is the Economic and Social Research Council (grant numbers: ES/P00198X/1 and ES/X000761/1), thanks to whom I led two projects: "The Appropriateness, Usefulness and Impact of the Current Urban Planning Curriculum in South African Higher Education" (2016–2019, aka SAPER) and the "Adaptations of Young People in Monetary-Poor Households for Surviving and Recovering from COVID-19 and Associated Lockdowns" (2022–2024, aka PANEX-YOUTH). Third, the British Academy awarded me funding for the project "Adaptable Cities, Pandemic

Mitigation and Crisis Preparedness" (2023–2024). Fourth, the Engineering and Physical Sciences Research Council (EPSRC)/ São Paulo Research Foundation (FAPESP) supported the project "Re-inhabiting the City: Bringing New Life to City Centres of Emerging Economies in a Changing Climate" (led by Lucelia Rodrigues and Joana Soares Gonçalves). And finally, thanks to the University of Birmingham and University College London (UCL) for several internal funding sources that allowed scoping projects to be conducted. During these projects, hundreds of individuals were interviewed and took part in the investigations. Thank you to all participants.

Such a journey would not have been possible without the insights, support, mentorship, and advice provided by colleagues and friends. I would first like to express my gratitude to Martin Vanier, Gilles Novarina, and Marcus Zepf, who helped kick-start my academic career back in France. Rachel Rodrigues Malta, your kindness and intellectual sharpness were exceptional. You left this world far too early. Many coauthors and research partners along the years should be mentioned here: John Bryson, your support along the years has been exceptional, and I am hugely grateful. Phil Jones, your backing, and always sharp advice have been invaluable. Mike Raco, your encouragement and support played a key role in leading this book to completion. Paul Moawad, Peter Kraftl, and Stuart Denoon-Stevens, our research collaborations have been inspirational and opened new and insightful enquiries. Rotem Shevchenko, I deeply miss you, and I wish you could read this book you so often enquired about. Thank you too to Hakeem Bakare, Leandro Giatti, Oleg Golubchikov, Boris Grésillon, Martin Lewis, Lochner Marais, Abraham Matamanda, Lorena Melgaço, Verna Nel, Francis Pope, Lucelia Rodrigues Francesco Rossini, John Round, Joana Soares Gonçalves and Elsona Van Huyssteen. My two employers in the

United Kingdom are to be acknowledged too for the way they fostered a nurturing research environment: the University of Birmingham (School of Geography, Earth, and Environmental Sciences) and UCL (Bartlett School of Planning). Thank you to Diane Bowden, too, for your sharp eyes and your flexibility. I would like to thank Jennifer Clark for her academic advice but also for recommending Columbia University Press. I am also grateful to the two anonymous reviewers for their very supportive and sharp comments. Finally, Eric Schwartz and Lowell Frye, it has been a pleasure working with you. The support and care you provided throughout the writing process was highly appreciated.

This book wouldn't have been possible without the patience and daily support of my family, who provided me with strength, inspiration, and resilience over the years. I dedicate this book to my grandfather, J. You were my rock and allowed me to be where I am today.

ADAPTABLE CITIES AND TEMPORARY URBANISMS

1

WHAT IS THE ADAPTABLE AND TEMPORARY CITY?

WHY ADAPTABILITY MATTERS

Cities have traditionally been defined, regarded, and planned as more or less permanent urban structures with rigid frameworks to allow the circulation of people, goods, and knowledge relatively efficiently and smoothly. Disciplines such as urban planning, urban design, architecture, and civil engineering have been established to allow the development, management, and transformation of urban spaces. All have aimed to deliver key objectives including, for example, local economic development; various types of land use; street and network layouts; the provision of public spaces and facilities; public health, well-being, and safety; environmental preservation; and responses to specific religious, cultural, military, or political needs.[1] Such strategic thinking and ways of shaping cities have been fully embedded within medium- and longer-term perspectives. This frame of reference has focused on permanence and stability. This clearly contrasts with much more agile and flexible approaches to urban development, particularly when this thinking goes beyond the micro, that is, site level, and concerns larger-scale urban areas (neighborhoods and settlements, towns and cities, urbanized

2 • WHAT IS THE ADAPTABLE AND TEMPORARY CITY?

hinterlands, etc.). Peter Bishop and Lesley Williams in *The Temporary City* justly point out, referring to the writer Dan Cruickshank, that the West values the materiality of buildings and hence of cities.[2] This contrasts with Asian or Eastern perceptions, where the spiritual and therefore the less permanent are perceived as more crucial. Consequently, a country like the United Kingdom is characterized by an artificially imposed permanence, which has resulted in ignoring more adaptable ways of producing the city and making temporary uses slow to be recognized within regulatory planning and policy spheres. At the core of this can be found diverse power relationships in the making and remaking of cities.

The production, making, and remaking of cities is a highly complex task that focuses primarily on filling gaps, fixing issues, and trying to navigate among various power agencies and huge inequalities. It is, as I will develop later, about thinking about alternative and creative ways of tackling those gaps and needs, and thus reacting and engaging with disorder and (in)stability. Attempting to tackle the question of why adaptability in urban making and urban thoughts—and hence any thinking that embeds and considers the nonpermanent and the temporary—is crucial. What is referred to as "urban planning" in the English-speaking world, or more widely as "urbanism" in urban studies and theory, has from its origin been meant to address key failures in the urban system. This covers a range of imperatives, typically the provision of decent housing, sanitation, public health, coherent public transport systems, and local and national economic growth. Without doubt, significant progress has been accomplished in the ways cities function on an everyday basis, but it is also apparent that the contemporary urban machinery is still deeply broken. Around the globe, cities of all sizes face transformative challenges that are only partly unpacked and remain

WHAT IS THE ADAPTABLE AND TEMPORARY CITY? • 3

unresolved. This is ultimately reflected in the very lengthy list of core priorities displayed in the UN Sustainable Development Goals (SDGs) and recent calls to revisit them, particularly in line with the COVID-19 pandemic and other ongoing crises, such as climate change.[3] Cities are still and will continue to be characterized by entrenched intersectional inequalities arising from systemic political, economic, and social failures along with power manifestations. In parallel, they remain shaped by rigid urban making and urban development practices that are not malleable enough to embrace the need for more adaptability in both the permanent *and* the temporary city.

The role of cities in local, national, and global economies and the influence of the urbanization process in shaping people's lives will continue to grow, and so will the extreme difficulty in understanding and responding to the challenges characterizing highly complex, partly broken, and dysfunctional urban systems. Numerous factors contribute to this, including limited financial and economic means; political decisions prioritizing specific interventions and power dynamics; the nature of specific places and communities; the lack of flexibility in strategies aiming to tackle transformations; and the lack of attention paid to the everyday, organic, and informal dynamics fostered by individuals' practices and behaviors. It can only be assumed unfortunately that cities will continue to sustain and foster severe inequalities embedded in path-dependent dysfunctions and intersectional burdens (typically poverty, socioeconomic inequalities, segregation, oppression, and abjection but also colonial legacies). This means that many urban residents will continue to struggle to live decently and access key services. Such challenges illustrate why adaptability matters for places and urban dwellers. Adaptability still suffers from partial engagement, both in thought and practice, even if significant progress has been made in the way built environment experts think about a more flexible urban development process.

Such preliminary statements shouldn't give the wrong impression to readers that the aspiration for more adaptable cities is new; adaptability and the various temporalities of the urban have always been part of urban dynamics. In changing and often disrupted urban contexts and despite being framed as permanent institutions, cities have always adapted to address specific needs, gaps, and challenges. Individuals, groups, communities, activists, and built environment experts have been at the forefront of those adaptations, shaping and enforcing the right knowledge and skills about what works, what doesn't, and what needs to be changed. Adaptability depends on how cities have evolved and is a core component of how their inhabitants use and transform the urban environment. It is a testimony to how cities and urban spaces may and will evolve in the future and survive. The COVID-19 pandemic was the latest (and certainly not the last) example of why adaptable and flexible urban environments are important to allow coping, forms of recovery, resilience, and possibly longer-term sustainability.

Still, there is probably a fundamental misconception that has fostered the general assumption that adaptability may not matter *that much*, particularly in the urban planning field. Cities and policies are shaped and planned thanks to data (e.g., traffic flows, housing needs), targets (e.g., economic development goals, the number of housing units to build, etc.), and wider political agendas. Those rely on financial calculations constructed on predictions and modeling. Such data inform decisions, policies, investment strategies, and financing and funding mechanisms. These shape the built environment along with people's lives and livelihoods. However, cities in essence will never be finished.[4]

Lars Lerup in *Building the Unfinished* in 1977 developed the argument that "unfinishedness" is not an imperfection but a creative and conceptual resource.[5] Unfinishedness matters because it prompts differences and allows creativity and experimentations; it triggers disruptions of existing modes and practices while allowing innovation when facing disruptions. Adaptability is thus integrative and part of the unfinishedness of cities, and this is why it is so important. Following the same line of argument, cities and individuals are intrinsically and constantly driven by uncertainties and the unknown. This is a lesson from the recent pandemic but also of any understanding of how people and places have evolved throughout history.[6] The unfinished nature of cities along with the obligation to account for uncertainties make the paradigm of the adaptable city even more fundamental in urban theory and research but also in practice. Indeed, designing disorder is crucial,[7] and so are experiments and disruptions in the city. It is very much within this experimental approach to urban making and urban thinking that this book engages with the ongoing debates about what makes cities and how they will be shaped in the future.

Dealing with uncertainty means tackling, understanding, using, and embedding adaptability in thinking about cities but also in their design and making. It also requires engaging with time and the various rhythms that characterize cities; this means recognizing the various temporalities of the urban condition, from the transient to the seasonal and those related to economic cycles or to periods of disruptions and crisis. Such heterogeneous temporalities can be related to various rhythms, routines, adaptations, and improvisations that are constantly engaging with permanence as a condition and interrogating permanent materialities as constitutive elements of urban spaces as well as power relationships in the production of urban spaces.

THE IMPORTANCE OF TEMPORARY URBANISM AS A CONCEPT AND FIELD OF RESEARCH

The making of cities isn't only about the planning of cities but involves a thorough understanding of how people live (and should live) in urban spaces. This resonates greatly with how *urbanisme* is used in French to refer to the process and dynamics entrenched in the aim of creating livable places (rather than regulations and control that, in essence, have been all about permanence and stability). The most contemporary French interpretation of urbanism derives from how urban making and urban development has been tied to the "School of the Urban Project," closely tying it with architecture and hence to the "fabrication" of the city.[8] More important, urbanism is a commonly used concept in urban theory when referring to the grammar of the city and the reading of the urbanization process.[9] The term "urbanism" (rather than "urban planning") will thus be widely used throughout the book in order to engage theoretically with the grammars of adaptable cities but also develop an integrated reading of adaptability moving beyond disciplinary silos and with a focus on the process of *urban making*.

Querying and stressing the importance of adaptability leads to embracing an *urbanism* lens rather than a sole *urban planning* lens. For a long time, the planning discipline within its Anglo-Saxon tradition has mostly failed to engage with the idea of adaptability: in essence, adaptability is not easy to regulate and plan. As a result, the planning discipline has paid little attention to the more creative and experimental ways of thinking about cities, with the exception of scholars who are embedded into more interdisciplinary fields of enquiry. This has been reflected in practice and in how urban planners have mostly handed over to urban designers or architects, but also to geographers, the task of engaging with adaptable approaches of (re)making cities. For many years, understanding the adaptable nature of cities and also their temporalities have thus been scrutinized within the fields of urban studies and urban affairs (here, integrative of architecture, urban design, sociology, or geography). This has led to (too) many concepts and theoretical lenses that have tried to tackle a diverse, complex, although actually similar phenomenon, hence blurring further any attempts to read the complexity of adaptable and temporary mechanisms systemically and exhaustively.

This is where the concepts of *temporary urbanism* and specifically *temporary urbanisms* come into play. Along with Peter Kraftl, and building on the work of Peter Bishop, Lesley Williams, and Ali Madanipour,[10] we called for using "temporary urbanism" as a unitary concept to refer to "processes, practices and policies of and for spatial adaptability, allowing the transformation of spaces in transition along with changes of use to tackle specific needs with the optimal objectives to create, provide and sustain liveable spaces."[11] The concept of temporary urbanism as a primary driver of adaptable cities is crucial because it allows us to unpack everyday dynamics and power relationships in the agile and flexible production of cities. While temporary urbanism in the past ten years has progressively been elevated as an overarching concept, its acceptance in the grammar of cities— until recently—has remained extremely sparse.

Ideas and debates looking at processes of adaptability and forms of temporariness in cities commenced with a primary focus on temporary occupations occurring on vacant sites and providing short-term solutions.[12] Research focused on decrypting trajectories of transformation while trying to develop new concepts and theoretical framings.[13] Diverse terms including "ephemerality," "transience," "liminality," "pop-up," "tactical," and "do-it-yourself (DIY) urbanism" were used to characterize temporary projects.[14] Most of the examples studied have been initially located in Europe and North America; recently scholars have more thoroughly explored temporariness in less developed contexts, moving beyond a sole focus on informality and informal practices.[15] Again however, pursuing the argument made earlier, a significant amount of work has been produced by scholars of urban studies, architecture, and urban design with a focus on buildings and sites (i.e., microscale). The stellar work of Gordon Douglas in the *Help-Yourself City: DYI Urbanism and Urban Design* is important here, along with Mara Ferreri's *The Permanence of Temporary Urbanism: Normalising Precarity in Austerity London* and Quentin Stevens and Kim Dovey's latest *Temporary and Tactical Urbanism: (Re)Assembling Urban Space*.[16] Still, limited attention has been given to adaptability at city scale and ways of "thinking" about cities, globally, and their development per se.

Debates about the facets of urban temporariness have tended to be piecemeal, discipline-specific, and often case study–based; most of the discussions have been characterized by an interest in making intentional but temporary interventions in urban spaces.[17] The use of the common-ground concept of temporary urbanisms has allowed the unwrapping of complex and multitemporal built environments, particularly with a view to better articulating everyday dynamics with the wider social and economic process of urban placemaking (shaped around a vision for the future). This has allowed transferring the temporary urbanism concept to new fields of enquiry by providing a new framework to unpack the nature and relationships between the informal and the formal in less developed contexts.[18] Paul Moawad typically applied it in the context of refugees' encampments, focusing on socio-spatial adaptations in contexts of limbo; by doing so, he managed to "unmask and recalibrate current habitable and livelihood conditions"[19] tied to refugees' waiting experiences in contexts of transitions. His work among others testifies about the crucial interest given to the field of "temporary urbanisms" in various and diverse urban settings.[20]

Both temporary urbanism and adaptability are crucially important to decrypt the complex rhythms and routines that characterize cities. They can be found in all urban locations, in various manifestations, hence acting as a meaningful lens to understand the changing and eminently diverse urban conditions that characterize cities globally. As I will discuss throughout this book, manifestations of temporary urbanisms and forms of adaptability can be observed in vacant buildings, in open spaces, within streets or gardens, and in more marginal places such as refugee camps and informal settlements.

TIMELINESS OF A FIELD OF STUDY

Adaptable forms of urban placemaking and their delineation in various forms of temporary urbanisms deserve further attention and investigation. The COVID-19 pandemic has reinforced this need further. Temporary urbanisms have been spreading as an easy socio-spatial fix to tackle socioeconomic disruptions, foster resilience, and envisage ways of moving forward toward "normality" and possibly recovering. There is a need to understand how temporary urbanisms have shaped and will continue to shape adaptable cities. This resonates with the question of scale and power. Adaptation occurs at different scales, from the micro to the macro, to the meso. The meso may affect the macro, and the macro might hide the micro. All are tied to complex power forces. They affect the built environment differently: typically, macro-level factors are more likely to be about the physical environment and to result in semipermanent alterations to the physical environment. Again, all scales display various forms of owning, gaining, and exercising power. This is one of the key contributions of this book.

The debates and movements toward adaptability and flexibility in the built environment and, more important, in how cities need to be designed, planned, and managed are at a turning point. In the last decade, a shift toward incorporating temporary uses and projects in the urban making and fabric has occurred; this resulted in the emergence of much more planned (i.e., top-down) and regulated approaches toward nonpermanent uses and practices that were initially more incrementally driven. This has been reflected in the spread of meanwhile shops, temporary gardens, and playgrounds but also in the creative use of streets and other single-use spaces. This has concerned both developed but also less developed countries, here contrasting with but also complementing other forms of insurgent and informal uses.[21]

The number of tactical, temporary, and adaptable experts in the academic and practice fields has increased over the years, shaping interdisciplinary and international communities of practice. In parallel, temporary urbanisms are increasingly being "planned." and spaces for more incrementally driven forms of temporariness and adaptations are becoming less prominent. There is a risk here that adaptable practices become detached from urban "realities" and needs." This resonates with existing debates in development studies over state-led approaches versus the support of informality as a planning strategy.[22] It also echoes other debates, including a critique of the breakdown of the welfare state and the rise (and use) of precarity in urban development.[23]

The 2020 global COVID-19 health crisis followed by what is named in the United Kingdom as the cost-of-living crisis have accelerated existing trends and deepened intersectional inequalities. Small-scale adaptable strategies have been pushed further to the forefront of communities' and cities' abilities to cope and display resiliency. This has led to hybrid temporary strategies involving both communities and regulatory bodies, strategies that are positioned as city-scale solutions toward the transitioning of declining high streets and neighborhoods. These have been merged into other priorities, for example, shifting behaviors toward active travel and pushing a net-zero climate change environmental strategy. The ways in which built environment experts have been thinking about adaptable cities is thus undergoing a profound shake-up, with minor and major changes and disruptions still to come. While adaptability could be a response to tackle specific urgent needs, there is also a risk that it becomes another driver of gentrification and segregation. More control and regulation of temporary and informal practices—even within hybrid arrangements—is also expected. This will restrain the ability of the most vulnerable to cope. Adaptability may then end up being more exclusive than inclusive, with only those in the right place, with the right skills, power, and knowledge, being able to benefit from it. All these are important questions that this book aims to address.

This book is timely because future directions for sustainable and resilient cities are being queried in the context of postpandemic recovery, climate emergency, and accumulated socioeconomic crises, leading to rising inequalities. Any new directions will resonate with adaptability in some form. Such debates are global but need to account for the extreme diversity of urban landscapes and their very diverse "urban fragments."[24] The future of cities relies on temporary and adaptable environments; however, this can be achieved only by critically reflecting on the paths taken by temporary and adaptable thinking and practices over the past decades. This can only happen if a dialogue between

FOUR ARGUMENTS

Four core arguments structure the book's narrative. They function as pillars constitutive of any aggregated thinking about adaptable cities and temporary urbanisms.

Argument 1

Adaptation and temporariness are constitutive of diverse urban conditions, of how cities have been produced and reproduced over time, and of their everyday and longer-term rhythms. Their role in the planned makeup of spaces continues but is evolving; this will have a significant impact on how forms of adaptability and temporariness are produced, by whom, and their ultimate outcomes.

As outlined at the start of this chapter, adaptation and temporary processes are widespread in cities globally. They all connect with the different rhythms that characterize urban environments and individuals' living conditions and practices. Forms of adaptability are increasingly being detached from grassroots local needs and translated in neighborhoods or cities as ready-to-use solutions. Temporary strategies are becoming common and more frequently used as tool kits; their malleable and innovative mechanisms, based on improvised and innovative use practice and thinking, are thus at risk of being standardized and further included into neoliberal forms of urban development. Great care is needed here to avoid triggering additional exclusionary practices.

Argument 2

Cities, built environment experts, and urban residents depend on adaptability and have already been using it in various ways. This doesn't come without consequences and challenges. Visible and invisible as well as accepted and unacceptable forms of adaptability characterize cities globally, resonating with wider debates about sustainability, resiliency, informality, and survival. All challenge both governance arrangements, power, and state responses.

One of the complexities in unpacking adaptability and the numerous delineations of temporary urbanisms is related to the variety of contexts in which they have been applied. Improvisation and alternative practices that emerge from them can be beneficial for both communities or groups but at the same time challenge existing urban development models. They can be considered threats for existing policies and strategies. While some forms of temporary urbanisms are acknowledged as part of urban-making practices, others connected to informal practices tend to be seen as unacceptable even if they are based on survival. Any attempts to tackle diversity and inclusivity, with the ultimate goal of delivering sustainable and resilient environments, have to account for these approaches. Such ambition is mostly ignored, particularly in the less developed contexts. Survival-led improvisations hence remain and respond to the urban condition and its intersectional challenges.

Argument 3

Adaptable cities and temporary urbanisms are both policy and (non) policy problems embedded in strong power relationships and various strategies developed by key groups or institutions. This leads to contrasting mechanisms of inclusion and rejection.

Adaptable and temporary urban dynamics have a tangential position in policy framework, at least at the city level, in both formal and informal community settings. This gives rise to difficulties and paradoxes. Temporary occupations translated into adaptable ways of using the city on an everyday basis are anchored in spatial boundaries. They are concerned with tensions and conflicts linked to landownership or divergent visions and voices. Their ultimate inclusion in wider policy agendas can be problematic. Place and people matter here. Successful adaptable processes reveal a very high level of place-based strategic thinking and political support. This is an indication of significant power dynamics at play, putting at the forefront space users and urban makers through either convergent or divergent logics about how to transform spaces.

Argument 4

Adaptability is not a universal ability and relies on a set of abilities, knowledge, and skills. This has consequences for the (re)imagining of the adaptable city, for its understanding, and for defining where adaptability can spatially and socioeconomically occur. It has repercussions on how adaptability and temporariness can evolve, particularly toward forms of perpetuation and permanence.

The delivery of adaptable and temporary initiatives requires specific skills and resources. The increasing number of temporary and adaptable advocates and experts is gathering momentum, leading to the development of communities of practice at both the local and the national and international levels. This leads to the circulation of ideas, knowledge, and best practice, which informs debates in various arenas of discussion. Skills are related to personal interests, training, abilities, and networks but also to other strengths or social privileges. This relates to gender and particularly household responsibilities but also to the type of work performed by individuals, including working hours and where the work can be performed (from home, in a hybrid between home and workplace, or not). Adaptable skills are channeled toward those who can perform them, for their own well-being and the benefit of their community. This displays clear intersectional inequalities with crucial spatial manifestations and policy implications.

STRUCTURE OF THE BOOK

Chapter 2 demonstrates why adaptable cities and the future of temporary urbanisms need attention. It looks at how adaptability and temporary uses have been implemented and have evolved. The idea of adaptability contradicts and challenges many preconceptions about how cities are shaped, designed, and planned, even if cities have been historically developed and transformed thanks to temporary adjustments. Central to the discussion are the roles of upheavals, disruptions, and crises as they initiate transformative reactions and changes that are clearly visible in the processes of adaptability. This chapter also deconstructs the evolution of the temporary and adaptability narrative, how it has been implemented, and what this means for models of development and policy. It first develops a new framework to understand adaptability based on creative urban making, reaction, disorder, and (in)stability; it unwraps the key tensions between the adaptable and the nonadaptable along with the flexible and inflexible, and then turns to longitudinal historical snapshots to illustrate how adaptability processes have been used to shape and reshape cities. It finally zooms in on the most recent interpretations of adaptability and so-called temporary urbanisms, and points out the complex tensions linked to the dynamics of regulation and deregulation and hence the forces that allow malleability.

Chapter 3 focuses on two primary dynamics of the adaptable city: activation and weak planning. It analyzes how temporary urbanism has progressively been used to accompany (mostly) larger-scale regeneration projects that will take years to be delivered and hence how the idea and process of activation has been interpreted and applied. This has occurred in several ways: as a physical activation of spaces, at different scales; as an activation of ideas and visions (doing things differently and creatively); and as an activation of human resources and networks. Such processes of activation sit within contexts of so-called weak planning and connect to the rhythms of the production of space; they resonate with modes of producing and governing cities and hence embed power struggles and strategic relationships, all of which must be acknowledged and explained. The discussion builds on the first major temporary projects and how they have been developed incrementally as responses to crisis and periods of waiting.

Chapter 4 describes the other key characteristic of adaptable cities and temporary urbanisms: their ability to provide alternative tools, solutions, and responses to the specific needs of communities and places. It highlights how adaptability and temporariness can manifest in efforts to meet previously neglected specific rights in contexts of deep socioeconomic inequalities. It examines adaptability as a mode of coping and survival that cannot be dissociated from an in-depth discussion about the connection between informality and those left behind, along with the underpinnings of everyday resilience. It also describes how temporariness and adaptability manifest not only as ways to respond to everyday needs but also as an instrument to sustain the nonpermanent status of some communities and settlements.

Attention is given here to temporary and adaptable practices and uses shaped as responses to the failure of cities and their governing bodies to meet those needs. These are intrinsically embedded in intersectional inequalities while also connecting to wider responses to major crises, which are not only driven by large-scale interventions but can also be fostered by more incremental practices concerning local places, communities, and economies.

Chapter 5 focuses on the more contemporary interpretation of top-down temporary urbanism initiatives that have been included more and more often into wider strategies of urban transformation. Adaptability and temporary urbanism are mostly designed with the ambition of creating a buzz; hence, they incentivize specific trajectories of transformation, triggering activation and value extraction. These sit in a similar narrative to the one used for promoting creative cities but also, more important, within the experiential nature of cities (and the experiential discourse that has been built around it). In such contexts, adaptability tends to spread beyond the indoors toward the outdoors to include public spaces, streets, and portions of the city that are also undergoing regeneration. This chapter describes the mechanisms of adaptability and develops a critique of its neoliberal interpretation and monetarization, which tends to favor pastiche practices and results in a loss of meaning and scope with detrimental socioeconomic and urban consequences.

Chapter 6 describes the latest directions taken by adaptable cities in pandemic and postpandemic contexts. What happened between 2020 and 2022 constituted an exceptional and revolutionary moment, breaking some of the dynamics, processes, and narratives that used to drive how adaptable urban making is envisaged and temporary urbanisms implemented. The global state of emergency not only challenged the ability of cities to *effectively* and *promptly* adapt but also produced a pressing need for new forms of adaptability in more hybrid forms. The COVID-19 crisis led to an accelerations of existing trends, including expanding the use of temporary strategies, at city scale, within recovery strategies. It also elevated the importance of adapting indoor spaces and outdoor spaces (pavements, streets, sidewalks) with the view of following other major agendas (e.g., climate change and active travel) and/or being more resilient in the eventuality of additional pandemic episodes. The (perceived) lack of adaptability in the most deprived and unplanned settings because of overcrowding; lack of open spaces; and also water, sanitation, and hygiene (WASH) conditions emerged as a primary concern that led to several detrimental consequences. In high-income countries, it exacerbated further livability inequalities from one neighborhood to another, but in low- and middle-income cities it reinforced tensions and exclusionary processes, with the poorest and most vulnerable communities being further marginalized. This chapter deconstructs how various forms of reactive adaptations resulted from insufficient adaptability in cities and urban spaces, leading to very quick improvisations favoring agility and creativity but also a softening of the regulatory planning process. The chapter also looks at how the perceived necessity to control the nonpermanent in contexts where informal and unplanned conditions prevailed led to further processes of exclusion and abjection.

Chapter 7 focuses on skills and knowledge. From the premise of temporary initiatives, projects that succeeded and were then raised as leading examples have clearly been those that, despite being temporary, were thoroughly strategized and planned by highly experienced professionals. The diffusion of temporary models and ways of delivering adaptability and temporariness have been achieved through the transfer of ideas and the creation of dedicated communities of practice. More important, knowledge is connected to how adaptability has become a political matter; it is a fundamental lens to unwrap the trajectories of transformation of temporary and adaptable processes. The expansion, diversification, and manifestation of how "temporary" uses have been sustained are concomitant with a professionalization of adaptable urban making, including its monetarization as a profitable sector of activity. Here, of course, its recognition as a relevant policy tool has caused the activity to grow into an attractive market segment for both small and larger organizations. Knowledge and learning are important elements to illustrate how individual and community skills can converge in transformative actions, supported (or not) by nongovernmental organizations (NGOs) and international nongovernmental organizations (INGOs).

Chapter 8 returns to two fundamental questions driving future research directions: What is the future of adaptable and temporary urbanisms? And what does it tell us about key paradoxes impinging on the work of built environment experts and urban scholars when dealing with the constant tensions between permanence and impermanence but also certainty and uncertainty? These paradoxes share the commonality of embracing and interrogating how places, people, and also policies are tuned toward relying on highly complex and diverse adaptive processes. A return to the four arguments outlined in the book's introduction is provided, allowing me to question further the relationship between urban making, uncertainty, and complexity. Adaptable and temporary urbanisms are fundamentally fostered by two distinct but related processes: crisis and emergency (reactionary responses) and value and income generation (at various scales but through similar neoliberal and globalized narratives). Both share a common area of concern:

how to account for and deal with uncertainty. The key paradoxes of adaptability and temporariness are anchored within uncertainty: agility with permanence as a form of preparedness, latency, and creative stasis versus impatience and predictions, and finally permanence, comfort zones, and breaking boundaries to tackle endless crises.

2

THE FLEXIBLE AND INFLEXIBLE CITY

There is an ongoing tension in how cities are shaped and evolve over time. It revolves around their urban structures being mainly inflexible and thus nonadaptable and the simultaneous necessity to remain adaptable as a response to disruptions, crises, or communities' and individuals' needs. Providing an epistemological reading of adaptable cities and temporary urbanisms depends on understanding the historical roots that framed how cities have been envisioned, developed, planned, and transformed over time. Such longitudinal framing is crucial and contributes to the discussion of why adaptable cities and the future of temporary urbanisms need attention.[1] The idea of adaptability contradicts and challenges many preconceptions about how cities are shaped, designed, and planned, even if cities have been historically shaped and reshaped thanks to temporary and more permanent readjustments to face structural and conjunctural changes. Such conceptions differ significantly. They do allow us, however, to unwrap why certain cities, countries, or knowledge holders have been at the forefront of promoting more agility and creativity in the shaping of urban environments and why others have been more reluctant, which consequently led to more incremental processes and less consideration given to a more agile processes of urban making.

This chapter has a very specific role in this book. It aims to engage with how adaptability and temporary uses have been implemented and have evolved over time. Urban transformations are deconstructed through the lens of flexibility versus inflexibility and are situated within wider socioeconomic, cultural, political, and historical understandings. This requires a set of steps and lenses for analysis. First, it involves an interrogation of some of the core constitutive ideas that allow situating the tensions between the adaptable and the nonadaptable along with the flexible and inflexible, and involves a new framework of understanding around the core principles of creative urban making, reaction, disorder, and (in)stability. Second, a longitudinal yet succinct historical snapshot is needed to dig deeper into the tensions inherent to the adaptability process and how it has been used to shape and reshape cities despite being outside mainstream urban thoughts. Third, a contemporary reading of the most recent interpretations of adaptability and so-called temporary urbanisms is necessary. What is at play here is how the flexible and inflexible nature of cities is associated with complex tensions linked to dynamics of regulation and deregulation, and power dynamics and hence the ability to allow malleability. This has key implications for how adaptability and the ability to adapt temporally and improvise are delivered. Central to this discussion are the roles of upheavals, disruptions, and crises as they foster transformative reactions and changes that are eminently embedded in processes of adaptability.

THE FOUR COMPONENTS OF THE ADAPTABILITY PARADIGM: CREATIVE URBAN MAKING, REACTION, DISORDER, AND (IN)STABILITY

Cities have been constructed through the accumulation and evolution of ideas and thoughts that have evolved and matured through the centuries and have been translated into various forms of urbanisms, making them partly unfinished. The adaptable nature of cities, while not acknowledged as adaptable, has effectively been informing urban transformation narratives. Such narratives have been constructed upon visions and designs based in turn on principles that current urban forms and built environments did not match expected needs. The adaptable narrative has been framed according to four constitutive and complementary pillars: creative urban making, reaction, disorder, and (in)stability.

Creative Urban Making

Adaptability and the idea that urbanism can be flexible are driven by the fact that cities and portions of cities are not solely planned based on land-use allocation but carefully crafted and designed.[2] This resonates greatly with disciplinary understandings and positionings of urban making, specifically creative urban making. The latest is multi-scalar and relates, for example, to innovative ways of using buildings, streets, and open spaces differently but also correlates with more city-scale solutions or community-led projects that aimed to tackle vacancy. Engaging with adaptability, emptiness, or change of use fosters dialogues between all urban fields. This dialogue depends, however, on how urban planning per se has been constructed as a discipline and how its more contemporary interpretations have engaged with the idea of creativity in "design" and "project." It is embedded in the continental European aesthetic and morphological tradition of urbanism, and thus depends on schools of thought and subsequent modes of practice.

The physical development planning tradition specifically has been driven extensively by an artistic and creative reading and understanding of cities.[3] Although this approach has evolved significantly since its emergence in the early twentieth century, its orientation toward aestheticization reflects how creativity has been influencing the design of cities. Unwrapping the extent to which creativity has informed urbanism and urban planning practice and how it has shifted away from its artistic tradition are ways to question epistemologically the adaptability paradigm. Physical development planning has been correlated to spatial and social change with the ambition of creating "ideal cities."[4] Doing so rested upon interrogating the spatial design and structure of cities. This was considered representative of a dominant art form. Spatial considerations were merged with social considerations with the development of social utopias (garden cities, for example, such as Letchworth Garden City and Welwyn Garden City in the United Kingdom or Sunnyside in Queens, New York). These displayed new reenvisaged forms of living and interactions made possible through unique urban forms. The design of those new settlements was a reaction to chaotic, unhealthy, overcrowded (industrial) cities.

Such an artistic dimension applied to the design of cities was embedded in architecture because urban planners were trained architects. It relied heavily, however, on the use of regulations on land use and was blueprint-led; in other words, it promoted a very design-led but rigid view of cities, with no spaces for malleability (this was very visible in the Burnham Chicago Plan or post–World War II reconstruction plans in England). Design here served land assembly and the realization of new urban (master)pieces that were to be implemented in a very determinist way.[5] On the one hand, there was no adaptability per se in how urban making was envisaged; on the other hand, this planning tradition anchored creativity in planning thoughts. The aesthetic dimension of physical development planning was quite rapidly challenged by other traditions along with a more rational

THE FLEXIBLE AND INFLEXIBLE CITY • 25

and technical view of cities in the 1960s onward; these excluded artistic aspects and started to shift urban planning away from the process of artistic design, giving space for architects and urban designers to retain the aesthetic and artistic side of urban placemaking.[6]

Planning as a separate discipline started to include more duties primarily around balancing social, economic, and environmental changes in urban settings. This means that urban planning further distanced itself from other fields of practice. It became less open to creative readings of cities, which was reflected in distinct skills, training, and career paths. In parallel, and also dependent on the evolution of the planning profession, the term "urban design" was developed in the 1910s. "Harvard's Graduate School of Design popularized the term with a series of colloquia in the 1950s leading to the founding of the first professional program in urban design there in 1960."[7] Architects and urban designers have thus continued to engage with the idea of flexibility as eminently connected to creativity and experimentation. This was noticeable in the avant-garde architecture movement that, in the 1960s and 1970s, had a keen interest in flexibility and variability.[8] This explains why temporary uses and temporary urbanism emerged out of discussions and initiatives led by architects and urban designers, not by urban planners. These practitioners shaped and led new ways for thinking about creative urban making.

In the Anglo-Saxon context, this has had some important consequences for the shaping of an adaptable approach to cities development. This is where context matters because those precursory approaches have interfered in how the planning profession constructed itself. Such differences in traditions and types of planning have been influencing the process of adaptability in design and later what can be referred to as temporary urbanism.

Now, there is no homogeneity from one country to another, testifying to the range of ideal types of planning systems identified in the 1997 European Union Compendium of Spatial Planning Systems and Policies.[9] The United Kingdom and the United States have specialized in more narrow (although still porous) fields in urban planning, with a land-use planning focus to which other disciplines, including urban design, urban studies, and urban affairs, navigate. The term "town and county planning" in the United Kingdom clearly refers to the regulation of the land and development activities of both public and private developers, which has made it largely separate from distinct sectoral planning processes.[10] It has no or little space for creative, experimental, and less regulatory-led thinking. Other countries (for example, France, Italy, and Germany) have embraced the concept of urbanism rather than urban planning, which converged into a more integrated approach toward regional and local urban and economic development. This has allowed more dynamic dialogues between architecture and urban planning—through urbanism—linked to multi-scalar approaches to urban development going beyond land-use management. The French case here is an interesting illustration of this evolution.

Urbanism in France originally derived from the term *aménagement du territoire* displaying the administrative and political tradition of centralized and decentralized planning that characterized the country and its strategies of national, regional, economic, and infrastructure development. *Aménagement du territoire* and *urbanisme* are two complementary concepts, with *urbanisme* being more locally anchored (i.e., at the city and neighborhood levels). The practice of *urbanisme* has evolved and been influenced in the last decades by the *École du Projet Urbain* (School of Urban Project), anchored in both architecture and urban planning (urban design does not exist as a separate discipline in France). This latest urbanism tradition has been playing a key role in constructing a contemporary discourse on the transitionary and adaptive nature of cities, hence feeding into the narrative about temporary urbanisms (called *urbanisme transitoire*, i.e., transient urbanism, in France). A more creative dimension of urban thinking and making has been sustained and anchored in localized approaches to places and community needs, going much beyond land-use management and master planning, as in the United Kingdom or the United States.

This school of thought tends to be associated with the work of several architects, including Christian Devillers, Philippe Panerai, and Bruno Fortier in France, and Oriol Bohigas and Ignasi de Solà-Morales in Spain.[11] It was originally constructed, however, on the work of North American and European scholars and practitioners who reacted against modern forms of urban development, particularly processes of urban renewal and slum clearance that denied local contexts and identities in the 1960s. These practitioners include Jane Jacobs, Saverio Muratori, and Aldo Rossi, who argued for the need to account for existing urban forms and local communities' voices and needs.[12] The urban project approach is grounded in a typo-morphological reading of cities. It relies on the importance of urban history and the link between architectural and urban forms. A key component of this school of thought, which resonates greatly with the adaptable city principles, is its temporal and path-dependent reading of cities and their inhabitants. In other words, it embraces the present and its physical (local setting) and social (people) connections while acknowledging the past and building on what was there before and what will happen in the future.[13] It also relies on acknowledging the diversity of local contexts and their distinct temporalities; these differ from one project to another and from one site to another. This approach toward urban remaking has triggered more convergent approaches between urbanists, developers, and policymakers based on principles of interactivity and nonlinearity.[14] As the French urbanist Ariella Masboungi argued over twenty years ago, "time is the companion of the project . . . a city is only a set of evolutionary trends, and the work accomplished by the project in urbanism is not aiming for a solution but sits within an approach towards progressive improvement, always open. Time requires also negotiation, learning about sharing the culture of the project or also about confronting the other disciplines which hold powers."[15]

Such accounts of temporalities within the urban project constitute a more flexible and multi-scalar creative urban-making process. This flexibility not only connects to the actors involved in the process but also to technical creative tools and agile regulations that can match with specific places. This way of approaching urban development and transformation has played a key role in allowing, over a decade later, for transient urbanism to emerge as a relevant and acceptable practice based on nonpermanence and flexibility. As I will discuss later in chapter 3, creative urban making will inform how temporary urbanism becomes associated with 'activation' but also to principles of aestheticization and branding.

Reaction

The tension between cities' flexibility and their inflexibility has been nurtured by strong concerns about cities' problems and dysfunctions, which have been related to the inadequacy of urban forms and implications for the living conditions of their inhabitants. More important, it is also related to the ameliorative, grassroots, re-allocative origins and orientation of the urban planning profession. It is useful to remember that some of the early planning visions stemmed from anarchist movements.[16] This displays a strong connection between reactive thinking, adaptable cities, and temporary occupations that originally spread as forced occupations of empty buildings, which were justified by anarchist narratives.[17] Those movements inspired by social utopia (Ebenezer Howard, Patrick Geddes, or the Regional Planning Association of America [RPAA]) started to emerge at the end of the nineteenth century and the beginning of the twentieth. They converged in trying to merge new urban models with alternative ways of living, working, and shaping a new and better society. Forced adaptation and reuse were a reaction against those who held power (state and landowners). It was a response to claimed rights that are not addressed (i.e., the right of occupying a building to provide a roof over one's head). This preliminary engagement with forced use and occupation has important long-term consequences. Such alternatives were resisted for decades and seen as risky approaches driven by groups of individuals outside any planning or legal regulatory framing. It can be argued, however, that social utopias and wider anarchist-led occupations share some commonalities with the contemporary interpretations of adaptable urban making. All had been trying to overturn urban and social dysfunctions with a focus on individuals, communities, and particularly those in need. These reactionary thoughts have denounced the inflexibility and inappropriateness of societies, urban forms, and urban making while flagging the inability of planning systems to conceptualize and deliver urban environments fit for purpose (assuming this is actually possible). Their influence has never vanished entirely and remains part of alternative urban thought aimed at finding solutions to ameliorate living conditions and reallocate resources (including land), all often driven by community-led grassroot movements. Still visible in the European and North American contexts, they can be found around the globe, typically in situations where informality prevails, as in Brazilian favelas; here, reactive manifestations of adaptability are constitutive of how these neighborhoods function and survive, and are driven by very active alternative social movements.

Such reactionary thinking about cities not being fit for purpose resonates greatly with the need to acknowledge and facilitate adaptability in the urban realm. This claim has been elevated as a matter of international concern over the last two decades. The way adaptability and temporary urbanism have been positioned as creative reactions to dysfunctional cities is the starting point of Ali Madanipour's book *Cities in Time: Temporary Urbanism and the Future of the City*, the first book to spell out clearly temporary urbanism as a concept in the field of urban studies, planning, and design.[18] Madanipour links the origins of temporary urbanism to the multitemporal reading of cities proposed in the United States Pavilion at the Venice Architectural Biennale 2012. Labeled as "spontaneous interventions," it exhibited 124 urban interventions initiated by architects, designers, planners, artists, and everyday citizens and resonated with the practice of tactical urbanism that was spreading in North America at that time. Its primary focus was to bring positive change to neighborhoods and cities, with a focus on projects exploring how to improve amenities, comfort, functionality, inclusiveness, safety, and the sustainability of cities.[19] Temporary projects and uses were clearly advertised as solutions to deliver such improvements in a context where cities (at least portions of cities) are unfit for purpose. This included "parklets to community farms, guerrilla bike lanes to urban repair squads, outdoor living rooms to pop-up markets, sharing networks, and temporary architecture."[20] A similar call to embrace adaptability and flexibility was

THE FLEXIBLE AND INFLEXIBLE CITY • 31

reiterated at the Venice Architectural Biennale 2016 when the architect Alejandro Aravena led the curation "Reporting from the Front." Again, examples of temporary and adaptable initiatives were raised as models to drive urban transformation forward, with Detroit used as the inspiration for the U.S. pavilion. Urban dysfunction and vacancy were at the forefront of the displayed narratives.

While the intention here is not to give greater significance to those ephemeral high-profile (and mostly exclusionary) events, it is important to recognize their roles in shifting the act of reacting and denunciating from minority (anarchist) groups to much larger and institutionalized communities of practice that are strongly connected to the fields of architecture and urban design (hence to creative urban making). Those movements instigated the recognition of adaptability in urban thought. The attention these movements received demonstrated a shift in urban thinking that spread much beyond architecture and design because the role of temporary projects led by communities started being put at the forefront. Temporary uses of space, in a reactionary context, are advocated as responses to need but also opportunities for change. They are critical tools to challenge fixed rules, rigid master planning, and long-term strategies. This feeds and relates to the penultimate component of this framing: disorder.

Disorder

Adaptability resonates with disorders and the ability of cities, planning, and urbanism to account for and tackle dysfunctions. Disorder can come in various forms, but all have a strong spatial component. Disorder is linked to the structure of cities and their (in)flexibility. In other words, disorder questions the relevancy and appropriateness of urban visions founded through rigid regulation and control. They are connected to creative urban making and reactions. As argued earlier, the narratives leading to denouncing the inflexible nature of urban forms have been grounded in a critique of built urban models that failed to respond to people's needs. Those models have nevertheless often been supported by policy and policymakers. This was the case with how Le Corbusier's orderly principles have been (badly) reinterpreted and applied in cities leading to urban disasters.[21] This criticism can be translated to how urban thoughts have frequently struggled to engage with gaps, vacancies, and hence disorder, referring to Richard Sennett's concept from the 1970s.[22] The orderly modern city has since then been inappropriate because of its rigidity and overdetermined forms. This predetermination and fixity have had clear consequences because they limit "people's freedom to act, stifle informal social relations and inhibit the city's power to grow."[23] Discussing the case of New York, Pablo Sendra and Richard Sennett demonstrate the impact of strict and limiting land-use visions. They argue that "planners' prescriptive writing was seldom based on inductive experience of the city; their prescriptions were deductively formulated, with the division of labour as a model for the division of space: separate places for shopping, schooling, housing." Such models of urbanism have made a city like New York extremely rigid, which has been accentuated year after year. This situation can unfortunately be applied to most cities globally.

This process of caging, that is, separating different uses, places, and people and rejecting disorder, is inherently linked to the shift of cities toward neoliberal planning and the monopoly of power in urban making by a limited number of stakeholders. In most contemporary developments, this translates into a lack of diverse urban fabrics and environments, with wider

THE FLEXIBLE AND INFLEXIBLE CITY • 33

consequences. Planners' difficulty in providing less rigid environments is a paradox for Sendra and Sennett because planners have far more technological tools at their disposal to make and think about cities than they possessed decades ago. Those tools and resources are not used creatively, however, which results in an "over-determination of both the city's visual forms and its social functions."[24] They continue to argue that "the technologies which make possible experimentation have been subordinated to a regime of power which wants order and control; in the grip of rigid images and precise delineations, the urban imagination lost its vitality."[25] The problem, however, isn't only about power relationships; it feeds into the more complex epistemology of how planning has been elevated as a discipline and profession, and the extent to which it has been channeled through specific ideas and schools of thought.

Urban dysfunctions result from unequal power relationships and hinder creative thinking. This point emphasizes the determination that planners put into elevating order as standard practice and hence in rejecting any forms of disorder stemming from anything unplanned. Such an approach coincides with the tensions between planning for stability, for certainties, and for the long term rather than envisioning change (including disruptive change) and flexibility within simultaneous or alternative time frames. Those tensions are eminently political; they relate to power mechanisms, who is effectively governing, and who is investing in the making of cities and hence financing them.[26] These critical components that affect the (rigid) urban-making process connect directly to the issue of stability in urban development and how it contrasts with a more evolutive and transformative approach to understanding urban spaces. Order in such contexts means stability, whereas any forms of disorder involve instability.

(In)stability

The principle and idea of adaptability rest on an understanding of the urban condition as highly dynamic, subject to multiple temporalities and, to some extent, never fully stable nor finished. It is hybrid, involving constant stability *and* instability. This permanent status of (in)stability implies that the process of urban transformation is a hybrid trajectory of change evolving over time. Again, however, most urban models have been built on an account of stability rather than instability.

Precursory discussions about the unfinished nature of (and in) cities are blended with Lars Lerup's interpretation of uncertainty, which he situates at the interplay between people and the physical setting. In his interactionist enquiry, he connects architecture to the everyday experience. His vision for unbuildable architecture matured through the critical practices of postmodern architects and their interest in differentiation and diversity.[27] The principle of the unbuildable is fundamentally linked to a conception of the built environment (or at least of some of its components) as nonpermanent and hence instable. Scholars in human geography, including Nigel Thrift and Peter Kraftl, have drawn on such analysis to build a multitemporal and dynamic analysis of urban features that embraces ideas of everyday adaptability and flexibility rather than stasis.[28] "Rather than view objects like buildings as fixed, one can interrogate the conjoined technologies (pipes, bricks, cabling), practices (construction, inhabitation, even demolition) and regulations (laws, building codes, health and safety legislations) that ensure they stand up over time. The relations between those many, diverse technologies, practices and regulations change over time—buildings are renovated, bricks weather, occupancy changes, and so on."[29]

The relationship between the unbuildable, the unstable, and time is crucial. Such principles fit into a temporal trajectory, and stability is in essence concerned with changes (a form of instability) because any objects encounter a trajectory of transformation year after year. Accounting for the hybrid nature of adaptability allows us to recognize the nonpermanent and hence (un)stable dynamics of the urban, which, despite being mostly rigid, are effectively concerned with constant, minor, and major changes and disruptions. The use of a trajectorial lens goes beyond the temporal and engages with the materiality of places, along with their stable and unstable character. It can be understood as the path followed by spaces and objects concerned with a process of adaptation through various forces and dynamics in place (actors, planning policies, development strategies, etc.). This path may be linear day after day, but it is fundamentally iterative, adaptable, and dependent on changes and transformations that occur.[30] It is thus highly hybrid. The notion of trajectory is also attuned to the (possible) changes in everyday rhythms, socioeconomic contexts, and material circumstances of any place, and is linked to minor disruptions but also wider crises. It also engages with future perspectives of urban making.

The temporal trajectory contrasts with the principle of stability; it elevates instability as a way to engage with the creative approach of adaptability, the acknowledgment of disorder, and the integration of reactionary mechanisms to address diverse disruptions, needs, and gaps. Bringing the principles of creative urban making, reactions, disorder, and (in)stability together as core and fundamental components of the flexible and adaptable approach to urban spaces and urban making allows the reframing of this approach as a nonpermanent form of urbanism. The latest is intrinsically embedded within the evolution of cities and how they have always adapted.

REVISITING ADAPTABILITY THROUGH THE EVOLUTION OF CITIES OVER TIME

How can the adaptable city be enacted? Adaptability relies on the transformation of the built and the unbuilt. This is why and how it resonates with vacancy or emptiness but also with unlimited and/or limited use. Adaptability can be generated from either a temporary and alternative use of space (a use different from what the space was designed for) or a transformation of use (progressive, difficult, or more complex adaptations). There is an important paradox here. Cities have evolved over decades and centuries through processes of adaptation. Nevertheless, adaptation and flexibility were not thought to be variables of urban making. While urban makers and later urban planners have been regulating cities and their environment, counter-mechanisms, disruptions, and small and major crises led to forced and ad hoc adjustments and changes—hence fostering de facto adaptability. Two linked triggers can be identified here: (1) the empty spaces and the spread of vacancy in the existing built environment, and (2) the rapid need for a change in use, which often emerges from severe crisis or exceptional events.

Urban Adaptability Over Time

Adaptability is anchored in urban temporalities. Cities' temporalities have been covered extensively by historians, including those who have focused on the history of cities across Europe. Notable scholars who have deconstructed the evolution of urban and architectural forms include Leonardo Benevolo, Lewis Mumford, Christopher R. Friedrichs, and Peter Hall, and, in French-speaking countries, Pierre Lavedan, Paul Bairoch, Marc

THE FLEXIBLE AND INFLEXIBLE CITY • 37

Girouard, Marcel Roncayolo, and Michel Ragon, among others. Understanding urban forms, knowledge about how cities have been shaped, and how adaptability has been embraced rest on a deconstruction of how cities have been built and rebuilt over time because of urban, socioeconomic, and/or political changes. Reflecting on the postpandemic city, the Centre for Cities recently argued, "The lessons from the 6,000-year history of the city are clear: they survive, adapting to and overcoming the challenges of disease, conflict and economic change."[31] Cities survive and adapt partly because of their unfinished nature. Such a statement takes us back to the paradoxical question: Why hasn't adaptability been accounted for more extensively as constitutive of the urban condition?[32] As Peter Bishop and Lesley Williams note, "at one time, many European cities were, like the African and Latin American city of today, largely a complex overlay of temporary structures and uses.[33] Civic leaders and patrons established, or facilitated the construction of the essential infrastructure—the religious and administrative buildings, grand avenues and squares. This framework was then filled by everyday uses that developed in natural confusion and diversity at a liveable scale." Until the industrial revolutions, those changes were relatively soft and long, then accelerations occurred in parallel with the increasing rate of urbanization. Over the centuries, cities progressively moved toward formalization and permanence, with the archetypes being the cities of the twentieth and twenty-first centuries.

Such an historical snapshot is important to contextualize urban adaptability as a constituent of the urban condition in European cities. This historical reading starts with the moment medieval cities emerged, with their rigid frameworks for cities' exponential growth.[34] The nonflexible and chaotic nature of the medieval urban area was a vector of disease propagation that perpetuated over the centuries. This fixity prompted discourses about change and hence adaptability, with public health at the forefront.[35] The transition from Roman (antiquity) cities to medieval cities led to a complete structural shift fundamentally linked to new political, religious, and social structures.[36] Over time, this entirely changed the organization and shape of cities while triggering the first major processes of urban adaptability. When not destroyed, theaters, amphitheaters, and thermae were transformed, and, while stripped of their original use, were recycled for other religious or public purposes.[37] Such small-scale adaptations were rare, however, and the urban fabric was totally reconfigured. Overall, only a small proportion of the urban infrastructure was permanent because only essential infrastructure, such as street layouts and substantial administrative and religious buildings, were solid enough structurally to remain over time.[38]

This fact is reinforced with the spread of urbanization from the eleventh century onward. At that time, cities alternatively grew and shrunk within walled boundaries. This had two consequences: (1) it restrained urban sprawl, and (2) it triggered forced adaptability in a context of growth and lack of available spaces within a very dense urban layout. In periods of crisis (wars, famines, pandemics), dereliction and empty spaces spread because buildings were not maintained anymore. In Paris, for example, between 1420 and 1440, one house out of three was abandoned.[39] The question is, How were those empty buildings transformed and reused? In periods of revival and regrowth, the answer was primarily demolition and destruction because of the poor quality of building materials and the ease of the task. This early-stage response resonated with Sennett's contemporary reading of the extreme difficulties in tackling disorder in the urban landscape. Such mechanisms of destructive transformations started to shift with the rise of the classical city in the sixteenth and seventeenth

THE FLEXIBLE AND INFLEXIBLE CITY • 39

centuries.[40] Cities during the classical period were still characterized at first by their condensed forms because they were still walled. Walls inspired adaptability and flexibility in building design because floor elevations, extensions, and use of empty spaces were favored in periods of growth and extensions.[41]

Health and sanitation concerns led to the destruction of walls and the spread of cities away from medieval boundaries. This change constitutes a turning point in how adaptability was translated in urban settings. Cities in Europe started to sprawl with clearer but unwalled boundaries and use between urban and rural areas; the denser areas were concerned with higher-quality urban design, while the outskirts included facilities linked to nonresidential uses (associated with protoindustrialization). During this time, adaptations were linked primarily with socioeconomic and political mechanisms and still remained relatively small scale.[42] Prior to the industrial revolution, most European cities were still characterized by limited and soft adaptations attributed to do-it-yourself (DIY) practices. Adaptability was triggered mainly by individual actions, in reaction to inappropriate use or major cycles of urban and demographic growth and decline. The lack of any planning systems and the relatively small sizes of cities reinforced this. This situation changed dramatically in the eighteenth and nineteenth centuries with the industrialization process. A more planned approach to city development started to emerge alongside accelerated urban growth. More incremental adaptations became less dominant, leaving space for planned transformations for economic, aestheticization, and modernization purposes.

The industrialization process led to intense dislocations and transformations of existing urban forms across European cities.[43] It also fostered a new utilitarian perception of the built environment. Buildings were not perceived anymore as permanent end-products but as entities that were, in essence, provisional and that could be replaced if perceived as not profitable or not fit for purpose.[44] Adapting buildings, as an incremental solution, was not considered an appropriate answer to replacement (i.e., demolition). This continued to prefigure contemporary (neoliberal) thinking about urban development, and the primary focus was given to replacement and demolition rather than adaptation.[45] Industrialization was the catalyst to combined upheavals resonating with how cities were going to transform and adapt. It was associated with significant urban and demographic growth, which exacerbated issues arising from rigid and not fit-for-purpose urban forms. While industrial activities spread progressively in the outskirts of cities, poor workers were cramped into the existing urban areas, leading to poor and unhealthy living conditions.[46] Concerns about hygiene led to new urban visions for neater and more efficient cities. Again, these didn't rely on adaptability but on destruction (with the archetype being the modernist vision of tabula rasa later in the twentieth century) and blank canvas (i.e., building on undeveloped lands in a comprehensive, design-led way). Industrialization also, of course, led to the birth of planning as a discipline and consequently to the inclusion of the principle of permanence rather than agility. Increased regulation of safety, public health, conservation, and protection of green spaces pushed cities further away from adaptation. This process "solidified" the built environment.[47] As a result, it became more difficult for European cities to change. More attention and resources attributed to land-use planning "inevitably [act] as a brake on change and experimentation."[48]

The process of remodeling urban cores for economic and social purposes drove the reconfiguration of cities from the start of the twentieth century onward and was further reinforced after World War II. From that time, the process of urban transformation and any considerations given to (forced) adaptability became significantly more complex. On the one hand, planning systems became more regulated; on the other hand, the nature of public and private relationships were progressively reconfigured. While urban areas grew more complex because of ongoing changes, empty spaces reappeared, allowing for both incremental and larger-scale adaptability.

ADAPTABILITY AND FLEXIBILITY IN THE CONTEMPORARY CONTEXT

The acceleration of changes that characterizes cities in Europe and around the world from the 1960s onward have been part of major structural alterations to national and global economies, from deindustrialization and the rise of service economies to the spread of new urban models founded on experiential and creative narratives. Deindustrialization and the shift to tertiary economies have constituted a crucial turning point in the need to consider adaptability in urban making. Dereliction and vacancy spread quickly in a context of multiple protests (war, economic crisis, counterculture movements, environmental concerns, and rejection of the state). Contemporary adaptability is thus embedded in the significant and rapid transformations that have characterized cities as a result of capitalist development and global urbanism.[49] The way adaptability has been accounted for (initially rejected and progressively accepted) is therefore connected to the perception of risk. Risks here are financial (i.e., profitability) but also political. Adaptability becomes related also to trends, visions, and the rise of branding and city marketing for competition purposes. This relates to the evolutions of cities from places where individuals work and live to places where they live, work, and *play*. The play/leisure nature of cities is much more ephemeral and dynamic, and thus requires agility. The complexification of urban spaces while requiring agility is nevertheless still significantly constrained by rigid layouts, urban forms, and regulations. As a result, important tensions exist between agility and rigidity that go beyond urban thought and are connected to the materialities and practical realities of the urban. This means that adaptability is attached to specific spaces and hence is relatively spatialized at either the building or site level.

Adaptability and forms of temporary urbanisms that have emerged in contemporary cities have progressively evolved. Overall, there are three types of temporary urbanism displaying distinct but not antagonistic ways of envisioning and implementing adaptability.[50]

The first type is a so-called "bottom-up temporary urbanism."[51] It dominated the urban-making process from the 1960s to the 1990s and initially had some connections with the squatting process. Bottom-up temporary urbanism manifests as a reaction to and often denunciation of specific needs not being met. As an initially forced then more negotiated and accepted reuse of space led by individuals or collectives (e.g., artists, activists, community members), it concerns spaces of production and creative expression, or more environmentally and community-driven initiatives in both indoor and outdoor spaces. Inherently rooted in antiestablishment and anarchist movements, it is connected to the narrative about the right of accessing vacant spaces, to adapt and inhabit them, if specific needs are not addressed by relevant governmental bodies.[52] Thus, it relates intrinsically to the squatting movement. Such dynamics characterized London in the 1970s, when squats spread in the city as a way to denounce housing struggles.[53] In this case, the Greater London Council facilitated the transformation of squats into housing co-ops. This secured the tenancy of many of the people squatting but

THE FLEXIBLE AND INFLEXIBLE CITY • 43

also neutralized squatting to a greater extent in the city and the country.[54] In France, housing-led squats appeared as early as the end of the nineteenth century and then spread and diversified through counterculture movements that emerged across Europe.[55] Artists became squatters and in the 1970s, when several emblematic artistic squats emerged: the Albany Empire in Londres (1968), Melkweg in Amsterdam (1970), Die Fabrik in Hamburg (1971), and Les Halles de Schaerbeek in Brussels (1973). Beyond the cultural and artistic discourses they displayed, these squats embraced a narrative around revendication and community empowerment along with a vivid criticism of an increasingly dominant neoliberal agenda driven by globalization. Some were constructed on strong communitarian purposes embedded within a singular location and style of living. This was the case in Copenhagen with Cristiana, in Berlin with the various squats located in the Kreuzberg neighborhood but also at the Rote Fabrik in Zurich (figure 2.1).

Across Europe, the occupations of empty spaces spread further in the 1980s. Driven by ambitious artistic, cultural, and creative goals, squatters' demands denounce the lack of spaces for nontraditional cultural expressions (i.e., culture that cannot be produced in museums or theaters). Their messages and increased visibility attracted the attention of policymakers inclined to widen the scope of cultural policies to various forms of cultural expressions.[56] The precursory transformations of Soho in New York, Shoreditch in London, and Kreuzberg in Berlin influence this acceptance and illustrate how artists and alternative cultural practices can deeply transform (and gentrify) neighborhoods. This led to a change of perception and effectively to the rise of "bottom-up temporary urbanism." While radical squats are transformed into more negotiated (legal) occupations, bottom-up temporary urbanisms emerged as micro-scale solutions for local and community

FIGURE 2.1 The Rote Fabrik Cultural Centre in Zurich, which opened on October 25, 1980.

Source: Lauren Andres.

development, first in Germany and then across Europe (i.e., in cities that witnessed the transformative impact of alternative cultural and artistic places). This shift also concerns, at the same time, the spread of tactical urbanism in the United States.[57]

Bottom-up temporary urbanisms become pacified temporary occupations that are not forced and imposed (i.e. squats) but agreed to and negotiated with key decision makers (including the property owner).[58] As a form of community-led experimentation, they respond to specific community everyday needs. By the end of the twentieth century, Berlin had elevated itself as the most proactive and open-minded city in favoring bottom-up temporary urbanism on its numerous vacant spaces.[59] "Skate parks in abandoned industrial estates, ponies grazing alongside the Berlin Wall, flea markets in disused warehouses, music and fashion in hard to let stores and climbing walls in empty buildings lots—scarcely a city in Europe has been so radically characterized by temporary use projects as has Berlin."[60] As a result, bottom-up temporary urbanism sits outside the formal policy and planning process as a solution in the context of vacancy where no other options are offered. Such forms of adaptable use of space are diverse and can include temporary shops (sometimes called pop-up shops), temporary community or office spaces, and temporary playgrounds, gardens or beaches (figure 2.2). They all share outside-the-box thinking that challenges formal planning arrangements in contexts of transition.[61]

FIGURE 2.2 Berlin and its temporary beaches.

Source: Lauren Andres.

Radical temporary occupations (similar to squats) did not fully disappear. Those forced adaptations of space, although rare, are labeled "autonomous urbanism," and the "insurgent city" continues to be driven by a strong anarchist discourse.[62] Those spaces are "where people desire to constitute non-capitalist, egalitarian, and solidaristic forms of political, social, and economic organization through a combination of resistance and creation."[63] Peter Bishop and Lesley Williams refer here to Hakim Bey's essay on temporary autonomous zones (TAZs) that was widely seen as one of the countercultural bibles.[64] His ideas were picked up by several writers on temporary urbanisms—typically Urban Unlimited.[65] Their so-called freezones "have acted as places in which dissenters and free-thinkers have found protection and living space," hence informing bottom-up temporary urbanism in some ways.

Bottom-up forms of temporary urbanisms dominant at the start of the 1960s have progressively shrunk down and were replaced by top-down and more hybrid forms from the end of the 2000s. This evolution occurred primarily in Europe, the United Kingdom, and North America. In other less developed contexts, bottom-up temporary urbanisms directly resonate with informality and ways to tackle precarity. "Normal practices of renting are based on contracts and agreements that may be too rigid for a variety of experimental or casual practices. This is why informal use of space, such as the occupation of parts of streets by street traders, is a temporary use of space on a highly precarious basis."[66]

The second form of temporary urbanism, top-down temporary urbanism, is the result of the appreciation by those holding power of the value of adaptability in accompanying transformations. It reflects the latest trends in neoliberal planning and development supported by recent changes in the global economy, alongside new technologies, flexible working practices, and

FIGURE 2.3 Pop Brixton in London, a temporary retail, leisure, and community project constructed from shipping containers and developed in partnership between Lambeth Council and the private company MakeShift. Pop Brixton opened in 2015 on disused land awaiting redevelopment.

Source: Lauren Andres.

the advent of knowledge economies.[67] In this case, temporary urbanism is planned and constructed by those who hold the power in decision making (i.e., landowners, developers, local authorities) as in the case of Pop Brixton, in London (figure 2.3).

Temporary initiatives are not merely seen as informal responses to urban challenges; they form part of more formal reimagining of cities and neighborhoods, within wider strategies and visions of urban transformations.[68] This significant shift in how adaptability is approached and valued connects directly with how cities are viewed as places of buzz and encounter given the density of flows (people working, living, visiting), interactions, and activities that characterize them; this resonates with the rise of the so-called experience economies and the notion of the creative city.[69] More important, it is also placed in the context of shrinking resources for local authorities and municipalities where the capacity to act is limited. Favoring temporary, community-led uses through small funding schemes is seen as an acceptable and attractive solution.[70] Ali Madanipour summarizes this phenomenon accurately: "The temporary use of space takes place in this context of a mismatch between supply and demand and a structural crisis of the economic development model. The recent global crisis [the Great Recession starting in 2008] and longer-term structural changes in urban societies have created spatial, temporal and institutional gaps, which are sometimes filled by temporary interventions, in search of interim solutions until the crisis is over."[71]

The third type of temporary urbanism is a combination of both bottom-up and top-down mechanisms; it can be labeled hybrid temporary urbanisms where the boundaries between the top-down and bottom-up are blurred.[72] A significant amount of small-scale temporary projects is based on processes of bricolage and initial improvisation among key stakeholders, both those holding decision-making power and those able to envision and deliver such initiatives. From improvised practices, temporary initiatives then start to structure themselves, with the support of those holding power (landowner and/or local authorities). Hybrid temporary urbanism is about local empowerment and rapid transformations; it is a form of adaptability in the process of making spaces viable and livable. It also displays a relatively immediate win-win situation for all in situations where there are very limited possible downsides identified (typically conflicts and strong oppositions). The improvisation

FIGURE 2.4 Hybrid temporary transformations of streets during the pandemic in Upper Manhattan, New York City.

Source: Lauren Andres.

component that characterizes this type of temporary urbanism is particularly remarkable in the context of significant upheaval and crisis, for example, the COVID-19 pandemic which led to hybrid temporary transformations of streets as in New York City (figure 2.4). While hybrid temporary urbanism needs to be embedded within a "crisis" context, it also displays the latest and more recent trend reflecting how adaptability is commonly embedded in urban thought, practice, and policy and where agility becomes a way to drive change forward.

While they are distinct in how they emerge and when, all three types of temporary urbanisms refer to temporal and multilayered discontinuities characterizing cities. They are "better than nothing solutions" but also represent "citizen-led visions."[73] Whatever the scale of those interventions, individuals and communities are the main drivers and targets.

CONCLUSION

Reflecting on the evolution of temporary urbanisms and the narrative of the adaptable city, attention needs to be given to various analytical lenses that will be decrypted and discussed further in the following chapters.

The progressive adoption of temporary and adaptable urbanisms as forms of urban making results from a new grammar and narrative of how changes can be activated. Such a new grammar of approaching urban development has been progressive and was led initially by a couple of experiments that gathered significant attention and visibility. This process directly connects with alternative narratives about cultural and artistic practices, community engagement, and urban development and is built on the principle of offering new opportunities for citizens to be urban makers. It connects ultimately with neoliberal and entrepreneurial planning interpretations of urban development, hence to city branding and city marketing strategies. Mara Ferreri summarizes this well when she argues that temporary urbanism practices have shifted "from marginal, adhoc and experimental practices still shrouded in imaginaries of illicit urban countercultures to their celebration and appropriation by urban policymakers and planners at a time characterised by reduced public resources and regulatory powers."[74]

There is also a clear relationship between adaptable and temporary practices constructed as responses to gaps, needs, crises, and overall needs for everyday coping and survival. This connects to forms of informality and insurgent practices that are visible in the less developed urban contexts but can also be found in developed cities. While such processes have been mainly examined separately, it is crucial to connect them in a wider deconstruction of adaptable urban making, which means examining the role of adaptability for urban dwellers who rely on adaptations and improvisations daily for survival and resilience.

What is at play here is how the spread and internationalization of temporary and adaptable practices and policies became progressively recognized for their role in the urban-making process from design, planning, and also political perspectives. This raises significant questions about situating the conceptual and theoretical underpinnings behind such recognition and, as a result, unwraps the complexity and diversity of temporary and adaptable practices. Those interrogations will continue in the forthcoming chapters.

3

ADAPTABILITY, ACTIVATION, AND WEAK PLANNING

Temporary urbanism, in all forms, and the way it has been constructed and elevated in the past ten to fifteen years as a standard and popular practice have very explicitly been dissociated from forced occupations (e.g., squatting). This disconnection materialized with adaptability being associated with processes of negotiated activation. Over the years, temporary and adaptable strategies have then diversified with top-down and hybrid forms increasingly spreading alongside community-led, bottom-up strategies. All have steadily increased in number from the end of the 1990s to 2008 and further accelerated with the COVID-19 pandemic, embracing adaptability even further. This chapter explores the dynamics of the adaptable city through two core concepts: activation and weak planning. Activation relates to the physical activation of spaces, at different scales, as an activation of ideas and visions (doing things differently and creatively), and as an activation of human resources and networks. Weak planning is understood as the incubator for temporary and adaptable urbanism. It relates to a context where mainstream development isn't happening because of financial, economic, planning, and political deadlocks; temporary urbanism emerges as an easy and cheap fix, requiring limited land-use management tools and regulations. It includes a period of waiting, of uncertainties, pushing the need to think about and use spaces in an alternative way.[1]

This chapter builds on the first major temporary projects that initially occurred in European and North American cities. It examines how these initiatives have been implemented incrementally and further developed as responses to major economic downturns prompting uncertainties and the need for alternative solutions. Temporary urbanism has been used progressively to accompany larger-scale (mostly) regeneration projects that will take years to be delivered. The combination of uncertainties and duration (expressed here in processes of waiting) is at the core of the idea and dynamics of activation. Such processes of activation sit within contexts of weak planning and connect to the rhythms of the production of space; they resonate with modes of producing and governing cities and hence include power struggles and strategic relationships that have to be acknowledged and unwrapped.

TIME, RHYTHMS, AND THE PRODUCTION OF ADAPTABLE AND TEMPORARY CITIES

The process of adaptability and temporariness is founded upon a reading of time as it relates to a trajectory but also to disorder, reaction, (in)stability, and creative urban making, which all share the commonalities of being specific moments in time. The process is highly grounded within the idea of offering an alternative (here linked to the process of activation described hereafter). There are important theoretical considerations to account for here. This involves situating the temporary and adaptable process of urban making in critical urban theories. A substantial number of urban theorists, from Michel Foucault, Gilles Deleuze, Yi Fu Tuan, and Edward Relph to Michel de Certeau and Henri Lefebvre, have been mobilized by scholars over the years (typically Ali Madanipour, Gordon Douglas, Quentin Stevens, Mara Ferreri, Panu Lehtovuori, and Sampo Ruoppila) to examine phenomena attributed to adaptability and temporary urbanism. Lefebvre in particular has inspired many working in the field. His contribution to the understanding of the production of the city, everyday practices, and the rights of citizens to intervene in urban making within so-called differential spaces is without precedent. This resonates more widely with more contemporary social and policy agency theories, typically the work of David Harvey, Peter Marcuse, and Neil Brenner. Temporary uses have been linked to the ability of giving power to citizens to promote counterprojects and ideas founded upon alternative urban futures narratives.[2] They have also been associated with contemporary paradigms linked to sustainability, democracy, equity, and social justice. Through Lefebvre's rhythmanalysis, the principles of adaptability and temporariness can be theoretically examined. For Lefebvre, as noted by Eduardo Mendieta, the "production of space" should never be dissociated from an analysis of the production of time, of temporalities that condition the experience of space.[3] Those are the moments to which I alluded, part of the trajectorial nature of adaptability.

Digging into this idea of time and duration is fundamental when trying to understand what constitutes the ramifications of the permanent and adaptable city. Madanipour, in his reading of cities through time, situated "temporary urbanism" and the forms of experimentation associated with it within the two concepts of Chronos and Kairos.[4] Informed by Foucault's work, he saw temporary urbanism as being embraced within a period of epistemic ruptures. "The distinction between Chronos and Kairos is

ADAPTABILITY, ACTIVATION, AND WEAK PLANNING • 55

between quantitative and qualitative time . . . While Chronos is slow and long-term temporality, Kairos is the 'opening of a discontinuity in a continuum.'"[5] Kairos thus represents "a particular and exceptional moment, a rupture or a turning point, either in the sense of the right or the favorable moment, to speak or to act, or with reference to a particularly decisive, fateful or dangerous situation."[6] History is then interpreted as a series of ruptures and decision moments rather than a continuous process of change.

Madanipour's interpretation of Kairos resonates immediately with the principle of adaptability and flexibility, and, more important, with the idea that such processes reflect moments of change, where space becomes affected by various rhythms, specifically everyday rhythms. This takes us back to the rhythmanalysis and its importance for reading adaptability. "The everyday is at the same time the space, the theatre, and the stake of a conflict between remarkable, indestructible rhythms and the processes opposed by the socioeconomic organization of production, consumption, movement and housing."[7]

It is, of course, within a critical understanding of cities and the nature of society itself that Lefebvre reconceptualized his analysis of urban dynamics with the everyday production of the city. Both are, for him, an epistemological and political precondition to understanding the nature of society. While it was too early for Lefebvre in the 1960s and 1970s to pick up temporary urban manifestations in their current contemporary forms (beyond more radical events marking the 1968 period of civil unrest and protests in France), his work engaged with contradicting traditional urban discourse and practice while putting equal significance on both people and place.[8] Temporary uses and the linked process of adaptability converge with other forms of appropriation *and* production of space. There is indeed a strong component about reclaiming the city from the state and from capitalism, which, of course, constitutes the precursory understanding of how and why temporary uses and occupations have spread in cities; this also allows the explanation of that bottom-up uses have been challenged and feared for years because of their narrative constructed on demand and protest, and a claim of the right to take possession of a vacant space.[9]

It is widely accepted that "temporary uses engage in conscious production of space, involving practices, conceptualisations and experiences" and enable "communal or group-based creation of value."[10] Value creation is strongly linked to activation.[11] These processes of value creation are intrinsically associated with citizens' rights to produce the city, even if those rights are exercised within highly political and conflictual contexts.[12] The process of value creation is also connected to time and the everyday, and time is a key component of the rhythmanalysis approach: "Time can be divided into usage and exchange. It has a use-value and an exchange-value; it is both lived and exchanged."[13] This resonates fundamentally with the understanding of the adaptable and temporary city, where the principles of adaptability rest upon diverse rhythmic use and exchange occurring in urban spaces. Temporary uses showcasing adaptable ways of using or reusing space differently are, in essence, an acknowledgment of the obsolescence of single-use space; this fits within wider criticism of defining the city and whether the city is obsolete or needs to be reinvented.[14] Following this line of thought, Lehtovuori and Ruoppila have argued that a reinvention of the city can occur thanks to temporary uses because they constitute an "important arena of such fundamental renewal and reinvention."[15] This is an important statement. While they engage with Lefebvre's initial right to the city, they also embrace David Harvey's view that it is more than just "a right of an individual or a group to access the

ADAPTABILITY, ACTIVATION, AND WEAK PLANNING • 57

resources that the city embodies."[16] Temporary initiatives "often become actively political spaces that show new ways to fill the 'empty signifier' of the right to the city."[17] With this in mind, any understanding of the adaptable city includes an examination of temporary uses but goes beyond it; it involves examining the process of adaptability through an epistemological interrogation of what is really "urbanism" and what and who it is for.

For Douglas, adaptability in the form of do-it-yourself (DIY) urbanism is an expression of how "relatively intangible factors such as economic development pressures, design cultures, policy ideologies, and the machinations of capital are experienced and understood in physical space and everyday life."[18] For him, Lefebvre's everyday analysis features in individuals' experience and responses toward "the conditions of uneven investment." He pursues this idea by hypothesizing that "DYI urban interventions were possibly examples of such Lefebvrian moments of critical awareness and transformative potential." Here, it is Lefebvre's tiny moments of subjective consciousness, what he called "partial totalities," like love, play, struggle, and creative activity, that provide opportunities for consciousness and agency. Such moments are part of everyday dynamics and rhythms, which take us back to Madanipour's definition of temporary urbanism as something that "may be interpreted as emphasizing Kairos rather than Chronos, formed of moments and ruptures rather than continuities and certainties."

For Lefebvre, "everywhere there is interaction between a place, a time and an expenditure of energy, there is rhythm . . . energy animates, reconnects, renders time and space conflictual."[19] Rhythmanalysis here, as a way to theorize adaptability and the process of temporariness and nonpermanence, goes much beyond duration in its connections to moments as episodes of crisis, rupture, or change. Rhythmanalysis is concerned with the process of urban making and particularly how the everyday connects and conflicts with the other temporal mechanisms affecting urban spaces.[20] The concepts of vacancy and obsolescence used by Lehtovuori and Ruoppila are important here.[21] They resonate with the impermanent nature of the process of adaptability. Impermanence is not only the trigger that attracts alternative uses; it also affects the social and spatial environment hosting temporary and adaptable initiatives.[22] Impermanence, while a trigger, is also a rupture to a "normal functioning." This dialectic relationship between trigger (alternative) and rupture (difference) converge with how Lefebvre reads rhythms in the cities. As he notes, "everyday life is traversed by great rhythms that are both cosmic and vital, such as the days and nights or the months and seasons. As a result, the everyday revolved around a conflictual unity between these biological rhythms and the repetitive process associated with homogenous time."[23]

Rhythms are connected to repetitions, which are recurring dynamics. Lefebvre asserts that there is "no rhythm without repetition in both space and time. These repetitions occur through 'returns' (reprises), that is, through measure."[24] From the point of view of the adaptable and temporary city, it is a matter of linking the rhythms of the quotidian, of the ordinary (playing, working, eating, gardening, etc.) to the needs of the quotidian, and seeing in the process of adaptability a way to fill gaps with regard to everyday needs. This is typical and can be observed in most types of (primarily bottom-up) temporary urbanisms, from pop-up uses, parklets, small parks, meanwhile uses, or other forms of DIY urbanism.[25] There is a real hybridity in the nature of rhythms that "fluctuate[s] between the cyclical, in which social organization manifests itself, and the linearity of the daily, which is the space of the quotidian grind."[26]

Two types of rhythms can be identified when applied to the adaptable and temporary city. First, the rhythms of life, which are those belonging to urban citizens but are often managed or controlled by the planning and policymaking process. City life is produced through crossings and tensions between the official and unofficial, the formal and informal; this is executed at different scales and through different temporal and organizational logics.[27] These are also informed by external factors and events (technological; environmental; socioeconomic; and, more recently, epidemiologic). For Lefebvre and Catherine Régulier, "there is a bitter and obscure struggle that involves time and the usage of time. The so-called natural rhythms are profoundly modified by technological and socioeconomic reasons, among others."[28]

Second, the rhythms of change (novelty) correlate with Lefebvre's view that "there is always something new that introduces itself into the repetitive."[29] Adaptability enables experience and creates opportunities for temporal experimentations, which themselves have their own rhythms within other cities' rhythms. These resonate with creativity and testing. "The repetitive movement associated with linear time is wearying, tiresome and tedious, while the movement of cycles has the allure of both an advent and an event. Although its beginning is just a recommencement, it has the freshness of a discovery or an invention."[30] Novelty is then linked to various dynamics of transformation: dynamics of acceptance, support, then rejection and conflicts within larger processes of urban transformation.[31] Adaptability and temporary urbanisms then take various forms, including temporary events in specific seasons (urban beaches during the summer), or they are linked to specific times (outdoor dining during the pandemic). Some, while starting as temporary, are sustained for longer periods and can even become permanent, in such cases participating in the character of a place and making it different.[32] When this occurs, it reflects an awareness of the importance of alternative rhythms that emerge as a result of "disorderliness" but also as a result of activation.[33]

ACTIVATION, ADAPTABILITY, AND RHYTHMS

Activation is the visible and positive narrative that emerged out of the genesis of new and nonpermanent uses. It is part of a process of unlocking change and new forms of valorization. Activation has progressively been raised as the key word used to defend any temporary urbanism ideas and attempts. It was the primary narrative for mobilizing temporary projects in the London 2012 Olympics Legacy strategy; meanwhile uses then spread in the city, strengthening value extraction processes for landowners and developers while matching experiential and branding purposes.[34] (I will develop this further in chapter 5.) Activation means that a building or an urban feature is not made for a single use and that vacancy can be tackled through alternative purposes developed on unfit-for-purpose spaces. Activation is about unlocking change with a view of promoting another, possibly better future. There is a strong experimentation and testing element that is part of this process; there is also an assumption that the process of transformation has snowball effects. This resonates greatly with the components of adaptability, in other words, creativity, reaction, disorder, and (in)stability. Activation is directed toward local communities, particularly those affected by declining and/ or unfit-for-purpose urban environments. It also targets those who may be attracted to live, work, and/or set up their business there in the future as a way to attract them to a place prior to its

FIGURE 3.1 La Friche de la Belle Mai in Marseille, a former tobacco factory transformed into an alternative cultural center.

Source: Lauren Andres.

final planned transformation. While activation has progressively shifted toward a more capitalist and neoliberal use of temporary urbanism, it is useful to point out the way it was expressed in some of the precursory leading examples. The example of the cultural center La Friche de la Belle de Mai (figure 3.1) is highly illuminating.

> The deal—that we made with the land and plant owner—was the following. We had a discussion with Mr M. who was responsible for the company assets and we developed the argument that such an agreement based on us using their site would help them handle and manage the problem linked to the transformation of the site.

62 • ADAPTABILITY, ACTIVATION, AND WEAK PLANNING

> We told them: Your image is disastrous—you have closed the factory and 700 workers are unemployed—so let us help you and the City to find a way to revive the site.[35]

This quote is from an interview conducted with one of the instigators of this project located in Marseille, France. La Friche is one or maybe the most well-known example in France of an initially temporary transformation of a vacant and derelict industrial brownfield into a complex and high-profile alternative cultural project that was eventually included in the long-term regeneration strategy of the city. I will explore its genesis and nature later in this chapter, but first there are several important components to highlight that are connected directly with the conceptualization and process of activation. There is a financial narrative, linked to the management (of an empty site) along with a social purpose constructed on the acknowledgment that people and place matter; there is also a clear negotiated partnership between different groups of actors playing different roles in the urban-making process. All those components constitute the activation process and how it has been used in early examples of transformation at the end of the 1990s until the end of the 2000s. This can be illustrated by another quote taken from an English planner reflecting on the evolution of local authorities' perception toward temporariness and activation in times of recession.

> I certainly noticed the change in tone and emphasis happening around 2008 when there was the crash, when all the developers were talking about "meanwhile uses" and I think it was because a lot of them had these big sites, had got planning permission but were suddenly facing the reality that they weren't going to be able to develop them straight away, so developers were becoming interested with what they can do with their sites in the meantime.

> Local authorities were also becoming interested in what was happening and the fact that sites were sitting there empty, when pressure was growing on houses and public services.[36]

Here is the idea of waiting and transition that resonates with the trajectorial activation process. It clearly displays how the temporary and adaptative narrative spread in Europe and North America in a context where local authorities were lacking "resources, power and control to implement formal masterplans" and as a result started "to experiment with looser planning visions and design frameworks, linked to phased packages of small, often temporary initiatives, designed to unlock the potential of sites."[37]

The process of activation is thus part of adaptable urban making and is immersed within a rhythmic analysis of the city. Starting with the standard definition of the term, "activation" refers to a process of making something active or operative. The underpinnings are transformational dynamics and the goal of generating new everyday rhythms in spaces that have lost their purposes and are not creating or extracting value. There is an assumption that activation can occur everywhere—in existing buildings and in public spaces; this goes beyond the perception that, "as public space is the most flexible space of a city, it is often, but not the only, the place in which this multiplicity [of uses] is made possible."[38]

Applied to urban settings, activation has a certain set of characteristics. It relates to a *physical activation* of a space (built or unbuilt) that changes the status and use of that space. This has some repercussions at various scales. The physical dimension connects to the idea of "spatial expansion" developed by Madanipour but also replacement.[39] Activation through new uses provides an opportunity for novelty as new uses spread into other (unusual) settings not designed for that purpose. "Temporary use of space may be seen a process of expanding space on a contingent basis, a process of creating a degree of flexibility in times of change."[40] Activation also has a social purpose when triggered by incremental and experimental projects. *Social activation* involves alternative urban players (citizens, community groups, artists) who have been given the responsibility for driving temporary projects. This resonates strongly with Douglas's DIY urbanism, which is connected with the principle of "participatory citizenship" but also with other work led by scholars on temporary uses who saw it as a new route for community participation at the neighborhood level.[41] Social activation is strongly embedded in the principle that it occurs through the novelty of the experimentation process related to trajectorial discontinuities, disorder, and creativity. Whatever the setting (either bottom up or top down), those who often set up, direct, or manage temporary uses have commonly not been "traditional urban makers." (I will discuss in chapter 7 the strong correlation between skills and knowledge and the professionalization of temporary and adaptable urbanism.)

Activation implies an *asset-based activation*: financial considerations along with land and real estate economics are always part of transformational dynamics. This type of consideration occurs in two ways. It can be a better than nothing consideration (temporary use is better than full vacancy). It can also be recognized that activation will affect land values and allow land either to sell at a decent market price or to generate more profit over the medium- and longer-term thanks to new flows of activities. Such strategic thinking was flagged in the early work on temporary uses in Berlin. "Interim use is always seen as a provisional measure rather than as a permanent solution, although it can be a way of demonstrating a concept's success in order to convince an investor that the chosen use could also provide a permanent solution."[42] The history and memory of a place is important because they can influence how users transform it, drawing on its atmosphere and remaining physical resources.[43] Asset-based activation is founded on implicit economic goals including, as John Henneberry highlighted, allowing cheap start-ups, showcasing creative talent, encouraging entrepreneurship, and contributing to economic development.[44] It also encompasses financial purposes, which typically translate into a reduction of the costs of vacancy (particularly empty property rates), the improvement of the physical condition of buildings and their security, or avoiding decay and vandalism.[45]

These different types of activation are linked to the everyday rhythms inherent in places *en devenir*; they are also connected to more important ruptures that characterize cities (typically deindustralization and urban shrinkage, decline of high streets and central business districts, the rise of e-commerce, etc.). Adaptability constitutes a response to the goals of triggering change and producing new alternative rhythms. It depends on a value-creation process. Processes of value creation relate to the trajectories (or paths) of change and their temporalities. "Activation processes through temporary urbanisms are localised and can be embedded—or not—within other paths of change. As such, they may occur irrespective of other forms of path dependency, in other words independently, or being connected to other paths of creation."[46] Path creation resonates here with value creation (both use value and exchange value) in the context of the production of space; again, it acknowledges the relationship between time and place within distinct disjointed or linked rhythms. There is significant diversity, however, in the material and immaterial changes and forms of activation and adaptability that each place and its surrounding environment can undergo, particularly regarding land value capture, among other factors.[47]

Activation constitutes a mechanism of "unlocking" through physical, social, and asset-based transformations that embrace different rhythms. The unlocking leads to a path of transformation stressing the process and dynamics behind changes, even if such changes are just ephemeral moments with no sustained impact or benefits. The result can be "alternative uses with different outcomes."[48] These outcomes testify to the diversity of adaptable and temporary practices that can be driven from the bottom up by citizens embracing their rights to unlock alternative outcomes to meet their needs and visions, or they can be driven in a more top-down process, "where the path creation process nurtures a wider path creation process built upon large-scale regeneration and land value capture."[49]

Path creation and activation are linked to adaptation and improvisation, also known as bricolage.[50] Bricolage leads to alternative solutions based on multiple actors who get together to "enable the alignment of heterogeneous actors, institutions and networks."[51] Bricolage is a subset of adaptability and reflects how actors engage in transforming a site in a nonpermanent and hence flexible way. Adaptability is the counternarrative to the "planned and the finished." It implies that hybrid, unusual, and alternative processes may occur, in contrast to what was envisioned and planned. The principle of bricolage is crucial in all forms of adaptability and enforces the novelty of temporary rhythms and their atypical roles in the production of the city. They involve less rigidity in how regulations are applied (which was true during the COVID-19 pandemic, as I will discuss in chapter 6). The path of change becomes immersed in a juxtaposition of bricolage and structure, through negotiation, consensus, and conflicts where agents of change play a key role.[52] The context, particularly weak planning, is crucial for this. Before discussing this further, I want to illustrate the process of activation a bit more through the example of La Friche de la Belle de Mai.

La Friche de la Belle de Mai is located in Marseille, the second largest city in France. From 1991, it was progressively elevated as one of the leading examples of the New Art Territories (in French, *Nouveaux territoires de l'art* [NTA]). The NTA label was newly used in the 2000s to identify the new spaces of artistic creation, the latest forms of cultural expression that marked the twentieth century. It was commissioned and launched by the French Ministry of Culture. La Friche was also included in a very large-scale regeneration program, Euroméditerranée, aiming to shift the shrinking city's economy and image away from its industrial character and transition it to service and experiential economies. The way activation occurred—but on very limited occasions at that time—was in line with how landowners used artistic projects to trigger value creation. As Juliette Pinard noted, in the 1980s in Paris, the *Société nationale des chemins de fer français* (SNCF), France's national, state-owned railway company, which owns a very substantial amount of land and number of buildings in the country, had already adopted this precursory strategy when it agreed to rent a former cold storage unit to artists known as the *Frigos*.[53] In this case, the SNCF adopted a "pragmatic wish to receive a rent, even a low one, for premises whose configuration is sometimes no longer adapted to regular rental. Through these legal temporary occupations, the owner's intention has also been to control the use of its buildings, for example, to avoid squatting."[54] This was the same approach used in Marseille. La Friche de la Belle is a perfect example of how rhythms of life and rhythms of change can combine, at different scales, leading to multi-scalar uses and activities that triggered processes of activation and valorization.

The occupation of the former tobacco factory occurred in a context of crisis for both the city and the neighborhood of the Belle de Mai, both of which suffered from severe socioeconomic decline and impoverishment because of the closure of most of

68 • ADAPTABILITY, ACTIVATION, AND WEAK PLANNING

the local industries from the 1950s.[55] The factory itself closed in 1990 and left many workers unemployed. The real estate market was on pause and was not able to deal with the oversupply of available spaces. "We could not see any cranes at that time, none. No one wanted to invest in the city."[56] This led to the multiplication of brownfield lands, which were estimated at around 600 hectares at the time.[57] The principle of activation was shaped through the vision developed by the deputy mayor in charge of cultural policies at the time, who decided to support the development of temporary uses on the city's numerous brownfields. Activation was here supposed to be achieved through "nomadism," with cultural projects being able to move from one space to another based on projects and needs.[58] His view was that, through those occupations, the impacts of the combined economic, social, and demographic crisis could be minimized.[59] To implement his vision, he contacted a local theater director who had developed a project on a derelict flour mill in the north of Marseille and then settled in the former tobacco factory in 1991. Activation initially materialized in securing the participation of the owner, the Société d'exploitation industrielle des tabacs et des allumettes (SEITA), who agreed to the temporary lease because it was a cheap way to secure the site and speculate about its possible purchase by the municipality.[60] The process of activation occurred progressively and at different scales. Physical activation started by progressively activating the three separate units of the factory. While the project initially started in unit 1, it then settled permanently in unit 3 (figure 3.2).

Physical and social activation was delivered through the successful development of a cultural project structured around the organization *Système friche théâtre* (SFT). SFT designed a strategy of cultural development based on multilevel processes of activation to anchor their project and hence sustain their presence

FIGURE 3.2 Unit 3, where La Friche de la Belle de Mai is located in Marseilles.

Source: Lauren Andres.

in the building. Part of the strategy was to build on the political vision of activation and argue that, through their own project, they could promote an alternative economic cultural development; the latest was based on the potential of cultural uses and activities to foster local economic development.[61] Activation went in hand with the recognition of La Friche as a leading cultural entity for the city, which not only should be financially and politically supported and sustained but also included within the large-scale regeneration scheme, Euroméditerranée,[62] launched in 1995. This is how the asset-based activation happened. For the owner, this process finally led to the former plant being purchased by the city. For the municipality, site-based activation

FIGURE 3.3 La Friche de la Belle de Mai, a cultural and community hub in Marseilles.

Source: Lauren Andres.

was transferred at city level. They used La Friche (figure 3.3) as their flagship project for promoting culture-led regeneration and investment in the cultural and creative industries sector. Unit 1 was transformed into a hub for activities dedicated to heritage preservation, while Unit 2 was redeveloped as a new hub for creative firms with a focus on the audiovisual, cinematographic, and video game sectors.

Activation mostly skipped the neighborhood per se and didn't lead to gentrification. Path dependency was key here, along with how use and exchange value were mobilized. The Belle de Mai district followed this trajectory of decline, rising unemployment, and increasing impoverishment. Many residents left to find jobs elsewhere and were replaced by a more vulnerable community of migrants who found the neighborhood affordable because of its poor-quality housing. The Belle de Mai district was not included within the perimeter of Euroméditerranée, and it was also excluded for over fifteen years from other city-led urban renewal programs. As a result, the neighborhood was split in two, with the former tobacco factory, once it was activated, seen as a highly valuable asset while the district was considered of much lower interest and value for both public and private actors.

From the lens of activation processes, La Friche de la Belle de Mai shows how different forms of activation occur at various scales, pushed by adaptability, as a vision, a principle, and a practice, but with various degrees of impact. Such processes of activation reflect how creativity, reaction, disorder, and (in) stability can generate positive transformations. Accounting for a variety of rhythms and hence temporalities is part of the narrative of activation; so is how the cultural project is shaped and implemented at site level with a focus on temporariness within permanence. A meaningful agility is thus made possible by relatively flexible regulations in a context of transition that, in turn, is inherent to the context of weak planning, to which I now turn.

WEAK PLANNING AS THE
SETTING FOR ACTIVATION

The concept of weak planning was initially used by Urban Catalyst, with a focus on Germany and Berlin and with the view of positioning temporary uses as core planning practices to deal with vacancy and the need to revisit traditional planning practices.[63] These were seen as not fit for purpose and unable to cope with disruptions and disorders. Weak planning is grounded in the transitory nature of temporary and adaptable urbanism and is tied to waiting, uncertainties, and a lack of resources and vision about a future development. Alternatives are thus sought to tackle dereliction and situations of transition, which was the case in Marseille, as previously discussed. Weak planning can help in periods of deep uncertainties and crisis where transitory solutions are sought. It is a stage in the planning and development process where rigid regulations are put aside to allow adaptable practices, uses and thinking.

Weak planning is part of the wider disruptions affecting cities and urban economies from "the relocation of activities, the cyclical nature of capitalism and its recurring crises of overproduction, made more frequent and magnified by globalisation. Changes in technology and the global division of labor have exposed local development processes to the wild moods of a blind force, creating long-term vulnerability and emptiness."[64] To this, we can add supplementary social and community movements pushing for social and environmental changes along with unprecedented shocks. Weak planning also has a more micro application. It is a stage in the development process where a space is taken out of a rigid and regulated planning process to allow adaptable practices, uses, and thinking. For Henri Lefebvre, there is a strong correlation between weak planning, the production of the city, its rhythms, and so-called differential spaces. Such spaces demonstrate a nonorderly vision of the city and a claimed right for city users to be different.[65] Their differential nature and hence differential everyday rhythms resonate with the concepts of spontaneity, difference, and disorder.[66] They emerge in contexts of weak planning.

Weak planning is in line with how some scholars have approached temporary urbanism as low-cost, informal urban interventions responding to community needs and addressing the issues of an inappropriate planning system.[67] In the early years of temporary urbanism (in other words, when bottom-up

ADAPTABILITY, ACTIVATION, AND WEAK PLANNING • 73

temporary approaches mostly prevailed), weak planning was an opportunity for users to react against a wider system that ignored their right to "produce" the city and to embrace both rhythms of life and rhythms of change. Weak planning can thus be characterized as a type of distinct planning context during which daily rhythms can embrace novelty and experimentation as the process of transforming places (and the wider planning system) are less prescriptive, interventionist, and planned. The temporal element of weak planning is important here and again resonates with a rhythmanalysis perspective. Weak planning is not a state characterizing the planning system. It is a temporal moment—of several months or, in some cases, years—where the rhythms of development and transformation are altered and partly broken; it is a moment of transition inherent to the waiting aspect of spaces that are underused or vacant or to a context of crisis where bricolage and improvisation are dominant ways of producing the everyday city. These fit into diverse strategies on how to manage stock supply and vacancy; deal with reactivation; and embrace more generally principles of innovation, fluidity, and flexibility inherent to twenty-first-century cities.

The situation in Berlin in the 1990s is a good example of weak planning.[68] The transformation of the city is intrinsically linked to its cultural renaissance thanks to temporary artist-led uses that began just after the fall of the Berlin Wall in 1989. The rapid spread of vacant units (primarily factories but also residential buildings) was unprecedented and led to collectives of artists investing in abandoned places; year after year, significant urban activation and hence transformations occurred, including gentrification.[69] These spread thanks to new forms of urbanism that differed from conventional state- or market-led development processes, which were dysfunctional and unresponsive to high levels of vacancy and dereliction.[70] These processes pioneered experiential approaches to alternative uses of public spaces and hence embraced adaptability thanks to prompt changes and temporary uses.[71]

Weak planning is valid for all cities, although resonates most significantly for cities with a strong planning system. Disruptions and the absence of "planned" alternatives mean that weak planning can be understood as a shadow planning subsystem based on its temporary status along with its fluid, flexible, and permissive character. Its fluidity involves fewer strict regulations and less control, which are fruitful for the appropriations of differential spaces. Boundaries between legal/formal and more informal/alternative activities are blurred, as are the distributions of power between the different stakeholders. The alternative rhythmic nature of being on standby (awaiting redevelopment) means that there is a temporary transfer of power from local authorities and market operators to users who take ownership of the place in an ephemeral way. It is important to reiterate here that this relates to situations where the temporary transfer of power is negotiated and agreed to among all parties. Behind this transfer, activation, specifically asset-based activation, with an overall goal of profit generation and value creation is very much present. The process of urban transformations is viewed through two distinct but related processes: "place-shaping" and "placemaking."[72] While place-shaping is in the hands of temporary users and draws on an adaptability narrative, placemaking refers directly to the master planning process, which in turn draws on the design and negotiation of a more rigorous and planned vision for a site or area. As the temporary opportunity for alternative uses fades away, formal place making starts to take over. The latter is informed by entrepreneurial and neoliberal planning visions and has a direct impact on how and if temporary uses will have a legacy for the transformation of the site.

The process of place-shaping is an exemplar of how the idea of temporary and adaptable urbanisms have started uprooting the policy process of urban development. Temporary uses are explicitly used as tools in the process of urban development and are viewed as capturing or retaining value—as the concept of activation was described before. This was one of the narratives developed by German scholars in Berlin when they shaped the concept of weak planning and argued for the importance of temporary urbanism. "For some time and with increasing frequency, temporary use has turned up in the discourse on planning as a new concept, as a new urban planning method. This temporary use falls outside of the normal economy. In order to create room for such activities anyway, more and more frequently, particularly in the context of art and culture, legally precarious situations are being tolerated that on the basis of their contracts alone represent only temporary use."[73]

The principle of place-shaping as a tool and as a precursory principle of master planning also means that a range of principles (of dos and don'ts) are related to it. A set of restrictions and incentives include cheap rents, few constraints in terms of maintenance, flexibility of use, and modularity of space all based on a DIY and a no-investment approach for the landowner (typically for electricity, insulation, maintenance etc.); it is also associated with specific temporary leases based on the ease of ending the contract, with no risk for the temporary tenants to remain locked into a long-term contract. This coincides with Madanipour's argument that temporary urbanism is a way to expand the use of space while also responding to specific needs. It provides "the possibility of multiple uses for the same space, a kind of inward and on-site expansion through multiplication. This is particularly the case with events that unfold in public spaces."[74] With regard to shorter ephemeral changes of use for buildings and open spaces, it relates to a diversification of possibilities embracing the complexity of urban life and its rhythms: "multiple use of the same place for different purposes in different times of the day and night expands spatial affordance, offering new possibilities for a variety of activities within the same place, none of which is allowed to become permanent."[75]

There is, of course, a risk of romanticization here. Although this risk will be discussed further in chapter 5, it is crucial to see, in the adaptable and temporary thinking between place-shaping and placemaking, a way to justify and encourage reinvestment from landowners and public authorities through the devolution of space transformation to users. "Temporary urbanism redefines modes of relation to the city and to urban dynamics through an entrepreneurial gaze that sees places as underused assets—or as 'windows of opportunity'—while deep transformations are occurring in the land and real estate ownership structures and in the mechanism of value extraction in urban places, leading to ever-increasing precarisation."[76] This quote refers specifically to London, but it resonates strongly with many other urban settings, as I will discuss later in chapter 5.

The transition from place-shaping to placemaking ultimately raises questions about the way cities are produced and how stakeholders navigate among the various arenas of policymaking and urban development. It raises the need to better recognize local knowledge by "widening stakeholder involvement beyond traditional power elites."[77] At the core is the distribution of power and, more important, a subtle relationship between tactics and strategies among urban producers who are involved in the contrasting rhythms constitutive of a flexible everyday versus a more structured planned temporality.

ADAPTABILITY, STRATEGIES, AND TACTICS

For Lehtovuori and Ruoppila, temporary uses can be viewed from two perspectives: as instrumental tools of urban planning and management or as intrinsically valuable spaces and processes, often with political and emancipatory connotations.[78] Those two perspectives are linked to the diversity of stakeholders involved in the process of adaptability, including those who hold official, legally binding power (landowners; developers; politicians, and local authority representatives, including planners) and those who acquired temporary power in shaping a place in a context of weak planning. It is too simplistic to assume that the scene is divided into only two groups, first, planners (and sometimes developers) who see temporary uses as a way to activate change and generate new exchange and use values, and second, the temporary users waiting for their fate and the continuity of their activities. Temporary and adaptable urbanism practices are characterized by the combination of multiple strategies and tactics that are naturally complex and defined by context. De Certeau's everyday life theory is useful here to cast light on this process.[79] It also complements the use of Lefebvre's insights into the production and temporalities of cities.

De Certeau's work has been widely used to explore how "tactics" developed in the context of everyday actions can resist the "strategies" of the powerful. Strategies and tactics are very different, particularly regarding how power is used and exercised. Defensive and offensive strategies are developed within a process of calculation or manipulation of power relationships and are related to determinism and regulation—which translate into formal planning (i.e., master planning).[80] They have an explicit aim in the production of space. Strategies are linked to the longer term, to planned visions and objectives. In other words, they inform and guide the master planning and placemaking process. On the other hand, tactics are "calculated actions" that "play on and with a terrain imposed on it and organized by the law of a foreign power." They need to justify their purpose and use. "A tactic is determined by the absence of power just as a strategy is organized by the postulation of power."[81] Tactics are more fluid and spontaneous and are not fully coordinated; they have "no proper locus" reflecting the everyday needs and rhythms inherent to adaptable place-shaping. Tactics "take advantage of opportunities and depend on them."[82] Flexibility is one of the key features of tactics because they must be mobile but also adaptable. A tactic fits more with what temporary users develop when they shape places through creative adaptations.[83]

Such a differentiation of strategies and tactics seems unliteral, matching Lehtovuori and Ruoppila's perspectives.[84] This doesn't offer the full picture, however. Strategies are much more complex than most interpretations. Looking back to some of de Certeau's early work, he represents strategies as being single and coherent ("univocal"), whereas in fact the interests of different powerful actors frequently come into conflict and must be mediated in order to secure changes in society.[85] This is a crucial point when trying to understand the complexity of temporary and adaptable urbanisms and their progressive diversification. There is a much wider argument to make regarding how both place-shapers and placemakers use strategies within temporary and adaptable urbanism. The strategies of the powerful are both *polyvocal* and subject to *negotiation*. This was clear in the examples of Marseille used earlier and can be seen in the case of the Flon in Lausanne, which will be discussed later in this chapter. Applied to temporary and adaptable urbanism, this is a crucial lens to investigate the complex multilevel governance systems associated with it. de Certeau talked about strategies emerging from a *"lieu propre"* ("proper place"), which formed a metaphor for institutional authority.[86] The narrative around temporary and adaptable urbanism is clearly constructed on a combination of different *"lieux propres"* that have become progressively more complex. This is one of the main reasons why temporary urbanisms are distinct and explicitly separated from any use that could be related to squatting. Temporary uses are constructed and strategized by the combination of actors who hold power in transitioning spaces from place-shaping to place-making. This distribution and transition of power is subtle and made even more complex the more the "temporary" is sustained. It rests upon the juxtaposition of Lefebvrian rhythms of life and change that are shaped by all actors but translated into visions and places differently.

De Certeau uses the term *lieu propre* to argue that a strategy comes from an appropriate and therefore authoritative place. It is a place of order, a fixed territory that serves as the origin point for power. This is important in the context of temporary and adaptable urbanism and takes us back to the contextual and path-dependent argument. Adaptability is a response to the rigid and fixed nature of the city, so *lieux propres* derive from the tensions inherent in rigid planning systems and regulations along with market dynamics. This primary *lieu propre* is then complemented and challenged by supplemental *lieux propres*, and while still being authoritative in setting ground rules for temporary uses also challenges any attempts to maintain a status quo for the primary *lieux propre* (which at that time had failed). The way temporary urbanism has evolved isn't only because of tactical acts of resistance (that is, DIY urbanism) toward traditional and fixed forms of planning. It is the result of a range of actors (landowners, developers, local authorities) operating from their own powerful *lieu propre* who saw the strategic benefits of pursuing their own agenda with and thanks to temporary uses and users. Here is a very utilitarian approach to precarity for those who hold regulatory powers;[87] however, temporary users also benefit from such arrangements. Looking back at the example of La Friche de la Belle de Mai, SFT key members managed to create their own *lieu propre* and strategically positioned themselves within various arenas of influence and decision making to drive their project very successfully. Before settling in the tobacco factory, they spoke with the former workers' unions and mobilized the relevant regulatory tools (i.e., they signed a rental agreement of precarious occupation—in French, *convention d'occupation précaire*) to ensure that the occupation wouldn't be associated with a squat. "We always respected the rules and we were always in a legal situation."[88] The person I interviewed continues by insisting that La Friche "was never a place where messy things could happen . . . We were not marginals, nor squatters, nor alternative users. We always fought against the image of the underground place or squat. This allowed [us] to position our project and legitimatise it." As I will discuss in chapter 7, this *lieu propre* is related to specific skills, abilities, and knowledge that have been crucial in constituting the relevant community of practice around La Friche and enlarge it further, along with securing financing from various agencies.

The action of SFT is what de Certeau calls *"Espace,"* which is a place defined by the strategies of the powerful.[89] The *Espace* is affected by different strategies constructed in distinct *lieux propres*. This means that the strategies SFT developed to secure and sustain their project can be very different depending on the scale of the interventions, their time space, who is involved, and how the temporary users gathered and constituted themselves as place-shapers. There is an important degree of responsiveness

FIGURE 3.4 The Flon neighborhood in Lausanne, Switzerland, and the variety of temporary occupations in derelict warehouses prior to redevelopment.

Source: Lauren Andres.

that emerges from those shaping the tactics. They show an ability to adapt and improve within their highly adaptable and nonpermanent setting. Tactics remain very much in the hands of temporary users but, as seen in the Marseille example, they can become strategies per se; as such, they act as an extremely powerful tool in shaping a larger vision of redevelopment and then leading into the permanent transformation of spaces.

It is useful in this discussion on activation, weak planning, strategies, tactics and *lieux propres* to bring in another example: the Flon in Lausanne, Switzerland. The Flon (figure 3.4) is a former industrial district in the city center that started to be underused in the 1950s and became derelict.[90] It was erected initially as a storage yard and thus had several warehouses of various sizes and architectural characteristics. Its transformation was constrained by planning restrictions that prevented any change of use without the approval of a new master plan. For almost fifty years and for various political and socioeconomic reasons (including strong opposition from the local population and key tensions between the owner—the Lo Holding—and the municipality), three master plans failed to be voted through.[91] The district waited with a great deal of uncertainty, which prompted weak planning. Activation became a de facto option in a situation where disorder and instability prevailed. It translated into the spread of "temporary" uses, signed off by the owner as alternative solutions even if they were not aligned with land-use regulations because they were nonindustrial. These became a financial alternative to the status quo of the estate but also an opportunity for a range of businesses and artistic-minded individuals. Galleries, artists' workshops, restaurants, clothes and shoe shops, and nightclubs, among others, settled in.[92]

As noted by one of the tenants, "the landowner was OK to rent some units at very interesting prices as long as people agreed to do up their spaces [installing heating]."[93] Temporary activities were considered a way to trigger an asset-based activation because they brought short-term income to the company at almost no cost. It also led to physical and social activation because the lack of regulations allowed units to be adapted based on everyday needs but also creative ideas. They had the benefit of complete freedom, for example, buildings were painted different colors, and social events, including barbecues and open cinema evenings, were organized during the summer.[94] Disorder and uncertainty created opportunities to experiment and were strongly valued by those who settled in the district. "When I arrived in this district,

ADAPTABILITY, ACTIVATION, AND WEAK PLANNING • 83

FIGURE 3.5 The Flon neighborhood and its open-air cinema in Lausanne, Switzerland.

Source: Lauren Andres.

I felt in love. It was an atypical neighbourhood, not really ordered, not Swiss in other words. A controlled anarchy was in place and this attracted a lot of interesting people."[95]

The district (then called Flon-Flon by the tenants and also named the little Soho of Lausanne by local media)[96] emerged through the creation of a new and unique community of creative users who benefitted from the flexibility of the district to make their businesses grow and also participated in the full activation of the site. Before that, few people would cross the neighborhood because of personal safety concerns, the district's appeal grew with temporary users. It became well known for its alternative character and its nonconformist activities (figure 3.5).[97]

The Flon started to change significantly, becoming a very visible and attractive area of Lausanne, but its future depended fundamentally on the adoption of a new master plan and hence new planning regulations. This is where the temporary tenants' *lieux propres* emerged, which were aligned with the different tactics they used to be heard; both their tactics and their *lieux propres* became crucial in how weak planning ended. While the owner had no goal of sustaining such temporary occupations, particularly under the cheap and very malleable rental conditions, they nevertheless had to work with and around them in order to allow a smooth approval of a new master plan. Representatives of the Flon, through their strong and visible, even if temporary *lieu propre* (which received significant recognition from the local population, media, and politicians) navigated subtly in order to ensure that the district would keep its "alternative" character. This involved retaining most of the buildings and the urban morphology, layout, and mixed-use nature of the area. This plan respected "the double vocation of the district: a perfectly central area and a slightly unusual space with a particular cachet, its own style and way of evolving."[98] The Lo Holding company used the asset-based activation strategically in two phases. While the master plan's vision was founded on the physical and social activation triggered by the temporary tenants, it then turned it toward a much more commercially driven and high-end strategy. The approved master plan was designed with enough flexibility to allow the company to reshape the district, including attracting new tenants (global brands) and push for a new range of customers. This ultimately led to a complete rebranding of the area, its neoliberal transformation, and gentrification (figure 3.6). A representative of the landowner explained how this was handled and strategized: "we collected enough benefits from the traditional Flon that we can still sell it with this identity which is

ADAPTABILITY, ACTIVATION, AND WEAK PLANNING • 85

FIGURE 3.6 The Flon neighborhood in Lausanne, Switzerland, today: a gentrified, high-end, and creative neighborhood.

Source: Lauren Andres.

now more and more declamatory and less a reality."[99] In effect, the Flon was sustained solely in a temporary artificial way, which included a progressive dissolution of the tenants' alternative *lieux propres*.

From 1999 onward, the full benefits of the long trajectorial activation process could be observed. The alternative image of the district had been used to shape the area into a trendy destination based on the use of iconic architecture and urban design. It also included a shift toward top-down, commercially led, temporary uses developed on open spaces (events, exhibitions, ice rinks, etc.). As a result, many of the Flon tenants left, either because they were unable to afford the rental increases or they were just not interested anymore in staying. Those who stayed longer recognized how they benefited financially from the progressive creative rebranding of the Flon. "I am disappointed about the district. It is becoming sterilized and looks 'has-been.' However, from a commercial point of view, I have no regrets."[100] Over the longer term, the Flon is more financially profitable to the owner (noting that Lo Holding merged with Mobimo Holding in 2009 to expand its portfolio), and the area still benefits the city and local municipality, and also some of those who initially settled in the now trendy, expensive, and bohemian district.

CONCLUSION

The development of the Flon is not unique and reflects many of the trajectories of the transformation of spaces of various sizes that evolved thanks initially to bottom-up forms of temporary urbanisms shaped by contexts of weak planning. They reflect a general trend that encompasses the progressive adoption of temporary urbanism as a form of planning, specifically in contexts of disruptions and crises, and hence the need for regeneration. Adaptability in a context of weak planning is highly localized, however; it concerns specific cities and neighborhoods. From a political perspective, it does not constitute a citywide strategy or a generalized approach to alternative urban making. This is an important point that places both weak planning and activation as relatively singular and exceptional processes focusing on specific sites and projects. Weak planning is associated with long time frames. Transformation is progressive and is linked to various types of activation. It contrasts significantly with the types of reactive, prompt, and unprecedented adaptations emerging in the context of a major crisis: a natural disaster or a pandemic—as I will discuss in chapter 6.

Activation is key in deconstructing adaptability along with the power relationships translating into strategies, tactics, and primary and alternative *lieux propres* that contribute to shift spaces from place-shaping to placemaking. Disruptions leading to weak planning and adaptable and temporary processes that emerge out of them connect with creativity, reaction, disorder, and (in) stability that are linked to rhythms of life and change. More important is that activation is about triggering transformations: this involves new uses (from vacancy to occupancy), a shift in how a place is perceived and valued and hence a return of financial values. Activation during weak planning is a precursor for how adaptability will shift and be embedded in the re-imagining of cities and the development of cool and artificial urban spaces, as explored in chapter 5.

Activation and weak planning can be translated beyond the contexts of crisis and industrial transitions that have been illustrated with the examples of La Friche de la Belle de Mai and the Flon. Adaptability and forms of temporary urbanisms shape spaces and people's lives in contexts where planning is inherently weak (where it is under-resourced and has limited land-use management tools and regulations) but also where adaptation is part of the everyday through coping and survival mechanisms. This is what the following chapter will explore.

4

EVERYDAY ADAPTABILITY, COPING, AND RESILIENCE

U ntil now, most of the discussion in this book has focused on transformative changes situated within a prospect of longer-term change. It is crucial now to turn to how temporary and adaptable practices and urbanisms manifest and operate to meet everyday needs. Doing so allows us to question how such practices are recurrent moments shaped as responses to the failure of cities and their governing bodies to meet those needs. These moments materialized spatially and thus are non-permanent, or at least authorized as such. They are embedded in intersectional inequalities and display the need of the most vulnerable to find ways of altering and using space differently and thus tackle everyday basic necessities. They also connect to wider responses to major crises, which are not only driven by large-scale interventions but can also be fostered by more incremental practices. Such moments and related temporary and adaptable practices feed into three contrasting although complementary ontologies: the planned and the unplanned as creative and reactionary responses to disorder and instability; the common and the uncommon, in other words, what is already on offer and widely available in contrast to what is more rare; and the politically and socially acceptable versus the unacceptable, with the last being characterized by its unstructured and perceived chaotic nature.

Debates have often categorized temporary and adaptable practices based on where they took place, in other words, in low- and middle-income countries versus high-income countries. Of course, such a distinction is still valid from the perspective of distinct planning and regulatory systems but also in relation to the deep socioeconomic inequalities, political instabilities, and overall lack of resources affecting the ability of people to cope and survive every day in low- and middle-income countries. Despite being very different, all temporary and adaptable mechanisms share similar dynamics. They are entrenched into modes of coping and survival favoring diverse improvisations. This resonates with and feeds into Henri Lefebvre's interpretation of how individuals and collectives express and defend their rights to exist and produce the city in the way that matches their own existence and needs.[1] In this configuration, citizens, but also built environment experts, see the principle of temporariness and adaptability as a way to claim, tackle, and address social and spatial rights. These moments are part of the rhythms of ordinary lives and how respective routines and repetitions can be challenged by alternative responses to dysfunctions. Adaptability thus sits within a wider agenda of resilience, and particularly everyday resilience.

Adaptability as a mode of coping and survival cannot be separated from an in-depth discussion about the connection between informality and those left behind. It cannot be separated either from how temporariness and adaptability manifest, not only as a way to respond to everyday needs but also as an instrument to sustain the nonpermanent status of some communities and settlements. In some cases, it manifests as an expression of purposely neglecting specific rights. This has significant implications not only for how those individuals and communities survive but also for built environment experts who have to navigate within such complex urban settings and conflicting policy agendas. There is no attempt to romanticize temporary urban solutions and interventions in contexts of disempowerment, poverty, and informality; instead, we must insist on the everyday crucial role of these temporary uses and solutions and hence need for recognition. The conditions for adaptability and creativity take various forms; the driving forces of informality are not only shaped by power but are also deeply embedded in colonial histories, poverty, economic inequality, and other cultural processes (e.g., stigmatization, violence of different kinds). These will be alluded to in our discussion. I will focus primarily on cities and urban contexts still in transition, but the wider underpinnings for all urban settings are hereafter unpacked. Such insights lead to an examination of the various forms of adaptation as ways to claim rights in producing the city (clearly influenced here by tactical urbanism practices) but also as alternative responses to real estate leniency and waiting, with vacancy being the manifestation of economic downturns. I will return to the more developed contexts toward the end of the chapter, with the aim of deconstructing how temporary uses have been elevated as opportunities to provide spaces for local business or cultural and artistic activities at below-market rates. In these instances, disruptions are more structural (linked to large-scale economic crisis), and survival translates beyond the individuals to include local places, communities, and economies.

ADAPTABILITY, TEMPORARINESS, AND EVERYDAY RESILIENCE

Coping and survival mechanisms materializing in temporary and adaptable ways of using urban spaces are immediate emergency responses to daily problems and needs. Everyday adaptations are temporary because they fluctuate based on individuals' singular needs along with the rhythms of everyday activities and how they started. Everyday adaptations are moments of resilience. They manifest as modes of claiming or defending specific rights attached to coping and survival, for example, in generating a small income, accessing food and water, or finding shelter. Other claimed rights connect to livability and urbanity needs: for example, the right to green spaces, the right to play and exercise, the right to learn and access information. Adaptations and improvisations are reactions to a "system" that does not meet needs and expectations; in other words, it is dysfunctional, disrupted, and in crisis. This is where everyday resilience comes into play as an important lens to engage with the adaptability of both people and places.

Resilience is a common concept that is alternatively or simultaneously connected with sustainability and diverse forms of survival. Resilience isn't sustainability, however, because it clearly includes the idea of dealing with, recovering from, and bouncing away from disruptions or shocks. It has been applied to various objects, from infrastructure and ecological systems to places, cities, communities, and local and regional economies. It has followed a path of multiple disciplinary interpretations, starting mostly in ecology, engineering, disaster management, and psychology. Resilience here has been solely interpreted as a process of bouncing back with the aim of reaching another equilibrium after a major shock.[2] It is thus connected to vulnerability reduction approaches with a focus on places and community as well as on policy and practical solutions.[3] The process of bouncing back implies a return to a path-dependent re-equilibrium where the focus is placed on avoidance, survival and recovery.[4] Re-equilibrium is founded upon a "return or displacement to single or multiple equilibria and upon internal and external factors that either strengthen or threaten systems, either contributing to or weakening their resilience."[5] In this context, adaptations include temporary and more permanent solutions, with temporary urbanism in the form of temporary shelters or hospitals being exemplars of disaster management responses. The term "adaptation" and not "adaptability" is important, as will be explained next. Similar approaches have been used in studies opting for a social and ecological focus examining the resilience of social groups or communities when they are threatened by major disruptions and crises affecting their environmental resources and livelihoods.[6] In such studies, adaptations have been understood as a "movement towards a pre-conceived path in the short run, characterized by strong and tight couplings between social agents in place."[7]

The shift to shaping resilience as a process of adaptability rather than adaptation occurred later, once scholars in economic geography, urban studies, and planning used the concept as a lens to explore the transformations of local and regional economies, cities, and also vulnerable communities.[8] This new interpretation criticized the principle of bouncing back, which doesn't align with what communities and places are seeking or what they need. The return to a pre-shock condition is understood as being undesirable because it does not address the (often intersectional) inequalities, vulnerabilities, and dysfunctions that led to (or cumulatively increased) disruptions and shocks faced by communities and places.[9] This is why adaptability, rather than adaptations, matter and why it connects directly with rights, moments, and a rhythmanalysis understanding of temporary practices. Bouncing back implies the return to a certain routine that may have been exclusionary for many and that mostly ignored and only partially accounted for the everyday diverse rhythms of the most vulnerable. An adaptability-led interpretation of resilience

EVERYDAY ADAPTABILITY, COPING, AND RESILIENCE • 93

relates to more diverse time frames, with some being longer while others are shorter and ephemeral. The process of developing resilience is here both physical and psychological. It relates to behaviors, memories, and sense of place. This temporal drift of the concept of resilience toward adaptability has allowed scholars to anchor resilience in the everyday and within anticipatory approaches of coping and survival.[10] It has been applied spatially, looking at how physical design and planning interventions can affect the ability of place to be resilient for security, terrorism, disorders, and antisocial behavior threats and in connection with local, regional, and national economies.[11] It has also been used to assess how vulnerable communities improvise to mitigate socioeconomic pressures. By doing so, adaptability has been viewed "as the dynamic capacity to effect and unfold multiple evolutionary trajectories, through loose and weak couplings between social agents in place, that enhance the overall responsiveness of the system to unforeseen changes."[12]

Recognizing this connection between adaptability and everyday resilience is crucial for examining adaptable and temporary urbanism practices. It allows us to define everyday coping and survival mechanisms. This resonates greatly with how Simin Davoudi and colleagues engaged with the concept of evolutionary resilience, applying it initially to climate adaptations and later to adaptive planning practices.[13] By doing so, she insisted on its anticipatory, future-looking, and transformability character across multiple scales and time frames.[14] Evolutionary resilience strongly resonates with adaptable and temporary urbanisms; it is indeed a condition and a response—in all types of urban contexts—to the gaps created by a broken system. As a result, temporary reactive (often improvised) adaptations arise as a form of resistance. Such resistance, when linked to daily coping and survival, reflects processes of "persistent resilience," in other words, "everyday coping practices and behaviors toward ongoing and changing everyday pressures."[15] These forms of persistent resilience can be immaterial, relying on informal arrangements and networks that can "take place in the sharing of knowledge and/or the mutual exchanges of everyday life—all of which are extremely ephemeral processes that states find extremely hard to observe and conceptualise."[16] They can also be highly spatialized, however, in the form of adaptable and temporary uses of spaces.

Temporary and adaptable practices in the context of persistent resilience are triggered by deficiencies that are not linked solely to dysfunctional urban environment and planning systems. Adaptability in the context of the survival and coping of marginal communities is a transformative process that is fundamentally disconnected from activation and other processes of value creation and extraction (this point differs when "survival" is applied to places, for example declining high streets, as it refers to economic survival and ways to boost local economic development). The process of adaptability and its spatial implications share similarities with the activation process because coping and survival mechanisms rely on innovative and creative improvisations arising from uncertainties and (ongoing) persistent social and monetary crisis. Improvisations rely on "agents of change," who can be individuals, communities, or external agents (for example, local nongovernmental organizations [NGOs]). As a result, adaptable practices and temporary uses developed by agents of change are highly incremental and mostly sit outside formal governance structures. Improvisations can be considered "tactics" according to Michel de Certeau's reading.[17] Such agents of change do not hold official decision-making power or the right to represent others (democratically speaking). Despite this, by investing time and resources and adapting spaces temporarily, they do play a key role in shaping places, allowing

EVERYDAY ADAPTABILITY, COPING, AND RESILIENCE • 95

individuals and households to cope and have some of their basic rights addressed (even partially or ephemerally). Such processes and mechanisms are universal, even if they manifest differently based on diverse places, contexts, and living conditions. They can reclaim spaces for temporary gardens, for temporary playgrounds, for growing food or interacting socially; they also relate to informal activities (for example, food or clothes stalls) and informal shelters (typically informal tented settlements [ITSs]). Persistent resilience and adaptability disproportionally appear in cities characterized by weak and under-resourced planning systems where uncontrolled and unplanned settlements and arrangements prevail. Forms of so-called temporary urbanisms and insurgent planning manifest in the outskirts of cities where integrated planning solutions cannot be implemented.[18] These are entrenched in colonial legacies as in Africa, where cities' development was guided by race. The best resourced and areas were given to and occupied by the (white) colonialists initially (and subsequently by whites in South Africa during apartheid) and became the most affluent, resilient, and in less need of adaptations. The others, far less attractive and further away from core urban services, were first used to relocate colonized urban dwellers as well as Brown and Black communities during apartheid. Today these areas continue to host the poorest settlements that are occupied primarily by households of Black ethnicity. These areas are where temporary urbanisms and insurgent planning occur most often, a testament to their colonial and racial legacies of inequality and socioeconomic segregation.

Adaptability, resilience, survival, and forms of temporary occupations are all entangled with a strong spatial component: they predominantly occur where available land is inexpensive, unattractive, and in or close to natural hazards (e.g., flooding, motorways, landfills, etc.). They concern locations that are perceived as

96 • EVERYDAY ADAPTABILITY, COPING, AND RESILIENCE

not fit for planned development of higher standards. As a result, they are often off grid and detached from access and proximity to transport networks, making improvisations even more important in daily survival and resilience. This applies to many cities but is more acute in some, typically African cities: "everyday living in hyper-growth cities is supported by blending citizen-led interventions with continual chronic and acute shocks. These are persistent shocks that result in continual citizen and household adaptation. The outcome is survival, but this is an inequitable process based on household location, capacities, capabilities and access to resources."[19] The temporary nature of such places is entrenched in the nature of those settlements, which can be dismantled, displaced, destroyed, and reconstructed easily; these often occur through violent processes of (often racial) rejection by those holding power and resources. Prior to examining this point further, it is important to examine how temporary urbanism, everyday coping, and persistent resilience can converge by looking at the example of the Teatro de Contêiner Mungunzá in the Luz district of São Paulo.[20]

São Paulo is a perfect example of a city in transition, where severe intersectional inequalities combined with one of the fastest growing metropolitan populations globally converge to make the city a very diverse and fragmented metropolis. Poverty levels are high, with around one-third of the population living in slum conditions combined with widespread squatting and hence illegal use of empty buildings.[21] The informal economy plays a key role for the vulnerable population, with many open spaces, streets, and pavements in the city center used for informal (food) trading. Although not fully regulated and licensed, these activities, as in many cities in less-developed contexts, are tolerated. An important and more unique challenge faced by the city of São Paulo is drug dealing and drug use, with the neighborhood

FIGURE 4.1 The Teatro de Contêiner Mungunzá in Luz neighborhood, São Paulo, Brazil.

Source: Lauren Andres.

of Luz, where the Teatro de Contêiner Mungunzá (figure 4.1) is located, being one of the primary hot spots (Luz's nickname is "crack town").[22]

Luz is located close to the city center. Despite hosting a range of cultural facilities and being well connected by public transport, it is very deprived and rundown, with high levels of vacancy and informal and illegal activities (including the reselling of stolen goods and drugs, too). As the primary area of dealing and consumption of crack and cocaine in the city, a large proportion of its residents either consume drugs or live on the proceeds of drug dealing. Consumers lie on pavements for most of the day. To respond to the issue, Luz was provided with a number of treatment/rehabilitation centers, many constructed on vacant lands using temporary structures (i.e., prefabricated construction). Because of its central strategic location and severe socioeconomic issues, Luz has been at the center of the municipality's attention. Regeneration plans have repeatedly failed, however, because of strong opposition from the local population and local businesses, who fear gentrification and increased control exerted on their (informal) activities. In this very complex context of weak planning, the Teatro de Contêiner Mungunzá was set up, initially as a temporary project. This example is of interest here because its implementation is effectively contributing to a wider attempt to tackle everyday coping and persistent resilience.

Teatro de Contêiner Mungunzá (figure 4.2) was developed in 2016 on a public plot of land originally used as a police carpark.

FIGURE 4.2 The Teatro de Contêiner Mungunzá is a social hub for the local community in the Luz neighborhood of São Paulo, Brazil.

Source: Lauren Andres.

The company was initially given permission to use the site for temporary uses, for a festival, for two months. In one night, they installed eleven containers and built the theater structure; in a weak planning context, they were then granted approval to stay for a three-year period. Everything on the site is temporary and adaptable, including the building (made from recycled shipping containers) and materials, the community playground, the gardening and food-growing structures and siting areas. While it was supposed to be a nonpermanent project, the municipality renewed its agreement authorizing the use of the land at the end of 2018. While no end date is indicated, the company, as of now, still has no guarantee of being able to stay on-site indefinitely.[23] The theater hosts performances in the evening for an external public, and during the day, it provides free artistic and educational activities for the local residents. Some of those activities target the homeless community specifically (including drug users).[24] During the pandemic, when the program had to be stopped, the place became a social hub to provide support, masks, and food to the most vulnerable. Social enterprises were also set up on the site in support of the local community (figure 4.2).

Although enclosed, the site and its grounds are kept open for locals who can use it to socialize, rest, or access the bathroom for nondrug use. For residents, particularly children and mothers, the theater has become a safe place where they can play and socialize without fear of violence. The community garden allows food growing. The theater hence acts as a hub to change the dire living conditions of those living in this neighborhood; it constitutes a space for temporary escape from the everyday pressures, where rights to play, socialize, learn, and feel safe are exercised. In this example, persistent resilience and adaptability rest on fuzzy and blurred boundaries between the acceptable and unacceptable. Through trust, tolerance, and mutual support, everyday resilience occurs in this context, which is atypical. I now turn to discuss more commonly found adaptable and temporary urbanisms in the context of widespread informality.

ADAPTABILITY AND PERMANENT IMPERMANENCE

Responses to everyday coping through adaptability and temporary urbanism are connected to the issue of sustaining livelihoods in informal settings and allowing the poorest communities to survive every day, which means accessing food and water and some form of income. This refers primarily to fast-growing cities in low- and middle-income countries, although informal practices and mechanisms are to be found everywhere, including in global cities like Paris, London, and New York City. As Ali Madanipour notes: "the use of public space for informal trade is a prime example of temporary urbanism by the poor in many cities around the world. Here ephemerality is a sign of economic weakness, an attempt to cope with the lack of jobs and the inability of the authorities and their regulations to control the development and use of urban space." For Madanipour, such urban contexts are characterized by a range of failures that trigger adaptable practices ever further because the "financial and institutional capacities of the local and national authorities are limited."[25] Failures that are the result of colonial and contemporary socioeconomic inequalities and entrenched in poverty and various manifestations of rejection concern planning and the built environment discipline, which to date have not succeeded in providing sustainable livelihoods, particularly those of the poorer communities.[26] Understanding how adaptability and temporary urbanisms manifest in such disrupted settings is crucial. While pinning down the discussion to a couple of examples, it is worth reflecting upon how built environment experts engage with such dynamics. The view of planners and built environment experts in South Africa is useful here to bring another layer of analysis: "People must, within limitation, be able to explore how to survive and how to create livelihoods for themselves."[27]

This meaningful statement takes us back to the social and spatial rights that are part of temporary and adaptable urbanisms. These are people's responses to detrimental disruptions and an unfit-for-purpose system and living environment with dramatic socioeconomic consequences. Adaptability as a mode of persistent resilience is delivered in two ways: (1) in the form of various coping mechanisms and practices used by vulnerable communities to sustain informal uses, and (2) in the responses constructed by decision makers and planners that translate to navigating, tolerating, or trying to formalize informal processes of placemaking. Informal placemaking is the primary manifestation of adaptability and temporary urbanisms in deprived settings. This statement is not an endorsement of the state's inaction toward the urban poor. It is a matter of arguing in line with other scholars like Faranak Miraftab, Phil Harrison et al., and Vanessa Watson who do not aim to formalize (and often criminalize) informality as the appropriate response.[28] The nonrecognition of informal placemaking ultimately ends up by solely benefitting the elites. Agility and adaptability are key both in how such places and communities exist but also in how they are addressed. "There is a tendency, inherited from colonialism, to artificially control urban dynamics, uses and practices through strict regulations and plans which in practice cannot be enforced. These are 'bad' plans and 'bad' regulations."[29] This tendency, which can be observed in many cities globally, doesn't match the realities of how urban spaces—where the affluent live—function or any attempts to account for the intersectional inequalities and layers of vulnerabilities that characterize them. The criminalization of informality is a political issue for planners. It requires them to navigate very carefully.[30] Informality isn't a choice and is part of persistent resilience. "For the group or the society to survive, it needs to fill the gap that has been created through the mismatch between a rigid constitution and a changing context. The disruption caused by non-routinized events may be interpreted as an essential ingredient in the process of adjustment to the environment."[31] Madanipour's point here converges with how built environment experts perceive informality in South Africa (typically referring to townships– figure 4.3). "Informalities are

FIGURE 4.3 Township in Cape Town, South Africa.
Source: Lauren Andres.

EVERYDAY ADAPTABILITY, COPING, AND RESILIENCE • 103

very cut to the bone economics; it's about survival, and I think it responds to whatever it presents or whatever opportunities presents itself [*sic*] for greater survival."[32] Such informalities are constructed upon adaptability, which can be considered a state of permanent impermanence.[33]

Permanent impermanence is strongly connected to the issue of rigidity in managing and regulating land uses (as already discussed in chapter 2). This core problem is exemplified in the context of resource scarcity as noted in South Africa. In an interview, one public-sector planner revealed: "We don't know how to plan with more flexible standards. The designing schemes have not been amended to take account of informality."[34] Another planner commented: "So, government gets swamped by the enormity of the problem that is identified . . . And then tries to do everything by the book and doesn't get anywhere, you know and then wonders why . . . The country's whole system has been developed around that."[35]

The lack of flexibility and the status of permanent impermanence are combined with a limited account of the realities of how low-income settlements actually function. This prompts more informality and adaptability. In South African cities, commercial lands are not included in strategic visions, and thus large businesses are not allowed to settle in townships. This reflects a lack of understanding of local settings and realities because allowing businesses to settle in townships would provide jobs and also enable dwellers to set up their own activities.[36] This lack of formal business opportunities, combined with the cost and bureaucracy around change of land use, means that local businesses are run informally from home. This explains the development of backyard shacks. "The owner of a (typically subsidized) formal house rents a portion of his yard area to occupants who live in a dwelling constructed either by formal or informal methods, thus gaining access to the house's water and electricity connections and to an outside toilet."[37] Such backyard dwellings can be used for commercial purposes or to accommodate a growing family. They are unplanned and are sources of health and safety concerns, including fire risks, impact on the electrical grid and sanitation, and serving as a source for the spread of communicable diseases.[38]

Some cities, typically Cape Town and Johannesburg (which have the most well-resourced planning departments in the country), have recently developed more progressive schemes to try to navigate within the subtle needs of those living in townships and thus acknowledge the importance of adaptability. This means that adaptable place-shaping has been accepted as part of authorized, permanent arrangements. Those progressive schemes include:

> an appropriate designing category for informality which allows more flexible, and standard regulations for home-based enterprises . . . So, that allows the notion of back yarding . . . This speaks to the vulnerability of communities in informal settlements. People would much rather rent a backyard shack in a property within an established township, than to live in the precarious living conditions in informal settlements where crime and safety are of major concern.[39]

Such schemes based on an adjustment of regulations are very rare. In most impoverished settings, improvisation and adaptation remain crucial, sometimes leading to innovative do-it-yourself (DIY) solutions that can expand to include entire settlements. The Hope for Communities aerial water project in Kibeira, Kenya, one of the largest informal settlements in the world, is an excellent example of an alternative DIY solution to water provision in an unplanned impermanent/permanent context.

EVERYDAY ADAPTABILITY, COPING, AND RESILIENCE • 105

It was designed in 2016 by a national NGO as an elevated system extracting water from a borehole (deep well) and providing it to kiosks. This engineering bricolage reduces breakage, vandalism, and contamination while making access to water easier and safer. The water is treated to make it drinkable, and the project employs local residents to sell it at an affordable price.[40] Another form of DIY adaptations can be found in Marikana, outside Potchefstroom in the northwest province of South Africa. This case is remarkable in a severe and distressing context of poverty, inequality, and injustice because it showcases the abilities of communities to address their own needs and develop adaptable tactics in light of the absence of appropriate answers from planners or relevant authorities in a context of permanent impermanence.

> Residents made their own water channels and own water systems because of the lack of authorities to provide in their need. So it's an informal settlement that is actually very much formalised, but they can't be formalised because of policy restrictions. So, yes, these people are located there and they are living there and they've got basically all the services that they need, but it's still informal. And for me our policies are not equipped to include that and it's an issue at the moment. You can't . . . In practice it's real and it's happening, but in policies it's not allowed.[41]

Marikana shows how such DIY adaptations leading to concrete transformative changes align with tactics of "DIY formalisation" favoring persistent resilience and survival.[42] These tactics are grounded in skills but also in how the community empowers itself to claim and defend its rights. Although very different compared to the processes of adaptability noted in Marseille, France, and in Lausanne, Switzerland, it nevertheless demonstrates the strengths of such tactics. The DIY watering system has become an "acceptable" solution for planners and local policymakers who are not able to implement other "planned" solutions because of a dysfunctional system.

In addition to the use of adaptability as a means to survive and to meet basic needs, adaptability can also be seen in more micro forms of temporary urbanisms that contribute to individuals' livability and everyday mental resilience. As noted by a South African planner: "To people who live in informal settlements, that's their homes, that's their pride and joy."[43] This statement is important because it illustrates planners' responsibilities in acknowledging and accounting for place attachment in any thoughts given to informal settings. The interviewee continues: "I think that as planners we need to make informal settlements as livable as we can and there's no reason why we can't do that." Resilience and adaptability here merge through subjective perceptions including identity, memory, and happiness, which are activated by temporary installations. Sheds, tents, and shacks in informal settings are effectively more than temporary structures with a roof. They are living spaces, homes for those living there.

I want to turn to Paul Moawad's work on ITSs in the Lebanese-Syrian borderscape (figure 4.4).[44] Such ITSs host impoverished Syrian refugees who fled Syria in 2011. Located on former agricultural lands, ITSs are off grid and are evidence of the legacy of geopolitical instability, stigmatization, and abjection.[45] The temporary nature of these ITSs is reinforced by the rules that affect them with the aim of sustaining permanent impermanence despite little prospect of the refugees returning to their homeland.[46] Since 2019, to avoid any attempts of permanent settlement, shelters need to be easily dismantled. This means that using concrete masonry systems and metal sheets are deemed illegal and are at a risk of being demolished.[47] The condition of physical material impermanence is anchored in everyday life.

FIGURE 4.4 Informal tented settlements (ITSs) inhabited by Syrian refugees, Beqaa Region, Lebanon.
Source: Paul Moawad.

It is imposed by regulations anchored in a condition of ongoing (permanent) waiting.

Despite this, refugees, particularly women, have transformed these precarious settings into "homes" as part of wider forms of persistent and mental resilience (figure 4.5).[48] Homes are created through the use of specific furniture, objects, colors, and room arrangement (typically the central *Soubia*, that is, a traditional stove area, where households gather together). All these details refer to their lives back in Syria.[49] Permanent impermanence goes beyond the home setting to include informal business activities, which are set up in tents to generate small supplemental incomes. The refugees use the same skills from their lives in their home country.[50]

FIGURE 4.5 The creation of homes in refugees' ITSs, Beqaa Region, Lebanon.

Source: Paul Moawad.

While all these practices are informal and unregulated, they show, as they did in South Africa, the crucial importance of adaptations and improvisations in contexts of waiting, uncertainty, and dire socioeconomic situations driven by former colonial, geopolitical and political, and sociocultural (including race) forces. The case of Syrian ITSs reinforces how manifestations of temporary and adaptable urbanisms inform a much wider resilience, where psychological resilience is expressed in material and subjective traces reflecting feelings of hope and memories.

These diverse manifestations of permanent impermanence allow us to question the nature of adaptable and temporary practices, how they constitute lived experiences for informal dwellers, and how they are perceived by built environment experts. What is apparent in the various examples used to illustrate the dynamics of permanent impermanence is how they lead to many tensions. At the core of those tensions is power, particularly how power is expressed by some and taken by others as reactive coping mechanisms. Power can be grasped by communities, households, individuals, and also NGOs. It can also be transferred by planners, as in Marikana. These power dynamics resonate with wider debates about the failure of the state, the lack of any welfare safety net, and the inability to govern with equity as a primary goal, specifically when people are still suffering from colonial legacies and diverse manifestations of segregation and injustice. Adaptability in this respect is a peaceful display of anger against inequality, poverty, exclusion, and other forms of violent rejection. The failure of the state results in privileging some (the elite) under a capitalist-led narrative of profit-making urban development. Central to this argument is that adaptability occurs as a response to the absence and failure of "robust accountable institutions and transparent planning processes and frameworks," thus enabling those in unplanned settings to "take ownership of places transforming informal settlements into liveable places."[51] Adaptability in situations of survival and (persistent) resilience also materializes in the re-creation of positive memories of the past, giving sense and meaning to the living space. Of course, persistent resilience and adaptability are demonstrated in very chaotic and complex settings. Such demonstrations are not specific to low- and middle-income countries. They occur differently, but with some commonality, in high-income country settings.

SPACES-IN-WAITING, RESILIENCE, AND EVERYDAY ADAPTABILITY

Adaptability, temporary urbanisms, and survival are strongly connected with socioeconomic factors. Urban dysfunctions are connected to the spread of vacancy and hence the survival of places, buildings, streets, neighborhoods, and what characterizes them (i.e., their identity, dynamics, and sense of place). They relate to tackling the survival of places that is closely intertwined with people's livability, livelihoods, and well-being. Adaptability in these circumstances is concerned with everyday rhythms and relatively minor disruptions, but it is situated in more structural ruptures (i.e., economic crisis and periods of downturns). These disruptions have spatial and socioeconomic consequences. They break existing routines and long-term development processes, allowing for more diverse alternative temporary solutions at a micro level based on the existence of in-between spaces that do not have a primary use or are vacant and can then be occupied. In this context, boundaries between the planned and the unplanned, the common and the uncommon, and the politically and socially acceptable versus the unacceptable remain blurred as various forms of adaptability and temporary urbanisms spread.

Referring again to tactical urbanism is important. As Gordon Douglas points out, DIY urban design activities are linked to failures in the official planning and development process; tactical "vigilantes" by their actions try to enforce laws that are not being enforced to respond to specific community needs and gaps.[52] They are driven by goals of promoting civic-minded improvements that are delivered through adaptable ways of transforming spaces. These demonstrate the existence and importance of "constructive forms of informality." Douglas notes that, in

New York City, "the making and remaking even of something as regulated as a NYC [New York City] street is still the result of a web of formal and informal practices: city developers under varying degrees of regulatory scrutiny, elected representatives and community groups, and everyday citizens with all manner of motivations and no particular authority."[53] In the United States, micro DIY temporary transformations have included the setup of benches, micro libraries, cycling paths, or small gardens. Those interventions are eminently anchored in the core pillars of adaptability, in other words, creativity, reaction, disorder, and (in) stability, while specifically connecting to vacancy in the urban fabric and everyday resilience. They relate to forms of "creative transgression" therefore questioning the governance of urban making, particularly "who is acknowledged as an actor who may change urban space."[54]

Such micro-scale temporary and adaptable interventions take us back to the everyday rhythms and the experimentations that penetrate daily routines within communities to ensure their survival in terms of livability. In his interpretation of everyday urbanism practices featured in the appropriation of spaces for informal commerce and festivities, Kelbaugh tackles an important aspect of everyday adaptability that effectively celebrates "ordinary life, with little pretense of creating an ideal environment."[55] Such activities often occur in spaces-in-waiting, where survival and coping can occur; this resonates with the concept of margins and how the most vulnerable navigate within them as part of their ordinary everyday lives as alternative rhythms and routines. Adaptable ways of using space, as modes of survival and everyday resilience, show how the "abilities to fly below the organized financial radar and work in the gaps and on the margins have allowed it to empower disadvantaged people and disenfranchised communities."[56]

FIGURE 4.6 Mobile and temporary gardens on derelict or underused land, Loughborough Junction, South London.

Source: Lauren Andres.

Access to food growing and gardening as a way to use spaces-in-waiting and respond to unmet community needs is an exemplar of adaptable mechanisms and the rhythms of life and change that characterize them. This concerns cities globally. In London, temporary gardening initiatives (figure 4.6) have for several decades spread outside traditional and planned allotments that blossomed in the city at the end of the World War I.[57] Loughborough Farm was launched as a community initiative in 2013 in a context where meanwhile leases and temporary urbanisms were spreading in the city. It is located in Loughborough Junction in South London, a deprived and diverse neighborhood. The project was developed with the ambition of creating "a patchwork of community

EVERYDAY ADAPTABILITY, COPING, AND RESILIENCE • 113

growing spaces on pieces of derelict or underused land" through mobile and temporary gardens.[58] Mobility is achieved by using builders' bags as growing patches; these are displayed on small vacant, sometimes polluted lands. This impermanent-permanent and highly flexible technique is authorized by the landowners, Network Rail and the Lambeth Council.

Food is grown by volunteers and local residents in the mobile gardens and made available for free to volunteers and sold to residents through small donations. It is also used in the community café set up in a nearby vacant building. The project has been driven by a key well-being narrative in a neighborhood lacking places for social interaction and physical exercise, but it has also expanded to other social goals. Training sessions on food growing and horticulture are organized for community members (particularly those seeking employment opportunities) along with a variety of social events allowing participants from different backgrounds and cultures to meet, interact, and support each other. Until recently, the project was based solely on temporary use of vacant lands, but it has now received permission to stay on a council-owned, underused site where some of its operations were already located, hence creating a new, mixed-use, affordable business and community space.

The example of Loughborough Farm shows the crucial importance of spaces-in-waiting as pockets of unused lands providing livable settings for those in dire socioeconomic situations. Adaptability is a tool for community mobilization and everyday coping while serving wider social and well-being needs. In such a configuration, coping and survival are more complex and hidden compared to such traits in low- and middle-income cities. Spatial and socioeconomic coping are connected to poverty but also to mental well-being, with adaptability being a tool for community-level and household-level resilience. This manifestation of coping

114 • EVERYDAY ADAPTABILITY, COPING, AND RESILIENCE

and resilience through the use of temporary uses goes further when they are applied to places and local economic survival. London again serves as an excellent example. Since the global financial crisis in 2008, temporary urbanism and meanwhile uses were seen as solutions to rising levels of vacancy. In 2009, 10 percent of commercial properties in London were empty and "boarded-up shops and fenced-off construction sites were visual reminders of the sudden slump in fortunes."[59] This crisis was combined with significant funding cuts. These affected all central and local governments and snowballed to affect small community organizations (particularly those in the culture, the arts, and creative industries) and small local enterprises, which saw support and funding schemes shrink. Adaptability and temporary urbanism became part of spatialized survival and resilience visions. The incentive here wasn't value extraction per se but the prospect of mitigating shocks and uncertainties. Adaptability as a mitigation strategy is based on the assumption that occupying spaces-in-waiting is better than nothing and, in a best-case scenario, can lead to positive transformations at very micro scales. These transformations match processes of urban, economic, and community resilience for those with little resources. The purpose of activation and value creation and extraction is secondary, even nonexistent. Adaptability is a reactive solution to try to alter trajectories of decline and enable micro transitions at unit and street levels; these occur during a waiting gap, through temporary transformations. Vacancies are "wasted resources and . . . it is better to use empty spaces, even temporarily, than to let them lie empty."[60]

Meanwhile strategies, and particularly the spread of meanwhile uses (figure 4.7; also called "pop-ups"),[61] are contextualized in the report *Looking After Our Town Centres*, which was published by the Department for Communities and Local Government (DCLG) in the United Kingdom in April 2009. This report

FIGURE 4.7 Meanwhile uses in London.

Source: Lauren Andres.

argued for making temporary leases easier but also safer, legally speaking, for the owners. It led to the Meanwhile Use Lease Contract that was designed to avoid being associated with mechanisms of squatting. This marked the beginning of a period characterized by a "combination of vastly different legal, institutional, economic, social and political conditions" supporting the spread of temporary urbanism and adaptability as an in-between planning solution with a focus on survival and resilience.[62] "Central to this is a clear and mutual understanding that a temporary use is just that, and that it will grow and move on, or fail and disappear. One of the key success factors is certainty around repossession dates. With exit strategies agreed in advance, temporary occupiers can plan rationally regarding the write off time for their up-front investments."[63] The main principle is that vacancies had to be filled because they were a burden for owners who are still paying taxes on empty properties despite having no financial return. Addressing the interests of owners and temporary users by enabling them to rent those working units at nonmarket rates (e.g., £100 to £300 a month) is a win–win solution.

In the early years of meanwhile uses, "pop-ups were very definitely compensatory forms of place-making. Their ad hoc decorative strategies, such as stringing up bunting or turning discarded crates into seating, only thinly veiled the dereliction of the properties they popped up in. Typical pop-up places included charity shops, community projects or volunteer-run services that replaced overstretched or closed-down council provisions, such as HIV testing clinics or temporary community libraries."[64] Local and everyday resilience is underpinning these strategies, especially in the most deprived neighborhoods with few alternatives.

Survival through temporary urbanisms and meanwhile leases retains the sense of space and former dynamism of a place and street. One meanwhile tenant, referring to one of the streets where he set up his temporary shop, said:

> In H. Street all the buildings were boarded up. But there was one pub next to us and it was about to get run-down, the owner was about to do a runner, then somebody else bought the pub

and then we had a few events and some people did say, even the pub, we are really glad you guys are here because together we are changing the landscape on the street. We had events in the shop where 100 people would come out and then they would come to that part of London. So you want to engage in an area, but also not change something too much because that is insensitive, but the shops are all empty, so the community definitely want something going on.[65]

This interpretation of adaptability in terms of resilience and a survival perspective has been sustained in a city like London and reinforced further as a result of the pandemic (see chapter 6). The purpose of adaptability for survival has recently been further expanded to include controversial solutions to address major societal projects, typically homelessness. The PLACE/Ladywell project in Lewisham, led by RSHP architects, used a prefab design to create a temporary structure made to be dismantled after no more than four years and put up again elsewhere based on needs and projects.[66] Implemented in 2016 and owned by Lewisham Council, it provides twenty-four temporary homes to local families in high-priority housing needs, in other words, in desperate survival conditions. The ground floor has sixteen commercial spaces for small and medium-sized local businesses. The PLACE/Ladywell project, while demonstrating a survival tactic, also shows how adaptability is pushed toward its boundaries, as an architectural but also political gesture. This feeds into a wider criticism of how survival-led adaptability has been used in the last decade. "If pop-up, in its early days, was an arena in which charities provided services that replaced retracted state welfare, this compensatory format of service provision is now being mimicked by government itself."[67] This area is problematic and illustrates state failures to provide for basic needs.

CONCLUSION

Adaptability and the temporary city have been examined in this chapter through the lens of everyday resilience, survival, permanent impermanence, and spaces-in-waiting. Adaptability has been approached as part of alternative rhythms and moments but also as everyday practices of individuals and communities coping with and surviving in dire living conditions entrenched in waiting, uncertainty, and disruption. These are linked to long-lasting inequality and forms of exclusion inherited from colonial pasts as well as geopolitical, political, and cultural forces. Adaptability is also associated with wider structural shocks, with survival being spatialized to specific places. Nevertheless, everyday adaptability, coping, and resilience concern all cities, despite needs, uses, and practices being highly contextualized and place-based. They all relate to basic needs, to rights, and to wider ambitions to address key urban, social, and economic issues.

Adaptability isn't solely informal and unplanned. It is also situated within the planned, either as a contrasting response to dysfunctional planned settings or as a crucial component of the planners' approach to urban development. In contexts of crisis and significant turbulences, but also in cities where informality and insurgency prevail, adaptability and temporary uses are part of the everyday landscape; they are common features of how people, communities and places survive. This takes us back to power and politics when such commonality is not accepted; most of the time, it is severely rejected, leading to detrimental consequences that planners and built environment experts have to navigate within, particularly in low- and middle-income countries.

Countries like the United Kingdom or the United States are quite different compared to South Africa, Lebanon, or Brazil (where informality is rejected by those holding power) with, on the contrary, an acceptance of adaptability as a community response to fill specific provision gaps. This acceptance raises significant concerns and has been widely criticized.[68] It shows how local and national governments' shift away from accounting for public good, from trying to address everyone's needs, and transfer responsibilities to local communities to find solutions for everyday issues and to improve the livability of their urban settings. This key criticism is embedded in how temporary urbanisms and the idea of the adaptable city have progressively transitioned to being used in strategies focusing solely on value extraction and branding within neoliberal planning strategies.

5

ADAPTABILITY AND
THE "COOL" ARTIFICIAL CITY

Over the past ten years, top-down temporary urbanism initiatives have been included more often in wider strategies of urban transformation. This is the result of a widespread recognition of the role of adaptability and temporary urbanism as triggers for activation and hence value extraction. Occurring at both meso and macro levels, they are primarily driven by top-down, public-private arrangements involving a previously planned allocation of roles, duties, and power among the actors involved, with landowners at the forefront. The process of adaptability, although it includes some form of agility, is highly thought through and strategized, which means less improvisation and more regulatory framing, all driven by neoliberal and entrepreneurial planning practices merged with adaptability.

This chapter discusses and engages with the latest trends that have embraced the use of adaptability and temporary urbanisms as ways to promote "cool" and "fun" moments in cities. Those sit in a narrative similar to the one used for promoting creative cities but also, more important, within the experiential nature of cities (and the experiential discourse that has been built around it). Temporary projects and initiatives are designed mostly with the ambition of creating a buzz and incentivizing specific transformations (including rebranding and planned gentrification). Such processes take us back to the rhythms of the city and specifically how everyday rhythms emerging out of temporary projects are enmeshed into mid- and longer-term prospects of value creation and extraction. In such contexts, adaptability tends to spread beyond the indoors toward the outdoors to include public spaces, streets, and portions of the city that are also undergoing regeneration. This chapter describes its mechanisms and develops a critique of its neoliberal interpretation and monetarization, which tends to favor pastiche practices resulting in a loss of meaning and scope with detrimental socioeconomic and urban consequences.

TEMPORARY USES IN THE NEOLIBERAL EXPERIENTIAL CITY

The rise of the adaptability paradigm and the spread of temporary urbanism and its inclusion within neoliberal planning find their roots in how temporary urbanism has been linked initially to arts and cultural practices. In other words, temporary uses are associated with cities being seen and advertised as cool, trendy, and creative places where people can be entertained. Going back to path dependency, their inclusion reflects how temporary and adaptable uses and practices became part of the creative city discourse.[1] This resonates deeply with how artists (often temporary space users) have been considered drivers of transformation and regeneration.[2] An implicit correlation exists between vacancy and artistic occupations viewed as temporary solutions to revitalize and transform neighborhoods. This is about value generation leading to gentrification, as observed in many capital and core cities, including, of course, London and New York, but also

Berlin, Marseille, Manchester, Milano, and Barcelona.[3] Ambitious regeneration strategies have included or have used the temporary reuse of empty buildings as vectors of activation, value generation, and rebranding. One example is La Friche de la Belle de Mai in Marseilles, France. Such spaces can be labeled as creative brownfields because they are aesthetically distinct, derelict, and flexible premises (often former industrial sites) that can attract and host artistic projects and hence rejuvenate places.[4]

In the past two decades, such creative brownfields have been part of the "creative city-economy."[5] Temporary projects, which often became permanent, have been merged within entrepreneurial strategies based on fostering the creative and cultural industry sector. The latest have sought to capitalize on the creative reputation of such alternative spaces, matching the wider narrative of the experience economy and of experiential cities.[6] In these instances, temporary projects are spaces of consumption and branding. The uniqueness of temporary initiatives includes place distinctiveness, diversity, and richness and is linked to spectacle, consumption, and entertainment. This has been explicit in how temporary (meanwhile) uses became a widespread strategy in a city like London and were supported and developed by key public organizations (for example, the Greater London Authority and London Legacy Development Corporation [LLDC]). As Mara Ferreri notes, "The original official narrative of temporary reuse hinged on a combination of 'creative city' discourses and policies and a new urgency to provide visual fixes to the effects of the recession on negative perceptions and experiences of urban spaces. Underneath the discourse of creative and community uses lies a strong need to mimic economic activity through symbolic public occupations that produce a sense of vibrancy and activation."[7] Key here is the importance of testing as a way to foster value creation but also to accompany transformations and deal

ADAPTABILITY AND THE "COOL" ARTIFICIAL CITY • 123

with asynchronous rhythms of transformations for places and people. This is expressed in the following quote, which reflects the approach taken by the Greater London Authority almost a decade ago.

> There will be lots of places that are going to have a lot of building work going on. These won't have the intended use until a long period of time, so it's how you manage that in places, in terms of having a temporary use. Given the amount of growth that is happening, as well as reinvigorating existing high streets, there is a need to foster emerging high streets. We are working in a couple of places with boroughs to try to see the uses that would work on an emerging high street and what doesn't work. In a similar way there is a growing concern over the fact that a lot of workspace has already been displaced by housing and a new way of looking at combining new workspaces with that, so again we need to test the limits of that. There are also lots of other things that can be tested, partly to convince people that it is possible.[8]

We can push the argument further by noting that temporary urbanism as a mode of production of cool places appears as a continuum of, but also a deviation from, the way in which culture and cultural facilities were used in the 1990s for community enhancement, rebranding, and urban competitiveness.[9] Such culture-led strategies have been revisited and diversified. This was partly linked to the costs of financing and then managing such projects, but it was also a way to address apathy from the public toward traditional cultural facilities and a call to provide new and more diverse places for entertainment.[10] The ephemeral, distinct, and experiential character of temporary projects elevated them as a new, alternative, and fun attraction that city residents can benefit from. Bottom-up temporary facilities (typically

Boxpark-type retail parks, which I will discuss later in this chapter) are based upon such marketing narrative and reinforced by their alternative design. The temporary space is a "brand" and a product of consumption, with a slightly edgy image; it offers a range of commercial and retail activities and is shaped as a "destination" where customers can experience something different.

Twenty years ago, Ann Markusen and David King referred to the economic benefits of culture as an artistic dividend. The recognition of the benefits of adaptability means that there is a "temporary dividend" that resonates with the process of value creation and extraction discussed hereafter.[11] This dividend derives from the ephemerality of the space and its ability to offer a different experience, similar to that of a show or an exhibition. The way local authorities and developers have embraced temporary uses converge with marketing strategies advertising cities as edgy and vibrant; temporary projects are seen as ways to attract customers and subsequently lead to other economic benefits.[12] This occurs at various scales (micro level and city level) and through various types of temporary uses. Typically, temporary gardens— known as pocket parks in the United States—have "inspired planning strategy for creating dynamic urban cultural experiences that foster economic development."[13] They have spread in many North American cities, from Montreal to Portland; San José; and Washington, DC, and they provide public spaces for people to interact. Parklets provide additional seating for restaurants, hence contributing to local economic prosperity and neighborhood branding. Thus, in British and North American cities, "politicians, developers and other elite interests attempt to mobilize and exploit grassroots popular participation like DIY [do-it-yourself] urban design in their favor, whether to claim community support and credibility or harness the cool factor of a trendy aesthetic. The embrace of public participation by elites coincides fittingly with the era of neoliberal policymaking."[14]

ADAPTABILITY AND THE "COOL" ARTIFICIAL CITY • 125

This evolution is well summarized by Nicholas Karachalis when he argues that "temporary use is not new, but over recent years it has gained popularity and become part of the images used in city marketing. It is celebrated as a policy tool to enhance public space and provide resources for the social and cultural economy to develop on a neighborhood level."[15] An important factor in this shift has been the increasing use of new technologies and social media to create buzz about specific places, businesses, or activities to generate attractiveness; flows; and, of course, financial returns. Such artificiality has been carefully picked up by local authorities and developers to take advantage of the role of influencers and shows how "social media provide both a near-real-time indicator of shifting attitudes toward neighborhoods and an early warning measure of future changes in neighborhood composition and demand."[16]

Within this experiential shift, temporary urbanism has been associated with the idea of the "creative milieu," and temporary users are considered "active players in the shaping of new urban spaces" matching a clear consumerism agenda.[17] This explains the global proliferation of temporary retailing initiatives from pop-up shops, restaurants, and galleries not only in places in need of transformation but also in existing hot spots (for example, Times Square or the Meatpacking District in New York City, or Regent Street or Shoreditch in London) as part of their global branding. A city like London has seen pop-up temporary projects ranging from temporary cinemas, malls, bars, restaurants or, miniature golf courses proliferate in recent years, thus making them mainstream, vacuous, and generic.[18] In such configurations, temporary uses and projects offer new services and goods and provide new ways to target customers and influence their behaviors and purchases. This explains why business improvement districts and local councils, typically in British, American, French, and Italian cities, have been active in temporary initiatives. The Meatpacking

FIGURE 5.1 The Meatpacking District in New York City and its temporary sitting installations and street closures.

Source: Lauren Andres.

District in New York (figure 5.1) is an optimal illustration of this trend: pop-up shops and sitting areas, temporary closures of streets for outdoor activities (including dining and events or festivals, for example, the L.E.A.F. Festival of Flowers) are part of its identity and trendy reputation.

Consumerism in this context is mixed with the experiential in cities as places of opportunities for "'not random, but not by accident either' encounters."[19] This explains how high streets and shopping malls have been transitioning away from places to purchase products to experiential spaces, or as playgrounds for conspicuous consumption based on hospitality and leisure experiences.[20] This isn't without consequences, and Ferreri summarized this correctly: "Far from being 'creative fillers' of vacancy in uncertain times, temporary projects have been incorporated into mechanisms of city revalorisation, often becoming sites of conflict as they reflect, in their origins, implementation and governance, the consensus of neoliberal urban development, with its uneven, boom-bust cycles of creative destruction, its loosening of regulations and its public support for private entrepreneurship."[21]

To illustrate the neoliberal shifts taken by the experiential reinterpretation of temporary urbanisms, a return to Berlin is important. As discussed in chapter 3, Berlin embraced temporary and adaptable uses of buildings as solutions for vacancy and then rebuilt the image of the city to attract external investors, entrepreneurs, and tourists. These included the multiplication of planned-on-purpose temporary projects (with some then made permanent), from beach bars, clubs, and artistic squats.[22] As Claire Colomb notes with reference to policy documents,[23] embracing temporariness as a development strategy showed a "broader shift in local policies towards the promotion of the cultural industries and the 'creative city,' accompanied by initiatives to encourage 'creative spaces,' of which 'interim spaces' reinvented by 'urban pioneers' were perceived as a key component."[24] This innovative and interventionist approach was made possible through the introduction of new regulations, typically allowing temporary rentals for nonprofit and community-oriented uses of public assets.[25] Such arrangements were better than no solutions in a context of real estate crisis and urgency to rebuild the reputation of the city. The focus was on creative entrepreneurs, community benefits, and the creative economy. Any references to previous squats or other illegal occupations, however, were carefully omitted from public discourse. "Squats or encampments associated with the radical Left and *Autonomen* movements—were left out of promotional narratives, and their existence was often repressed or suppressed by Berlin's successive governments."[26] Once the market started to pick up again in the 2000s, the supportive and flexible approach and policy toward temporary users changed significantly, with temporary uses explicitly acknowledged as "generating the right preconditions for further commercial redevelopment to take place on or around temporarily used sites."[27] Temporary projects, flirting between their adaptable status and a prospect of possibly staying, were terminated through evictions and nonrenewal of short-term leases, hence leaving way for formal redevelopment. Projects that sustained their activities underwent "expansion, professionalisation, commercialisation, and cooperation with or co-option by the local state and the market" aligned with a strategy of entrepreneurial gentrification and value extraction.[28]

The policy implementation observed in Berlin allows us to situate the emergence of the temporary dividend as a specific sector of activity participating in value generation and profit-driven urban development.[29] Berlin, followed by London, has seen this dividend translated into new but more pastiche interpretations of adaptability reflecting "subversive temporary place-making being increasingly drowned out by commodified and government-sanctioned pop-ups and meanwhile uses," even if those were initially initiated from grassroots alternative creative movements.[30] Such actions as in Berlin are not unique and are "harnessing and incorporating practices and strategies from urban social movements and the counter-cultural scene in the name of 'cultural creativity and entrepreneurial activation' while simultaneously dismantling existing social infrastructures and implementing stricter forms of urban policing."[31]

Engaging with this critique of neoliberal temporary urbanisms takes us back to Henri Lefebvre but also David Harvey and Mike Davis.[32] The contemporary deviation of temporary urbanisms toward branding and cool urban living shows a clear divide between, on the one hand, the rhythms of consumption and asset generation and, on the other hand, the rhythms of the everyday, particularly those immersed in more grassroots and alternative purposes. The immersion of temporary urbanism in consumerism has been an additional step in confiscating the experimental side of the adaptability paradigm and hence its association with coping and community tactics.

More concerning is how market-designed temporary uses have often been hidden under the umbrella of community benefits in areas undergoing gentrification. A "key advantage of temporary use is that it can be linked to forms of more participatory approaches to city marketing."[33] This has been explicit in the United Kingdom and typically in London in large-scale regeneration projects, such as in Croydon (South London) or Wembley (North London) but also, for example, in Brixton, a multicultural neighborhood in the London borough of Lambeth known for its bohemian and cultural character and for undergoing significant transformations for more than a decade. This neighborhood has hosted its core Pop Brixton (figure 5.2), a temporary retail, leisure, and community project formed of shipping containers and developed in partnership between Lambeth Council and the private company MakeShift. Pop Brixton opened in 2015 on disused land awaiting redevelopment, and while initially planned for only a three-year period, it benefited from several lease extensions (despite not being profitable); it should remain on the site until at least 2024 while new development plans for this central area of the district (Brixton Rec Quarter) are negotiated and despite the Pop Brixton company entering into administration in June 2024. Pop Brixton gathers independent businesses (mainly restaurants) along with a coworking space hosting social enterprises, a youth radio station, and other small

FIGURE 5.2 Pop Brixton in London: a place to be (for some).
Source: Lauren Andres.

businesses. It also has a small food-growing project (pop farm). The perception of the local authority when setting up the project reflected how temporary urbanism was approached as a form of development to support the community and also serve the transformation of the area.

> We as a local authority can be a more enlightened land owner because we have a different set of objectives and parameters. This project won't make any money until after year three, but that is not a problem for us because we can point to all the outcomes we will support, in terms of local businesses supporting, in terms of local people who will be working here, so we can be a bit more flexible in that regard now. I guess also we are working with a

ADAPTABILITY AND THE "COOL" ARTIFICIAL CITY • 131

private sector here, but here the private sector is also someone who has gone into this more out of interest than out of commercial imperative, perhaps that has caused us some problems as well because it hasn't been as commercially minded.[34]

Today, Pop Brixton is one of those love/hate projects: it is very popular among its users, but it has also been ferociously criticized for participating in the socioeconomic transformation of the neighborhood and its gentrification and for being extremely costly in terms of maintenance and not profitable. It is an example of the latest temporary urbanism entrepreneurial trends, and I will return to this example later in this the chapter. Overall, the advertised "community benefits" are a way to tackle (or hide) other social challenges and feed into more complex urban development models founded on assetization, value creation, and extraction.

ASSETIZATION, VALUE CREATION, AND EXTRACTION THROUGH TEMPORARY USES AND ADAPTABILITY

The process of value creation and extraction is part of the adaptable and temporary urbanism paradigm already touched on when we discussed the "activation" process in chapter 3. What characterizes the shift leading to a temporary urbanism dividend is that it is embedded in the process of financialization, in other words, another "stage of capitalism in which finance has become more dominant than hitherto, and that whilst the economic system remains capitalist a different form of capitalism has emerged (which at some stage will evolve into some other form)."[35] This is fundamentally part of the latest trends characterizing value creation and capital accumulation.[36] David Harvey was already emphasizing this process as the secondary circuit of capital, in which surplus value is monetized,[37] when the term "financialization" became a buzz word in 2010.[38] This is the same time that top-down temporary urbanism became a widespread solution to address vacant and underused spaces based on the goal of extracting financial benefits through an experiential and entrepreneurial narrative.

Financialization as a lens for reading the contemporary dynamics of the adaptable and temporary city is complementary to situating it within globalization and neoliberalism processes. It anchors the urban and hence temporary urbanism within a system of asset supply and value extraction, in other words, as a way to generate new income streams.[39] As Desiree Fields and others note, the "urban landscape makes an attractive escape valve for the finance capital that has accumulated globally in recent decades and is on a perpetual hunt for yield."[40] This means that plots of land have become assets and that landowners and landlords are the agents of neoliberal development. The mobilization of land as a financial asset has led to the development of various strategies to create exchange values from things that otherwise would not be saleable.[41] This is exactly where temporary uses come in, and they have been included in the dynamics of assetization, in other words, "the transformation of things into resources which generate income without a sale."[42] The generation of income is based on the assumption that temporary interventions are part of in-between solutions sitting within cycles of financing and investments (allowing the increase of land values but also generating rents from temporary commercial units in larger-scale developments). This also concerns the anticipated future income streams triggered by the activation process launched by temporary projects and hence the increase of land values across the neighborhood.

ADAPTABILITY AND THE "COOL" ARTIFICIAL CITY • 133

Assetization occurs in various ways, and significant concerns have been raised relating to its wider socio-economic impacts, particularly towards the most vulnerable communities and businesses already living and working in precarious conditions. Adverse consequences may include delaying investments to serve speculative future rounds of value creation, and fostering temporary initiatives for speculative value extraction.[43] The lucrative assetization of land through temporary projects has been characterizing the strategies of both private owners (typically landowners and developers) and also local authorities as landowners. Local municipalities have indeed become more reliant on monetizing land and infrastructure in a context of austerity and budgetary cuts. This has formed the context within which investment-seeking cities have become sites of neoliberal experimentation favoring adaptability in urban development and hence temporary urbanism.[44] It isn't, however, a brand new process.

The use of temporariness as a form of assetization is anchored in earlier work on time-space-structured transformations used to revalorize devalued landscapes.[45] It testifies to how capital circulates through the built environment through non-permanent processes. Weber notes that this circulation is highly dynamic and erratic being related to cycles of redundancy, abandonment, destruction, and reconstruction.[46] There is an explicit relationship with time and cycles of development which has been integrative of the urban development process (see chapter 2). Schumpeter's notion of "creative destruction" is still relevant,[47] as it allows capturing "the way in which capital's restless search for profits requires constant renewal through galelike forces that simultaneously make way for the new and devalue the old."[48] This is where temporariness and adaptability fit in and have been reinterpreted with further thought given to the assetization of land *and* temporary constructions. What is at play here is the nature of obsolescence and the link between obsolescence and landscapes being left behind by innovation. Temporary initiatives are by essence obsolete, at least in their most contemporary top-down interpretations. They have a clear end date (even if their initial timescale often ends up being extended). Redundancy is hence materialized in construction materials which are not meant to be durable without subsequent additional maintenance costs. While temporary projects are not supposed to be sustainable, their obsolescence isn't, however, linked to a displacement of interest or to dramatic economic or technological changes. Obsolescence is constructed as a trigger of value activation and (re)creation; it is part of the urban buzz and experiential narrative with the goal of moving towards a new cycle of value extraction through permanent constructions. If this cycle isn't completed on time the adaptable nature of the projects allows the initial temporary use to be extended. This occurs when the real estate market still hasn't picked up or a new planning application hasn't been agreed yet.

Such a reinterrogation of obsolescence and assetization takes us back to the financialization of the city and what this means for the next stage of capital accumulation. The latest manifestation "has been globally unfolding and locally evolving over the last three to four decades, and has now installed itself at all levels and dimensions of everyday life" based on a diversification of financial intermediaries.[49] Drawing upon Lefebvre and Harvey, Moreno argued that "financial capitalism was liable to mutate into a new urban form, based on the intensification of 'secondary' circuits of exploitation operating both inside and outside the realm of production."[50] This can be observed in the rise of urban forms of rent-extraction—particularly towards housing, but not only. It also concerns commercial units and any other innovative experimental spaces of encounters within which temporary

ADAPTABILITY AND THE "COOL" ARTIFICIAL CITY • 135

strategies have been stitched. Value creation here is arising from an agglomeration effect based on the activation process anticipated out of temporary urban transformations. This larger-scale process is, however, much more complex that a simple strategy of activation. It includes both monetarized and nonmonetarized values and assets, inclusive of encounters, experiences and intangibles closely linked to population density and of how the temporary dividend is manifesting. This inclusion of temporariness as illustrated by Harris through the recognition of pop-up uses testifies to what Harvey sees in the postmodern condition and how the experience of time-space is being compressed because of globalization.[51] This reflects "changing technologies and economic structures and instigating tangible changes in how places are felt and perceived" but more importantly a recognition of adaptability and the ephemeral in the production of postmodern experiential cities.[52]

A decade ago, Moreno hypothesized the existence of what he called a "new urban 'spirit' of capitalism" linked to the changes encountered by the production of space for financial profit and the changing role of postmodern cities.[53] "The city, comprising a fabric of social assets saturated with value, provided a space in which capitalism could re-fortify itself, through restructuring the ownership of the relations of production, consumption and collective consumption." The inclusion of the temporary dividend in the long-term vision of redevelopment and profit generation constitutes one of the latest trends of this new urban spirit. This is effectively materialized in how neoliberal planning has been driven forward thanks to more complex and diverse public–private networks influencing policy formation. These were triggered by increasing deregulation aimed at creating flexible, solution-oriented decision-making structures.[54] This neoliberal deregulation, for Ward, testifies to a "calculated informality" service and a solution-oriented policy innovation. Indeed, here, the temporary value extraction arises from a conglomerate of urban "buzzes" (architects, retailers, visitors, etc.) who participate in making the temporary project an income generator.[55]

There is another important factor to consider in the way temporariness became merchandised and assessed in the mid-2000s. This is intrinsically linked to how product selling practices were transferred to urban spaces, here territorializing further city marketing practices. The retail sector embraced pop-up technics to generate a 'sense of excitement' and attract specific customers allowing the sale of 'niche' products at a higher price.[56] Such practices, often used by major global brands, have correlatively encouraged temporary uses. The customer, or space user, by going through such a customer experience, is viewed as being offered a "time-limited exclusivity."[57] It is in that context that the 'pop-up sell event' was translated to 'pop-up' spaces, and specifically pop-up experiential spaces, typically pop-up malls with the first one, Boxpark, being set up in Shoreditch, London.[58] The temporary pop-up mall isn't a destination customers visit to find a product but primarily an experiential destination; the marketing rational behind the projects is about exposure, innovative experiences and testing, all with minimal economic risks.[59] The pop-up malls are strategically located in upcoming neighborhoods, undergoing transformations, hence matching a wider marketing strategy.[60] Such pop-up malls constructed by clustering shipping containers have spread globally. Several examples can be mentioned from TI:ME in Montecillo, Stackt in Toronto, Common Ground in Seoul and of course in London, Boxpark in Shoreditch (figure 5.3), Croydon and Wembley. Boxpark Shoreditch, the first project of its sort in the United Kingdom, "played a big role in asking questions on the use of urban vacant land, densifying short-term development and challenging

FIGURE 5.3 The pop-up mall: Boxpark in Shoreditch, London.

Source: Lauren Andres.

traditional planning approaches."[61] While criticized for its very commercial approach to urban making, it is nevertheless considered as a successful initiative with positive impacts on the local economy.[62]

The marketisation and assetization of the temporary dividend goes much beyond its translation into the model of pop-up retail parks. It has been manifesting in various ways, dependent on the developers'/local authorities' visions and ambitions. At site level, the strategization of temporariness as a process of asset and value extraction has been used by some small/medium size developers from the 2000s onward, specifically those specialized in redeveloping lands not seen as valuable assets for other developers. The quote below from a developer in London is an exemplar of how assetization through the temporary dividend is part of a complex risk management and financing strategy.

> Property development is nothing but a series of problems to be solved, of risks to be mitigated and managed right from the beginning: risk in purchasing land, risk in planning, risks in sales, risks in delivery, risk all the way through. All we do as property developers is manage that risk, bit by bit. So if you think about buying a piece of land that is dead and buried that nobody else wants, you need to do something more as the land is crying out for some sort of engagement . . . To mitigate that risk you have to show people they are wrong; you have to turn that place around in perception terms. You cannot do that by planning a scheme and making a nice brochure because people go 'yeah alright, nice picture, but what does that mean'. Even when you have the diggers on site and start to build people say 'yeah, good luck with that'. If you do things on that site, however, that means that 50,000 people arrive and have a really happy time and Facebook and Instagram and website it. A site that was dead and buried is now alive. By doing so, you can change the perception of a place. That is a huge tool in helping to regenerate and getting everybody else on board, the funders and the people that make it happen, to believe that that places can change, including the local authorities.[63]

The value of the temporary dividend isn't then only constructed upon the marketing of a standard product; it is constructed on testing ideas and uses but also through the galvanization of both political and community support. Temporariness here is a tool to embrace and benefit from the different rhythms of transformation and the wider challenges associated with urban development

ADAPTABILITY AND THE "COOL" ARTIFICIAL CITY • 139

(including of course its political dimension and community engagement imperative). The interviewee continued as follows:

> Politics sits across the top; there are always politics involved in every property development. How do you make that politics work in your favour? By putting yourself out there in the middle of the place and showing people your true intentions and persuading them that you are doing good. Local authorities aren't interested in buildings, they are interested in people who are working there, jobless people, socially disadvantaged people; so how do you contribute to helping people, to having better educated people, fewer that are jobless and more happy people in socially cohesive places? If you can show you can do all or part of those things, you are doing a good job and you will be supported and helped in your mission. In the type of developments that we do, that are difficult, you need all the help you can get.

Using temporary projects to revive a site, generate value and support isn't unique to the United Kingdom, but occurs in many other countries, including France. The examples of the Iles de Nantes and the strategy of the French national railway company (SNCF) are here worth referring to in order to continue the discussion.

Iles de Nantes is a large-scale regeneration scheme in the Upper Brittany region located in the medium-sized city of Nantes. It concerns the revival of a former industrial brownfield site situated on an island in the Loire River, adjacent to the city center. The project is led by a dedicated local public development company, the SAMOA, created back in 2003, at a time when temporary urbanism (*urbanisme transitoire* in French, i.e., "transient urbanism") started to spread in the country. What is of interest here is how 'transient urbanism' has been, from the start, an integral component of the redevelopment vision to support the rebranding, assetisztion, activation, and long-term transformation of the area. The temporary dividend is displayed with a focus on the cultural and creative sector. It is tailored around the collaboration between local authorities and communities, developers, not-for-profit groups along with small firms and businesses.

Until 2011, temporary projects primarily designed around cultural and artistic initiatives were used as experiential tools to re-brand the island and label it with a new identity and role in the city. Once the first development phases were completed, the SAMOA diversified the temporary urbanism strategy further and implemented a new real estate strategy which embraced the temporary dividend by renting spaces and units in vacant buildings awaiting demolition. Temporary tenants were targeted in the following sectors of activity: cultural and creative industries, multimedia and image, not-for-profit, arts, design and architecture.[64] The use of temporary uses has been further expanded in recent years to include wastelands awaiting development temporarily allocated to urban agriculture and logistics services. The approach taken at the Ile de Nantes is quite unique, particularly in the way it has been using the full-spec of top-down forms of temporary urbanisms with the goal of nurturing the wider marketing of the project to gather interest from investors and new residents. Clearly the temporary dividend has been a way to shape an innovative and distinct postmodern vision for the city and its city centre. As such, it has been sitting within a regional and national rebranding process differing but also complementing the way in which temporary urbanism has been embraced in the French capital itself.

The spread and professionalization (see chapter 7) of temporary urbanism in Paris occurred from 2012. It initially focused on specific sites (e.g. empty buildings) with the goal of developing cultural, artistic and community-focused projects.[65] It also concerned temporary outdoor projects in high-profile touristic areas (for example along the Seine River with its flagship project— Paris Plages). This ad hoc and high-profile strategy significantly expanded in 2019 when the city launched and adopted in 2021 a charter promoting the temporary occupation of buildings. This charter was signed by the largest real estate owners in France, including the SNCF.[66]

For almost a decade, the SNCF, through their dedicated real estate entity, has been at the forefront of embracing temporary urbanism to manage its property portfolio more efficiently and extract values from buildings and sites not on the market for sale in the immediate future. As in Nantes, assetization and value extraction aren't the sole goals. Reshaping the company's reputation, enhancing its heritage and positioning it as a key player in real estate development was central to the SNCF's policy.[67] Following this ambition, the group has multiplied the transformation of former empty assets through temporary uses, principally cultural and artistic spaces in Paris and the Ile de France region.[68] What SNCF has been doing here resonates to a greater extent with the strategy adopted by Network Rail in England and the way it has used meanwhile leases to find new tenants for its properties located next to or below rail tracks (i.e. under-arch units as in London, Loughborough Junction for example, or Birmingham, Digbeth). What is interesting in the French case (and not that valid—yet—in the United Kingdom) is how the temporary dividends have also been integrated into the transformation and renewal of deprived social housing estates. Here, the national agency for 'urban renovation' (ANRU) is now also starting to temporarily allocate new uses to empty spaces and buildings over the different stages of urban renewal.[69] Assetization is applied to sites and properties mostly owned by housing associations (OPH in France), hence considered as public assets. Alongside a goal of value extraction, temporariness is associated with social benefits and reputation: bringing inhabitants together, changing the very negative image of those estates and hence facilitating the transformation of those neighbourhoods, particularly in the outskirts. The temporary dividend is, therefore, associated with ambitions of beautification, securitization but also implicit sanitization.

Overall, commercially driven models adopted in French and British cities testify to how temporary urbanisms and diverse forms of adaptability have diversified beyond activation and testing to be integrated as core components of much more complex strategies of asset management, real estate development and planning. As a result, in such configurations, little nowadays seems to be left to spontaneity and significant concerns and criticisms are raised particularly toward the artificialization and loss of essence of temporary initiatives and the meaning of adaptability.

TEMPORARY URBANISM DRIFTS AWAY FROM AN INCLUSIVE ADAPTABLE NARRATIVE

Criticisms have been raised against the interpretations of temporary urbanism in terms of neoliberalism and consumerism.[70] These are grounded on four main issues: the primacy of top-down mechanisms that has led to a loss of meaning and freedom to experiment, particularly when temporariness is driven by artificial aesthetics rather than content; the tendency of temporary initiatives to trigger exclusion rather than inclusion; the use of

ADAPTABILITY AND THE "COOL" ARTIFICIAL CITY • 143

the temporary dividend based on value extraction and assetization being a factor of gentrification and displacement; and, the marketisation of temporariness displaying a perverse commercialization of precarity, with the latest not being tackled from a policy perspective.

Going back to Lefebvre, one of the greater values of temporariness in urban making is to offer moments of spontaneity, of difference, as part of the everyday production of the city. This used to materialize in alternative visions, projects, that embraced the temporary 'moment' of standby as a way to shape distinct rhythms and outcomes, contrasting with the planned routines and repetitions that constitute urban development and cities overall. As such, "there is always something new that introduces itself into the repetitive."[71] For Lefebvre, most rhythms in principle can coexist, testifying to what he calls "eurhythmia."[72] Eurhythmia is a process in which any rhythms can occur conjointly and effectively not clash. In some situations, though, discord can occur leading to arrhythmia and to rhythms damaging each other.[73] Building on this point, it is apparent that contemporary interpretations of temporary urbanisms and their neoliberal interpretations are now clashing instead of being complementary. These are due to discords related to meaning or purpose and specifically to whose needs they are serving. Indeed, the channeling of the temporary dividend for value extraction and selling strategies has resulted in temporary initiatives losing their experiential character and being rendered artificial as a standard product of consumption reflecting the nature of the neoliberal postmodern society.[74]

Temporariness indeed becomes artificial when the temporary dividend is solely set up to respond to economic and marketing purposes through artificial beautification (i.e. the trendiness of a place). In such circumstances, it follows a profit-making agenda without taking any account of people, places, and their localities.

Those projects, as a result, often fail and are vigorously criticized. Indeed, misinterpreting the wider ambitions of temporary agility leads "to a more sinister and cynical application"[75] of the adaptability narrative for which temporary uses "are in fact no more than another facet of the manipulation of the hapless citizen consumer. The subversive has been subverted."[76]

Such criticisms are to be merged with how these projects often contribute to accelerating gentrification, hence fostering exclusion rather than inclusion. Typically, Pop Brixton, alluded to earlier on, falls into this category of being strongly criticized by local community members, particularly those who have been living there for years, who saw the area changed, witnessed the arrival of new residents, with higher incomes, and have been impacted by increasing rents and higher living costs. Pop Brixton is viewed as a profit-making space (even if the project isn't profitable *per se*), aiming to transform the district and effectively displace its residents and small businesses, with such dynamics being shaped through public/private agreements.

> The problem is these spaces are not very civic at all. In initial cases, such as Pop Brixton in South London, this has seen a private entity take public assets and begin to profit from them by creating new exclusive spaces of consumption that cater predominantly to an external market rather than a local one. The private entity is not accountable to the public so has no obligation—the failure lies in the agreement between the council and this private entity.[77]

This artificialization and drift is also particularly visible when temporary uses are effectively imposed on developers, typically under 106 agreements in the United Kingdom. Artificialization here sits within the lack of strategic thinking put behind the delivery of the temporary dividend. The quote below is revealing.

ADAPTABILITY AND THE "COOL" ARTIFICIAL CITY • 145

It highlights how imposed temporary uses in a recent large-scale regeneration project in London are very carefully crafted with two main priorities: meeting regulations while ensuring value creation, but also anticipating any risks and possible conflicts.

> We are looking at a project that could still take twenty years; we have been on site for ten years already. It's a 30-year-long project. Some of those meantime uses could be quite a long time. We are very much conscious that it is much better to put the land in some kind of active use rather have it fenced off, gathering dust, empty fridges etc. We are also very conscious that if the meantime use you put into is so popular that sometimes you can have a bit of a backlash when you come to build the building you have permission for . . . One has to be very upfront as per the fact that it is a meantime, temporary use . . . I am not saying we cannot put temporary allotments for example, but if we do so, you are better off to use skips.[78]

The strategy displayed here is explicit: the purpose of temporary uses is to make the area more livable and active and to deliver this through the goal of benefitting existing and future community (as per 106 agreements). However, the way temporary urbanism is framed testifies to a very artificial and narrow interpretation: temporary uses are targeting specific age groups (particularly young people) and are shaped with a clear end date and through a process that is putting at its core discontent avoidance. This included temporary playgrounds, strategically located opposite a shopping mall, a social pavilion used for community purposes but with minimal amenities and service provision (e.g. no heating), temporary sports fields and retail parks, all complemented by temporary seasonal events (Christmas market, ice rink). This restrictive but very strategically designed approach to the temporary dividend aligns with Harris's point that temporary urbanism and the pop-up sector have become "big business."[79] It also complements Bishop's critique that "there is a growing tendency for city policymakers to ask for temporary buildings and interventions in the absence of how these may really contribute to addressing the underlying issues. The idea that they are interesting has got through, but the application into strategy has not."[80]

Going back to the point made on rhythms, a situation of arrhythmia thus seems to emerge here, at least for some groups of individuals whose everyday practices are effectively affected by temporary transformations instead of being positively impacted by them (or even being able to initiate them). Temporary urbanism in some of its latest and more perverse interpretations has, therefore, been exclusive rather than inclusive. It has been following a similar path to the one of the creative city and its cultural and creative quarters. Its latest interpretations have ignored the local character of places and their local needs to prioritize profit-making and consumerism. What is even more concerning is the extent to which temporary strategies have been fostering exclusion, and making socio-economic inequalities more visible. Retail and commercial-led projects but also many of those focused on leisure, culture or arts—all part of the experiential nature of cities—have been primarily targeting middle- to high-income individuals, often under the age of forty and holding a high education degree (hence fitting with the profile of the "creative class"[81]). Noting that many temporary projects are serving regeneration prospects, and are hence located in former industrial working-class and diverse neighborhoods, they do significantly contrast with the type of urban settings long-term residents are used to. As a result, they feel unwelcome and excluded from new temporary projects. This issue was the primary critique

ADAPTABILITY AND THE "COOL" ARTIFICIAL CITY • 147

that arose from the Friche de la Belle de Mai in Marseille which, as a project, never really integrated into its historical neighbourhood.[82] A similar observation can be made of Pop Brixton. As Douglas rightly points out reflecting on DIY urban making in England and North America, "There might also be a concern that the formalization of some projects or types of projects that best fit with white and affluent values could risk crowding out or further marginalizing ideas, uses and design sensibilities that do not match mainstream, market-based ideals. The problem isn't that these spaces are being created by educated, privileged people; it's that the opportunity to influence the character of one's community in this way is not open to all."[83]

Clearly, many temporary initiatives and hence assetization processes sit within wider dynamics of gentrification; these had often started to occur prior to the adaptable narrative being introduced and were an additional catalyst to encourage temporary projects.[84] Looking at NYC, Douglas demonstrates how the use of planned DIY tactics in Time Square led to a spike in retail rents in the area.[85] Similarly, it is not surprising that the Meatpacking District and its combination of high-end retail, cultural facilities, temporary installations and luxury new development make it one of the most expensive area in Manhattan. As mentioned earlier, Berlin has been in a very similar situation with some of its key (initially alternative) creative brownfields used as leverage for gentrification.[86] While an initiative like the Tacheles (figure 5.4) always rejected a shift towards a more traditional alternative space it ended up being fully part of the city branding strategy, being presented as "a set of spaces, courtyards and streets, providing a mix of traditional architectural elements, retail outlets and restaurants, a designer five star hotel, office space, apartments and a series of courtyards run by the artists of Art Forum Tacheles". The district now labelled 'Quartier am

FIGURE 5.4 The Kunsthaus Tacheles in Berlin, Germany: an iconic alternative space that led to the rapid gentrification of the neighborhood.

Source: Lauren Andres.

Tacheles' thus followed a rapid path of gentrification with the spread of high-end housing developments.

The contemporary directions taken by postmodern, neoliberal and experiential temporary urbanisms are, therefore, without doubt occupying much of the space that was previously given to emptiness, both as an opportunity to experiment but also as a manifestation of urban dysfunctions. Clearly "temporary solutions do nothing to alleviate the causes of a vacancy in the first place or prevent it from happening elsewhere. This explains the brightly colored, loud, and vibrant nature of 'pop-up' temporary urban interventions in London, where creators seek to distract onlookers from the crisis of displacement, by creating a spectacle

ADAPTABILITY AND THE "COOL" ARTIFICIAL CITY • 149

in the public realm."[87] The emphasis on spectacle creation and place beautification tends to hide the often dire realities of those neighborhoods undergoing transformations and particularly the everyday difficulties encountered by the most vulnerable residents and local businesses. This is where temporary urbanisms transitioned to being artificialized as 'just' a development tool, rather than, as discussed throughout, a way to deeply engage with the very diverse rhythms of the urban and the diverse and often harsh realities of its long-term residents. "Careless inclusion where they serve no purpose is likely to be at best counterproductive and even detrimental. Temporary interventions will not resolve deep-seated structural problems in the city. Half completed then abandoned projects can be an insidious form of urban blight, leaving behind cynicism in the communities where false hopes have been raised."[88] This is, therefore, where the introduction of temporary uses is failing as they are disconnected from the principle of adaptability per se.

In such a context, temporary urbanisms have been shaped and driven by those holding power, owning land, as well as relevant skills and education. In other words, they were developed by powerful rather than hidden voices, who are often those living in a state of precarity. The commercialization of precarity has also engineered a precarity of place and labor.[89] Materially and aesthetically, temporary projects have valorized nonpermanent structures that are effectively used in the context of crisis and disaster management, the most popular ones being containers. Such containers—in other settings—are where the most vulnerable are provided shelter (e.g. refugee camps) but also detained. Containers are now "no longer just used for their practical values in emergency conditions and uncertain times, but also for their cultural cachet."[90] In such a context, what has appeared is a banalization of the idea of the nonpermanent being fine, acceptable, and actually preferable to other forms of construction, as more profitable (or at least perceived as such). This reflects the drift of the temporary and adaptably narrative from its people-centric focus. Similarly, the glorification of temporary working, of temporary spaces and temporary modes of living in and experiencing the city has paralleled a process hiding the precarious working conditions of those employed to run those 'temporary' places (for example zero hours working contracts in the United Kingdom).[91] The test and experiential nature of temporary activities have been used to support an argument that the workforce needs to be adaptable and hence insecure, effectively meaning that the temporary material structure is easily removable.[92] In other words, while temporary uses have been keeping "vacant sites warm while development capital is cool,"[93] they have mostly served investors once they were ready to go.[94] Temporary urbanisms have therefore deviated away from a use of adaptability that enables the filling of gaps and addressing specific needs in an inclusive way.

CONCLUSION

Neoliberal, postmodern forms of temporary urbanisms that have widely spread in cities in the past decades, pushed and driven by landowners, developers, and local authorities, have thus led to the rise of a temporary dividend. Here the adaptable city has been envisioned in line with rationales constructed upon assetization, consumerism and marketing. The process of adaptability and its translation into various forms of temporary initiatives have fed and contributed to wider processes of privatization and financialization, through means of rebranding and reshaping areas as cool and trendy though often exclusionary places.

Here the principles of creative urban making, reaction, disorder and (in)stability have been to a greater extend artificialize to serve monetarized purposes.

Assuming that the most detrimental deviations of temporary urbanisms concern all forms of temporariness in cities nowadays would, however, be a misinterpretation and a more nuanced reading, as always, is needed to go beyond this general trend. Adaptability and temporary urbanisms do still have a clear purpose in many cases for urban development and urban living, leading to positive transformations. However, such new directions deviate away from an inclusive place-based purpose upon which temporary uses and adaptations have been founded. In addition, they make less visible and imperative the principle of adaptability as serving other needs beyond value extraction, branding, and the experiential nature of cities. There is a key tension here which till 2020 seemed to be following only one path.

This indeed changed with the COVID-19 pandemic. The unprecedented health crisis triggered a re-interrogation of why adaptability matters, but also of how temporary urbanisms can be used to serve new purposes going beyond a neo-liberal interpretation of the temporary dividend. It marks the beginning of a new and more hybrid understanding of the principles of creative urban making, reaction, disorder and (in)stability.

6

THE PANDEMIC AND POSTPANDEMIC ADAPTABLE CITY

Prior to 2020, the processes of transformation through temporary initiatives and uses were mostly either top-down or bottom-up, as discussed in the previous chapters. For the first time, because of the COVID-19 pandemic, adaptability became a core urban priority. The state of emergency didn't only challenge the ability of cities to *effectively* and *promptly* adapt but also produced a pressing need for new types of adaptability in more hybrid forms. The pandemic returned the focus to adaptability in open and outdoor areas rather than indoor spaces, reinterrogating their common single use and their role within neighborhoods and local economies.

COVID-19 led to an acceleration of existing trends, including expanding the use of temporary strategies at city scale, within emergency and mitigation strategies. The pandemic also elevated the importance of adapting outdoor spaces (pavement, streets, sidewalks) with the view of responding to new requirements (typically social distancing) and shaping longer-term urban resilience in response to new forms of working and living. The lack of (perceived) adaptability in the most deprived and unplanned settings because of overcrowding; lack of open spaces; and water, sanitation, and hygiene (WASH) conditions also emerged as a primary concern that led to several and detrimental consequences. In high-income countries, the pandemic exacerbated livability inequalities from one neighborhood to another, but in low- and middle-income cities, it reinforced tensions and exclusionary processes, with the poorest and most vulnerable communities being further marginalized. A key manifestation has been the attempt to take control over everyday adaptability and temporary uses, which has a direct impact on poor households' ability to access informal avenues to purchase food but also work, and hence to survive.

Substantial attention is given in this chapter to the latest directions taken by adaptable cities in pandemic and postpandemic contexts. What happened between 2020 and 2022 constituted an "exceptional" and "revolutionary" moment, breaking some of the dynamics, processes, and narratives that used to drive how adaptable urban making was envisaged and temporary urbanisms were implemented. The extraordinary nature of such a crisis will be debated, specifically how crises are common factors contributing to (in)adaptable urban making. What is apparent, however, is that various forms of reactive adaptations resulted from insufficient adaptability in cities and urban spaces, which led to very quick improvisations favoring agility and creativity but also a softening of the regulatory planning process. The pandemic also increased the perceived necessity to control the nonpermanent in contexts where informal and unplanned conditions prevail. Challenges related to COVID-19 also led to a reaffirmation of the crucial importance of community-led interventions fostered by hybrid arrangements based on coping, livability, and well-being (including mental health). Such dynamics led to questions about the evolution of the adaptability paradigm in such unprecedented contexts but also its legacy.

THE NONADAPTABLE CITY, AND THE IMPACT OF THE PANDEMIC-LED EMERGENCY RESPONSES

Extraordinary Versus Ordinary in an Unprecedented Context

The pandemic acted as a turning point, but a key question is. To what extent were such transformations extraordinary or entangled in the "ordinary"? By "ordinary," I mean everyday ordinary dynamics (including preexisting dysfunctions and inequalities) that have just been amplified and slightly tweaked because of unprecedented events. This is an important question, prompting a wider debate, particularly regarding how quickly cities and societies have tried to go back to "normal" and forget about the health crisis.[1]

In 2002, Jennifer Robinson referred to the ordinary when she tried to dig deeper into how urban theory had approached the reading of cities.[2] She argued that the diversity of cities was reduced for too long to a simplistic separation between "global cities" in rich and market economic countries and other "third world" cities in poor countries and emerging economies. Taking a postcolonial view, she defended the idea that urban theory should learn from a much broader range of urban contexts, based on some form of cosmopolitan comparison, into which the concept of "ordinary cities" would fit. Elevating the crucial importance of the diversity and complexity of the "urban" is the essence of any approach designed to understand and account for the ordinary. John R. Bryson et al. extended Robinson's argument by applying the "ordinary" to "all types of urban settlement including informal settlements, towns, and cities" to refer to "something that is 'normal' or common, with no distinctive or

THE PANDEMIC AND POSTPANDEMIC ADAPTABLE CITY • 155

unusual feature," hence, the opposite of the extraordinary.[3] Their objective was to acknowledge the ordinary in order to counter any attempts in urban theories to develop a unified approach and hence privilege exceptionalism rather than the ordinary and the everyday.[4] Doing so also made the point that the ordinary is effectively the most common type of urban setting that, for diverse reasons, may not be at the forefront of policy agendas or academic debates.

Building on Doreen Massey's reading of space, in which she insists on the intimately tiny "interrelations and interactions that shape space" but also bringing Georges Perec's insights on the media's attention to everything "except the daily," Bryson and colleagues continue their deconstruction of the ordinary by developing the term of the "infra-ordinary" to characterize and highlight the importance of the "accumulation of everyday activities and encounters in the creation of urban living, lifestyles, and economies.[5] These infra-ordinary activities and encounters reflect the diversity of people living within a place and linked to other places. It is these everyday activities that shape urban routines and the ways in which people negotiate the interrelationships between livability, livelihoods, and place."[6] This is where the question of the pandemic—exceptional or not—sits. The pandemic *was* exceptional and unprecedented. It significantly disrupted lives, economies, and urban systems around the globe, and such a global reach was without precedent. Most of the COVID-19 policies and strategies were driven by health concerns but also by the ambition of returning to normalcy as quickly as possible. Such placeless and peopleless approaches mostly ignored the ordinary, that is, the everyday practices, needs, challenges, and rights of all individuals. This led to significant immediate but also long-term dysfunctions. The pandemic and its impacts on people, places, and local economies weren't, as such, exceptional and unpredictable. It substantially reinforced the intersectional socioeconomic and spatial inequalities and dysfunctions that characterized all high-, medium- and lower-income cities.[7] The reinforcement of inequalities is related to the disruption of the ordinary: everyday lives, working patterns, education, food, play, leisure, and socialization mechanisms of individuals and communities. The ordinary of every day is both formal and informal. It includes diverse and dynamic infra-ordinary uses of spaces related to everyday necessities of adapting very quickly. Such everyday dynamics were mostly outside the scope of global narratives, which embedded another type of adaptability constructed as a response to the rigidity of cities.

Rigidity and Health Emergencies

Prior to 2020, adaptability and all forms of temporary urbanisms were not at the forefront of urban thinking and planning policy. They were used more as tools or solutions available to serve specific needs (as we discussed in previous chapters). Indeed, this non-necessity also resonated with the relative permanence of the urban fabric, making mainstream adaptability quite challenging. COVID-19 thus came as a brutal shock because it revealed the extent to which the built environment, both indoors and outdoors, was incapable of dealing with emergency health regulations, including social distancing. It constitutes a "temporal as well as a spatial epiphany" as cities "lacked preparedness for life to continue as normal."[8] This unpreparedness was the result of rigid urban morphologies and structures and regulatory systems perpetuated because of control and lengthy procedures rather than agile and prompt adaptations.

The thinking about pandemic cities led to a return to initial discussions in the late nineteenth century about miasma theories, the exposure to polluted air, and how to address disease transmission in the context of very densely built and populated environments. It "returned biological risk management (BRM) in urban environments to the planning agenda."[9] At that time, and noting the different state of scientific and technological advancements, ventilation was already positioned as the key response for urban environments. This concern led to the development of planning as a discipline but also to the first planning models that attempted to promote livability and well-being (e.g., garden cities). The issue for planners and any built environment experts was that, for decades, because of the lack of major global health crises, the thinking about cities had shifted from an urban health penalty to an urban health advantage.[10] In such contexts, public health concerns were no longer focused on infections and virus transmission but rather on "degenerative diseases and anthropogenic disorders."[11] The health narrative was displayed in a significantly different agenda, which made cities and dense urban cities totally unprepared for a global pandemic.

Encouraged by other agenda (e.g., sustainability or climate change) and the neoliberal planning process, urban development models were focused on land-use intensification and an increase of urban density, in other words, occupancy and usage.[12] The consequences of such models were harsh in a pandemic when a significant proportion of small residential units did not accommodate online working and schooling, open spaces (sidewalks, streets) were not wide enough for social distancing, and service facilities (hospitals, schools, etc.) were not designed for adaptability.[13] More important, the impact of pandemic restrictions on urban lives revealed further existing urban and spatial inequalities, particularly the ability of inhabitants to access open spaces, particularly green spaces, in periods of lockdowns or mobility restrictions.[14] Overcrowding and inadequate living conditions of the poor alongside existing health conditions came at the forefront of intersectional burdens that made specific communities more vulnerable and at risk. Helen Pineo correctly notes that the "pandemic's inequitable health impacts were predictable in the sense that these populations are generally likely to experience layers of disadvantage that make them more vulnerable to health threats."[15] This takes us back to miasma and ventilation as "low-income and minority ethnic residents are more likely to live in neighborhoods with high environmental burdens and they are also more likely to have noncommunicable disease (NCD), partly attributable to the poorer quality of their environment."[16] Such intersectional disadvantages characterize all cities, but they are, of course, even more visible and acute in contexts of informality (informal tented settlements [ITSs], townships, slums, favellas, etc.).

In the most marginalized urban settings, the issue (and "political" fear) of density and the impossibility of enforcing any form of social distancing also contributed to exclude those living in informal and less planned settings. It also reactivated colonial and segregationist approaches driven by principles of what is healthy and unhealthy; in such narratives, informal settings where improvisations and temporary adaptations prevail are abject spaces and those living in the poorer conditions are outpowered by decision makers. It is worth remembering that in colonial times and typically in Africa, the segregation of space was based heavily on eugenic theories driven by health and sanitation concerns.[17] More often than not, colonial planners used the pretext of protecting the health, safety, and welfare of the public to "craft spatial policies whose actual purpose was to buttress the power of the colonial state and to facilitate its efforts to effectuate social control in the colonies."[18] Such actions meant that sanitation was used as a "metaphor which colonialists first invoked to justify the establishment of segregated locations that facilitated the control of urbanized African workers."[19] The unplanned and thus temporary and adaptable settings were thus seen as having to be sanitized. In South Africa, but also in the wider African context, the mobilization of the dark side of planning had stretched beyond colonial and apartheid eras, with postcolonial and post-apartheid states still using it as a means to remove what the state sees as abject, and hence it was used to justify evictions, displacement, and slum clearance.[20] The pandemic effectively extended and reinforced such practices with abjection becoming a significant thread to justify further controlling, policing, and enforcing encampment of the most vulnerable under the credo of "national protection" and state of emergency. Racial and ethnic inequalities become even more visible as a result.

While various scenarios were observed around the world, all shared the commonality of informal settings being perceived as dangerous places where COVID-19 could easily spread and hence favor citywide contamination. Through a narrative about prevention, control of movements, including control over access to work and food, were enforced to the detriment of poorer communities.[21] This was the case in camps and informal settlements, typically in Lebanon in the Middle East (figure 6.1). Here, "the lack of infrastructure and facilities on site, the absence of adequate and healthy outdoor and indoor areas, the high number of households sharing one tent with no safe social distancing, induced confusion and fear amongst governmental and multisectoral agencies."[22]

South African townships were also subject to lockdown rules without any considerations given to livelihoods, leading to several

FIGURE 6.1 Dire living conditions in Lebanese informal settlements.
Source: Paul Moawad.

instances of tension and riots.[23] Survival struggles and anger led to "scenes reminiscent of apartheid protests . . . Communities queuing for undelivered aid have built barricades of burning tyres and fought pitched battles with riot police, and similar scenes have played out in Johannesburg and Port Elizabeth."[24] More importantly, and going back to intersectional burdens,

FIGURE 6.2 Informal sidewalk vendors on a street in Bloemfontein, South Africa.

Source: Lauren Andres.

the fear of going outside and accessing health facilities for non-COVID diseases meant that a significant amount of health conditions were ignored, as were early age vaccinations, with longer-term consequences.[25] Pressures to control informal uses and movements also led to trying to control informal street vendors in Africa (figure 6.2), South America, and East Asia, thus affecting food security.[26] I will return to this point a little later in this chapter.

In all cases, the chaotic nature of the built environment and living conditions was considered a health threat requiring specific actions and control. This led to two contrasting responses to adaptability, both questioning the issue of regulation versus deregulation and the problematic nature of the planning system in times of crisis.

EXTRAORDINARY, REACTIVE, AND DETRIMENTAL RESPONSES

To address the rigidity of the urban fabrics but also control people's movements within cities, (temporary) arrangements, improvisations, and emergency regulations were crafted. They resulted in two main responses in approaching spaces. On the one hand, there was a push toward agility and deregulated planning systems in many high-income countries, putting adaptability at the forefront of (emergency) planning practices. On the other hand, there was a turn against adaptability and common laissez-faire, with an increase of regulations targeting the unplanned, specifically in low- and middle-income nations.

Agility and Deregulation

Prior to the pandemic, any form of adaptability of the built environment—except for the purely tactical, microscale, and ephemeral—was heavily grounded in a step-by-step process; this included a set of regulations (including health and safety concerns and beyond) that were often connected to a compulsory consultation process with the local population. Gordon Douglas summarizes this well in reference to New York City and what planners from the department of transportation in that city thought about "city bureaucracy."[27] He says, "Trappings of institutional inertia were heavy in the air." The standard response to do-it-yourself (DIY) interventions, despite real interest, he argued, were quickly discounted on the grounds of the "importance of official processes and their own expertise, referencing specific regulations and technical terms. There are obvious reasons for this, including basic safety and orders."[28] This is a

THE PANDEMIC AND POSTPANDEMIC ADAPTABLE CITY • 163

common standard that characterizes all American and European cities. Such challenges arising from this rigidity were exacerbated further during the pandemic and showed why a city like New York was struggling to respond to new health requirements: the time and process associated with adapting uses and spaces. As mentioned by two built environment experts working in the city:

> It would be a lot easier if we had environments—at least regulatory environments—where in a very short-term way, we could do more experimentation. It doesn't have to be all permanent or nothing.[29]
>
> Prior to the pandemic, we had insanely bureaucratic rules around sidewalk seating. It was infamously taking a year or more to get sidewalk seating permits for restaurants . . . City planning was concerned about streetscape and urban design and wanted a ton of control. All went out the window and the city was able to say okay let's put this aside, this is an emergency so let's cut the red tape.[30]

Very similar points were made by planners in London who reflected on how the pandemic context differed and how, specifically regarding mobility issues, programs were delivered much more quickly. This was the result of deregulation and leaner processes, which involved scrapping community consultation.

> COVID happened. This allowed us to accelerate the projects. We probably did about eight years' worth of work in 10 months. We put in five low traffic neighbourhoods across the borough which was a lot and we fast-tracked a pop-up cycle lane in the space of two to three weeks.[31]
>
> We were basically told by central government that we shouldn't do any consultation and we just needed to do it in within a matter of weeks. That was the actual wording, a central directive. So we just went and did it, whereas, you know, we usually spend about

six months to a year doing community engagement and going through a political process. The legislation was also changed to allow for these schemes to go very quickly [i.e., temporary traffic orders].[32]

The pandemic transformed approaches to how the city is used—including its buildings, open spaces, and spaces of mobility (streets and pavements/sidewalks)—but it also transformed how the city as a whole is experienced. Radical changes occurred because of social-distancing measures and lockdowns, shifting the engagement of individuals with urban built forms, real estate, design, and streetscapes.[33] Adaptability and emergency-driven temporary urbanisms became common around the globe. "Governments, businesses and citizens have used temporary/tactical urban approaches to rapidly retrofit urban streets to take advantage of the temporarily reduced intensity of city traffic, to serve rapidly increasing needs for outdoor walking, cycling and dining and to provide the increased amount of space that such activities now require due to physical distancing."[34]

Prepandemic models of urban development and urban planning were thus momentarily scrapped to include much more flexibility and agility in an unprecedented emergency. These can be referred to as reactive adaptability to emergency, not properly planned-ahead adaptable dynamics. This led to an "intriguing combination of political and economic trajectories that are often seen to be in conflict—for example, deregulation and regulation, or laissez-faire versus government-controlled markets."[35] This process resulted in very rapid improvisations driven by health and safety concerns, mobility purposes but also economic goals. Such improvisations occurred at various scales, adjustments at the nano level (buildings) to microscale (street grids), to a stretched urban realm (at neighborhood and city levels).[36]

THE PANDEMIC AND POSTPANDEMIC ADAPTABLE CITY • 165

For planning systems, emergency temporary amendments were activated to make processes less rigid and allow very quick transformations. In England, for example, this translated into significant shifts in planning regulations. Such shifts were very similar to what was observed in some cities in North America and Europe. First, new time-limited permitted development rights were introduced to allow for the change of use and adaptation of existing buildings as well as new temporary modular buildings.[37] This included in the Town and Country Planning (General Permitted Development) (England) Order 2015, a new Class 12A of permitted development (PD) that enabled "emergency development by a local authority or health service body."[38] This was typically used in transforming London ExCeL, a convention center, into the NHS (National Health Service) Nightingale Hospital London, a temporary hospital, with similar projects conducted across the country. In addition, new time-limited PD rights focused on changes of use, temporary events, and temporary structures with the aim of helping food and drink businesses. This included a new permitted change of use allowing A3 restaurants and A4 drinking establishments to change to takeaway food and the right to add temporary structures and/or seating facilities for outdoor dining and activities.

In response to the need for temporary traffic arrangements and to facilitate social distancing, Experimental Traffic Regulation Orders (ETROs) were used and supported by the Emergency Active Travel Fund (EATF), a £250 million investment from the British government.[39] Implemented by local authorities, this translated into a variety of adaptations and arrangements, including widening footpaths to provide pedestrians with more space and thus enable social distancing; it also led to facilitating travel by segregating bicycle lanes from vehicle traffic on radial routes, creating pop-up lanes, and implementing schemes to reduce traffic volumes and encourage walking and cycling in residential areas (low-traffic neighborhoods). Deregulation and rapidity were achieved as such schemes were implemented—as stressed in the quotes below—without public engagement and consultation, which led to significant backlash.

Similar dynamics of deregulations and with less rigidity towards specific regulations (i.e. health and safety, accessibility access) were observed in New York City and in many other American and European cities (e.g., Milan, Rome, Paris, Lyon, Marseille, Barcelona, Berlin) with the emergency open restaurants and open street programs. What is clear is that temporary adjustments of space based on a temporary deregulation of planning procedures were justified through the umbrella of emergency crisis responses, resilience, and prospects of future recovery.

Numerous authors stressed the importance of temporary transformations during the pandemic, which went beyond economic and emergency rationales and resonated with other ambitions (tackling mental health, promoting social interactions and physical activities).[40] For public health purposes, stadiums, conference centers, and parking spaces were transformed into temporary recovery facilities and hospitals. Large green spaces were converted into emergency field hospitals in Vancouver and New York.[41] A significant proportion of hotels around the world were temporarily allocated to housing homeless people while also being used as quarantine centers.[42] In India, empty malls were turned into shelters for migrant workers who were unable to return to their villages.[43] Religious buildings were used as temporary morgues, as were ice rinks and aircraft hangars in the United Kingdom.[44] Shipping containers were used as intensive care facilities or drive-through testing stations in car parks.[45]

Adaptations and improvisations not only concerned buildings but also outdoor spaces (figure 6.3). To allow people to

FIGURE 6.3 Outdoor dining in New York City during the COVID-19 pandemic.

Source: Lauren Andres.

exercise outside, parks and street furniture were radically altered with wider pavements and footpaths to support social distancing.[46] To tackle the sharp decrease in public transport and need for alternative mobility routes, temporary and low-cost bike and running lanes were developed in cities in many countries, typically in Colombia, Germany, France, the United Kingdom, Australia, and New Zealand and throughout North America.[47] Adaptations thus helped with outdoor dining and entertainment, but temporary regulations also translated into temporary arrangements of the food supply chains. The temporary changes of rights of use allowed "struggling businesses to keep trading and hungry citizens to keep eating" by "adopting pop-up distribution approaches such as click-and-collect and/or take away delivery."[48] Adaptability occurred here not only by softening land-use regulation but also by adapting supply chain regulatory mechanisms, thereby seeking to safeguard economic value.[49]

Such shifts represent a move from urban planning that is focused primarily on conventional work and experiential places (e.g., indoor cafés) to alternative experiential places (e.g., sidewalk dining, streets changed to pedestrian walkways and recreational and noncar uses). Elevating adaptability as a planning solution also significantly blurred the conventional single use of spaces (particularly mobility spaces) and led to blurry boundaries between privately owned, for-profit and publicly owned, nonprofit spaces.[50] This differs significantly from reactive responses implemented in low- and middle-income contexts, which targeted individuals and settlements based on more informal arrangements.

Abjection and Encampment as Reactive Adaptations

The pandemic and the narrative about disease transmission and ventilation led to a stigmatization of everyday coping strategies built on informal and temporary forms of adaptations and uses (as explored in chapter 4) and on everyday living and survival. Informal settlements (townships, ITSs) but also informal activities (street vending) became the focus of a process of "regularization" and control, particularly—but not only—during periods of lockdowns. These processes were inherited from historical legacies, as discussed earlier, and were linked intrinsically to political discourses about who and what to prioritize. Thus, the increase in regulatory mechanisms regarding control and policing was driven by a narrative of fear of the other and a rejection of

THE PANDEMIC AND POSTPANDEMIC ADAPTABLE CITY • 169

unsanitary, hence, unsafe living. This led to explicit processes of abjection, in regard to the individuals inhabiting those spaces and their living conditions.[51] These individuals were often refugees or migrants (hence, those who are already suffering from rejection).[52] Control over mobility was exercised and justified by conforming to the World Health Organization (WHO) guidelines (for example, in sub-Saharan Africa or in Lebanon).[53] Thus, residents of informal settlements were forced to stay inside, despite their livelihoods depending on accessing the outside. This translated into various configurations where adaptability, nonpermanence, and unplanned strategies were considered unacceptable in order to enforce health emergency principles.

In southern Africa (i.e., South Africa, Zimbabwe, and Mozambique), encampment was motivated by confining "people in their homes to restrict contact among individuals, thereby slowing the spread of the virus."[54] In some cities, this meant using police enforcement, leading to protests and riots. Such measures were inappropriate and widely criticized as "enforcing lockdowns and community containment is next to impossible in informal settlements where households who lack direct access to services such as water and sanitation in their homes must access communal facilities, which can become hotspots for possible COVID-19 infection."[55] Such processes that did not account for local contexts and needs severely affected informal dwellers who relied on the informal sector to generate daily income and access food.[56] This deprived the poor from access to income and severely disrupted the informal food chain; informal dwellers access and purchase food mostly on a daily basis because they are not able to buy, store, or refrigerate large amount of supplies.[57] The pandemic thus led to deprived communities facing increased hunger.[58] The support from national and local governments, through grants, coupled with aid from international nongovernmental organization (INGOs) and nongovernmental organization (NGOs), were limited and too restrictive. Allocation was also challenged by limited social protection, nationality issues, and corruption.[59] Adaptability here was not only feared but also taken away from the poor, hence depriving them of a fundamental coping and survival tool.

Restrictive encampments were also implemented in refugees' ITSs, typically in Lebanon, during periods of national, on and off lockdowns and beyond. These encampments were associated with tailored preventive measures. Refugees in ITSs were perceived as high-risk transmitters of spreading COVID-19 to adjacent host communities.[60] A sanitization discourse based on fear rendered any form of temporary urbanisms unsafe. This was supported by the lack of infrastructure and facilities on site, the absence of adequate and healthy outdoor and indoor areas, the reliance on temporary materials, and the high number of households sharing one tent with no safe social distancing. Similar to what occurred in southern Africa townships, fear-induced strict mobility restrictions, curfews, and strict encampments significantly affected refugees' abilities to work informally and forced them to rely solely on international aid. Unlike townships, no riots or protests occurred in ITSs, however, because the fear of the "other" and the virus unnerved both host communities and refugees, who "locked" themselves inside the ITSs (despite the absence of physical barriers, i.e., walls).[61] This increased local tensions because local host communities felt left behind; while suffering greatly from the socioeconomic impacts of lockdowns, the aid wasn't initially directed to them. Similarly to African informal settlements, the informal food chain system was severely affected by lockdowns and inappropriate attempts to control people's movements, thus leading to an increase of hunger and desperation.[62]

In Africa but also in East Asia and South America, concerns about the nonregulation of the uses of spaces expanded beyond

THE PANDEMIC AND POSTPANDEMIC ADAPTABLE CITY • 171

informal settlements. Whereas informal street vending is a common characteristic of cities and often occurs within blurry boundaries between authorization and laissez-faire policies, national and local governments used the pandemic to attempt to control the informal street sector. Driven by (and hidden by) the narrative of imposing health regulations, it was part of wider political ambitions to "clean the streets." "In many cities, the rapid and radical response to this COVID-19 outbreak has been to enforce policies to crack down on street vendors and eliminate large numbers of such invisible workers from public spaces where they are no longer able to secure a job and earn a decent livelihood with a certain degree of autonomy in their working lives."[63] This happened in countries like Peru, Mexico, Ghana, Nigeria, Zimbabwe, India, and Thailand, among others, where specific restrictions strictly limited the activities of informal food producers and distributors. In South Africa, informal street vendors—often immigrants—were subject to having to apply for "business or asylum seekers' permits," which were extremely difficult or even impossible to obtain because of a lack of proof of official residence or right to stay in the country.[64] Many of them did not have a permit to operate as a business, which blocked them from setting up their shop. Such a strategy under the emergency health narrative effectively took away the unstructured nature of informal arrangements on which the poor rely. Such processes of sanitation, control, and regulation of the informal were not unique to the African continent. In East Asia, and typically Vietnam, the informal food market and street vendor activities were deemed as unhygienic and hot spots for virus transmission.[65] "The earnings of informal street vendors in cities such as Bangkok dropped by about 80 percent as a result."[66] In many low- and middle-income cities, the rejection of temporary urbanisms and lack of attempts to develop relevant adaptations of spaces, regulations, and restrictions had detrimental impacts on the urban poor and will have longer-term consequences.[67] While leading to an increase of poverty and hunger, long-term health implications are expected from an increase of tuberculosis (TB) and other diseases (including mental health) to consequences linked to the refusal to seek medical support for non-COVID-related conditions and undertake basic vaccination (typically among children and youth).[68]

Such a picture is gloomy and sad. There are a few exceptions, however, worth mentioning that demonstrate more attention and care given to the most vulnerable. In Central Java, Indonesia, and Kalaw, Myanmar, municipalities converted roads into fresh-produce markets.[69] Temporary adjustments were made to achieve this, including "repainting the road markings to demarcate trading sites."[70] In other middle-income cities, school fields and parking lots were converted into food markets to reduce the need to travel to supermarkets. In many cases, however, adaptations and improvisation with regard to access to food but also play, leisure, or any forms of socialization occurred through ad hoc community-led initiatives, displaying the struggle of state organizations to account for the need of the poor.[71] Such initiatives are examples of how forms of hybrid temporary urbanisms emerged as a result of the pandemic, particularly in temporary arrangements where boundaries between bottom-up/top-down mechanisms, along with formal (regulated) and informal (unregulated) practices, became more blurred.

THE EXCEPTION, THE CRISIS, AND A COMMUNITY-FIRST APPROACH TO ADAPTABLE ADJUSTMENTS

The pandemic triggered new forms of adaptability and led to new forms of hybrid and reactive temporary urbanism. The boundaries

THE PANDEMIC AND POSTPANDEMIC ADAPTABLE CITY • 173

between the traditional bottom-up/top-down approaches are blurred not only from governance, funding, and regulatory perspectives but also because of the extreme diversity of temporary urban changes and coping mechanisms that occurred. COVID didn't lead only to forced adaptations through deregulations; it also fostered and reactivated temporary forms of community "get-together" dynamics at the micro level, either supported or at least authorized by local authorities.

As explored earlier in chapter 4, adaptability is connected to well-being, hope, and also pride when it is related to "temporary" homes and communities' living environments. From this perspective, the pandemic leveraged additional mechanisms to further strengthening the relationship between adaptability, people, and place. Such mechanisms are crucial social assets in times of crisis, and this isn't unique to the pandemic. It is strongly embedded within the adaptability paradigm. Responses to natural disasters are always followed by temporary interventions focused around shelter, basic needs, and health.[72] Adaptability goes beyond the physical emergency response, however, and includes community (re)building.[73] In Christchurch, New Zealand, after the 2011 earthquake, there were small-scale and often innovative attempts to maintain community spirit, such as an urban living room featuring a book exchange inside a recycled fridge, or dance spaces on disused land with music from a converted washing machine.[74] During the pandemic, such adaptations involved both mitigation and prospective recovery. The need for alternative spaces combined with the need to work from home became the catalyst for community adaptations and temporary spatial adjustments and uses for very diverse types of urban settings. London and New York are examples.

While London had a long-standing history of using meanwhile uses to deal with vacancy in high streets, community inclusion, and reuse of empty lands, the city didn't adopt a very proactive strategy (from a built environment and planning perspective) regarding how to support businesses and communities during the pandemic, aside from adjusting spaces for prevention purposes and support for the food and beverage sector. Very little was done to target local communities. From the start of the pandemic, the approach was focused on looking ahead and recovering. Meanwhile uses were immediately embedded into strategic directions for the city of London, with the idea of "transitional urbanism" promoted as key for activating local economic (re)development.[75] No specific program or funding was attached to it, however.

In the absence of city-led initiatives, the use of meanwhile strategies spread in a relatively ad hoc way, often triggered at borough level, and led either by large consultancy groups (typically Arup) and smaller organizations specialized in localized regeneration strategies through meanwhile transformations. These small organizations saw their activities increase once lockdowns were over, with a focus on the reactivation of empty buildings and units and the rising need for new flexible working spaces. Such companies have specialized over the last decade in regenerating "scraggly bits of land . . . not really usable . . . and that maybe have never even been used before."[76] Their activities are heavily grounded in local economies and what is needed in specific (often socially deprived) neighborhoods to activate change. What is interesting here is the extent to which meanwhile transformation strategies started to address the lack of working spaces at home. "What we've seen massively come out of the pandemic is the demand for desks from people who wouldn't ordinarily need them. They don't run a business, they work for another organisation. They can't work at home because they are homeschooling."[77] This is linked to "all that kind of social change that happened" and thus increased the demand for flexible "office-studio type spaces, usually not much more than about 10 or 15 square metres."[78] These are microscale temporary transformations led by community groups and hence differ from other coworking models that were already spreading before the pandemic because they target other types of users. The pandemic elevated the issue of working space beyond large organizations to community groups and organizations in an unprecedented new, hybrid working context.

Working from home and tackling mental well-being was at the forefront of small and spontaneous interventions in London. These emerged outside any programs led by local authorities and were driven solely by communities feeling the need to get together. The Green Project in Shepherd Bush, London, (figure 6.4) is an interesting example of a community gardening initiative that emerged as a reaction to pandemic lifestyles. Many residents in

FIGURE 6.4 The Green Project SB in Shepherds Bush (White City), London.

Source: Lauren Andres.

176 • THE PANDEMIC AND POSTPANDEMIC ADAPTABLE CITY

the area didn't have access to their own gardens and were living in blocks of flats. The neighborhood was characterized by a set of rundown open spaces owned by the London borough of Hammersmith and Fulham (i.e. local authority) but left abandoned and covered in litter. Residents got together to use those spaces and beautify their neighborhood while creating opportunities to get together safely.

> Initially, I sent an email to the council asking them to clear out the area of all the rubbish. When we started, we were a little bit afraid as we didn't know each other. I received both positive and negative responses. I set up a pretty website, and an Instagram account. They were very successful and we started receiving replies which put a name to the group. At that point, we had the time because during the lockdown we didn't have much to do with social life, and that was the way that we started meeting this wonderful group of people.[79]

The need to get together safely in a period of crisis was the main trigger. Community members shared how this was a way to tackle their lack of socialization during lockdown, the difficulties of homeschooling and working at home, and the overall feeling of being alone and struggling mentally. The community has now transformed three spaces, gathering more support and members over the months and keeping a very agile approach to the beautification of the neighborhood.

Other forms of community mobilizations through temporary adaptations can also be related to the survival of small businesses. Some core intersectional issues here are valid across many cities. I illustrate this point with the example of Queens, New York. The Temporary Open Restaurants Program, as discussed earlier in this chapter, was launched during the pandemic throughout New

York City, but its implementation displayed some significant discrepancies with, unsurprisingly, the most affluent boroughs, that is, Manhattan and Brooklyn, benefitting widely from the scheme compared to others like the Bronx or Queens, or the neighborhood of Harlem in Manhattan. This is where community-led interventions and adaptations are important, even in a context of city-led deregulation. The borough of Queens is very diverse and includes core pockets of deprivation and poverty; typically, 20 percent of residents in the Elmhurst and Corona areas were already living below the federal poverty line in 2019, and those figures have increased.[80] Areas in the Corona district were COVID hotspots in terms of infections and deaths. These areas, typically around Jackson Heights, are also characterized by issues of safety, gangs, prostitution, and illegal selling.

Such districts include small nonprofit organizations focused on neighborhood development. These organizations, for example, the 82nd Street Partnership, work toward supporting the local business improvement district, particularly through a "range of local economic development programs, including neighborhood marketing, placemaking, streetscape beautification, supplemental sanitation, and advocacy."[81] Very small organizations, often characterized by one or two employees, had to improvise during the pandemic to support businesses with very little means. As noted by one of their representatives: "I have tiny restaurants; they might have two or four tables inside the restaurants and they do not have the resources to build the outdoor seating or don't have the language or computer skills to apply."[82] The point made by this interviewee is crucial because it highlights the deep inequalities characterizing local economic landscapes and how city programs were not enough to support all types of business equally because of a lack of resources or skills. Thus, their survival depended on other types of support and grants, typically those

FIGURE 6.5 Temporary installation in Jackson Heights, Queens, New York, to support struggling local business during the COVID-19 pandemic.

Source: Lauren Andres.

secured by the 82nd Street Partnership, which facilitated the building of outdoor seating infrastructures and organizing small events to allow restaurants to sell food outdoors and takeaway. Such mobilization didn't emerge only as a result of the pandemic. Before the pandemic, mobilization concerned the most vulnerable within the community, for example, the elderly and young people. The pandemic reinforced such mobilization. "What I am planning to do is reclaiming the Plaza [i.e., the Dunningham Triangle, a public space at the center of the neighborhood] for the community, for families and for workers. It needs to be a safe place for women who are harassed by drunk men and for young men because of the gangs."[83] Such initiatives were based on the assumption that spaces like streets, curbside parking spaces and sidewalks could be utilized beyond their mobility purpose.

Streets became the archetype of the adaptable city during the pandemic. Empty or partially empty streets were temporarily repurposed to allow social distancing, walking, and cycling and repositioned as a key material feature of place attachment in a neighborhood. As noted by a transport planner based in London, "throughout COVID people's relationship with their streets and the local area has changed because you know you're not travelling into Central London so much. People seem to be much more kind of emotionally attached to that [local] area."[84] In many cities around the world, various adaptation mechanisms featuring alternative mobility arrangements transformed streets and curbside parking spaces. Such schemes were run differently: some were driven and managed by the municipalities (for example, in Seattle, Washington, and Vancouver, British Columbia), and others were set up by municipalities but were run by organizations and communities, as in New York City with the Open Streets Program. This program was based on the existing (but small-scale) New York City (NYC) Plaza Program and was launched by the New York City Department of Transportation (DOT) in April 2020 to provide New Yorkers with safe, socially distanced activities during the height of the COVID pandemic. In 2021, it made the program permanent. The Open Streets Program is an example of the use of hybrid forms of temporary urbanisms. While supported by DOT through relatively little funding, it relies entirely on locally based, nongovernment involvement. Each open street results from a community or a community organization representative or organization application, which is then approved (or rejected in a limited number of cases). Unlike standard street closures (e.g., school street closures), the street is closed at different moments of the day, week, and year, and hence introduces new rhythms and routines based on what the community is willing to develop. There is a very strong degree of distinctiveness in the size, location, and nature of the activities; the types of organizations; and the success of the open streets. "There's definitely not a one size fits all approach. I think that's what sort of makes Open Streets unique; it is that we really empower the community to sort of take whatever kind of look and feel they want to develop for the Open Street."[85]

Adaptations and temporary reappropriations of streets are part of a combination of regulated and deregulated process but are based on more organic arrangements that can range from neighborhoods and community groups getting together to large organizations (typically business improvement districts [BIDs]) running this as part of their overall mandate. Organizations delivering these schemes are responsible for full programming and management; thus, they can shape the nature of the adaptations, changes, and temporary uses and their purpose. Open Streets Program initiatives reflect very severe discrepancies between boroughs, as they did for the Temporary Open Restaurants Program. Here again, Manhattan and Brooklyn have the most number of

THE PANDEMIC AND POSTPANDEMIC ADAPTABLE CITY • 181

open streets. A DOT employee recognizes that "such community involvement . . . has a lot of privilege attached to it."[86] Such privileges refer to the nature of the community workforce and their skills, available time, and knowledge (all related to training and job occupations). This means that hybridity and agility translate into how temporary uses and events were developed and continue postpandemic. Open streets led by BIDs are very structured and well resourced, and mainly rely on DOT for procedural and funding purposes. Those led and managed by small community groups require more innovative ideas and input from external parties, including DOT, that may need to step in to address maintenance issues, particularly traffic barriers and safety.

New York City is certainly an example of best practice compared to temporary transformations of streets around the world. At the city level, the overall success of the Open Streets Program is being debated. A lot of criticism has emerged because the program didn't achieve its yearly target number of open streets and because of strong opposition from car-owner lobby groups using concerns about safety and inclusive design to raise complaints. From an adaptability perspective, however, the program built on the legacy of New York City tactical urbanism approaches and expanded its scope much further with crucial policy priorities: community well-being, cohesion, and behavioral changes (particularly with active travel). New York City achieved what many cities haven't. It is worth focusing on three temporary full closure schemes, run by community groups, that emerged during the pandemic: Vanderbilt Avenue Open Street in Prospect Heights, Brooklyn; the 34th Avenue Open Streets Coalition in Jackson Heights, Queens; and Jennings Street Open Street (run by the Caldwell Enrichment Program Inc.) in the Bronx.

Vanderbilt Avenue Open Street (figure 6.6) is run by residents through a neighborhood development corporation, that is, a

FIGURE 6.6 The Vanderbilt Avenue Open Street in Prospect Heights, Brooklyn, New York.
Source: Lauren Andres.

community-focused, nonprofit organization that works to revitalize neighborhoods and promote sustainable development.[87] Vanderbilt differs from other open streets in Brooklyn that are mainly driven by BIDs and used for commercial purposes (for example, in Park Slope) or by communities for traffic pacification and creating pedestrian walkways (Willoughby Avenue Open Street and the Fort Greene Open Streets Coalition).[88] The core group comprises a dozen members and about forty volunteers. During the health crisis, when they were stranded at home, they met to enhance the livability of the area and community well-being while supporting their local restaurants. As noted by one of the members: "I lived for 18 years here and I saw nothing as

THE PANDEMIC AND POSTPANDEMIC ADAPTABLE CITY • 183

successful as this before. It came out of nowhere. Local was key, yes, as people were at home. And we have relevant expertise in the neighborhood: logistics, branding, event manager."[89]

The Vanderbilt Avenue Open Street started through an economic relief plan focusing on solutions to help the recovery of local restaurants on the avenue. It was then transformed into an open street proposal. The success of the plan led to a ramping up of its programming. This has included the organization of specific events during each open street day, from dance classes and family entertainment to bike classes and mobile curling workshops, and also spontaneous picnics and weddings. The temporary closure involves setting up ninety temporary barriers and amending the avenue layout by introducing alternative walking and cycling routes. The plan is funded thanks to a DOT grant and other nonprofit grants, in addition to fundraising and corporate sponsorship. While the first year was entirely run by volunteers, the group managed to hire two community marshalls starting in the second year to deal with security and safety. This was made possible by requesting a small contribution from restaurants.

The success of the plan has been the result of the residents' commitment: "You need to have a community with the right skills and keen to do things. The team is divided into four tasks: development and fundraising, communication, programming, and street safety, plus volunteers who play the role of executive directors. All the people in the team have the relevant professional experience."[90] The Vanderbilt Avenue Open Street is an illustration of pandemic-led hybrid adaptations driven by economic and social ambitions. Its diversity and success are based on its grassroots and formal nature even if, after three years, solutions are now sought to sustain the adaptable program into the future, with volunteers encountering difficulties in finding the time to manage the scheme and facing fatigue. This observation

184 • THE PANDEMIC AND POSTPANDEMIC ADAPTABLE CITY

resonates with the second example: the 34th Avenue Open Streets Coalition, the most visible and most politically and widely acclaimed open street initiative in New York City.[91]

The 34th Avenue Open Streets Coalition is located in Jackson Heights, Queens, in a very diverse neighborhood, where over one hundred languages are spoken.[92] While the upper end of the street hosts mostly very poor households with several families and/or generations living together. Many have emigrated to the United States quite recently (some still in illegal situations). The middle and lower ends are slightly more affluent. The avenue is bordered by dense housing blocks of rental and corporate housing on both sides. Aside from a church and three schools, the long avenue includes only housing units. It is also characterized by a lack of green spaces, open spaces (e.g., plazas), and playgrounds. The 34th Avenue Open Streets Coalition covers twenty-six blocks (twelve miles), with the avenue closed permanently between 7 A.M. and 8 P.M., every day, and activities running at different times of the day (figure 6.7). As in Vanderbilt Avenue Open Street, the trigger was the COVID pandemic. The 34th Avenue Open Streets Coalition started in May 2020. As pointed out by one of the group members: "People were locked. Some people hadn't been out for months. Everything was closed. We could hear ambulance sirens going all the time. People wanted to exercise, work out, do activities outside, the children wanted to play but there is very little open space around: one playground (very minimal) on the other side of the road, two housing blocks have small green spaces but they are all fenced with strict no play rules."[93]

The street was effectively the only available space for people to convene. The avenue at the time was dominated by cars. Speeding was an issue, and the school partial street closures were not respected. Community members who had been living in the neighborhood for over a decade started to talk to each other and

FIGURE 6.7 Open street on 34th Avenue in Queens, New York.
Source: Lauren Andres.

decided to apply for an open street designation. They were joined by the most recent residents, including recent migrants. The group quickly reached a dozen core community members who formed a committee and 147 registered volunteers. The primary goal of the 34th Avenue Open Streets Coalition was to "invite people to the street."[94] "COVID let us experiment."[95] There are no restaurants on 34th Avenue, so the program relies fully on allowing the community to live in the neighborhood differently, particularly to walk and cycle safely, play, socialize, and learn new skills. Activities include sports and dance classes for different age groups, arts, painting, gardening, children's races, and biking. "The scheme allowed people in this community to talk to each other. Before, some families were scared to ask, as also English isn't their first language. Now, they know who to ask and what to do."[96] Opening the community has been supported by English and Spanish lessons in the street and dedicated sessions on specific matters (e.g., how to register children at schools). Food poverty is a major issue in the area, and food distribution is organized every week to assist those in need. Food bank trucks also come in to complement the provision of food on an ad hoc basis, with residents queuing in the street while other activities are going on.

As in Vanderbilt Avenue Open Street, the 34th Avenue Open Streets Coalition is run thanks to DOT financial support, other nonprofit grants, and fundraising. DOT also supports the management of daily barriers, which quickly became unmanageable for the community group. The success of the 34th Avenue Open Streets Coalition elevated it to a flagship project for New York City and its mayor. As a result, it has been receiving significant political and media attention. Key to its success was that temporary street day closures, thanks to low-cost adaptations, could have a very positive impact on local communities when socioeconomic deprivation had several causes. It improved residents' everyday lives and provided major changes. Its success goes beyond its social and community benefits, with the 34th Avenue Open Streets Coalition also matching a wider active travel agenda for the city.

The 34th Avenue Open Streets Coalition (and the absence of a local economic agenda) is exceptional in scale. It resonates, however, with smaller schemes run in areas of severe deprivation, as on Jennings Street in the Bronx. The Jennings Street Open Street illustrates how a small organization managed to pursue its work with vulnerable young people during the pandemic thanks to hybrid temporary urbanism. The plan was developed in an area with no available community center or facilities for young people that would provide them with a safe place to stay after

THE PANDEMIC AND POSTPANDEMIC ADAPTABLE CITY • 187

school or during holidays and would also provide food. "The community is food starved."[97] The charitable organization ran its activities prior to the pandemic, but it suddenly faced real challenges because of the social-distancing rules that prevented them from using their existing indoor space. The Jennings Street Open Street was therefore a way to sustain its community role. "I heard about the scheme through word of mouth, and decided to apply and we were seeking for a solution to continue providing our support to our community of young people."[98] The program was thus transferred to the street and was complemented with other activities (e.g., Zumba, basketball), particularly during holidays, in order to keep young people busy, entertained, and hence out of trouble. It was very small and received less publicity, but this initiative demonstrates again the extent to which the street—as an adaptable space—can serve clear social purposes in an emergency.

These three examples point out how New York City used the pandemic to move beyond traditional approaches to temporary street closures, specifically those driven mostly by municipalities and local businesses rather than communities, as in Seattle, Washington, or Vancouver, British Columiba.[99] It shows how a different approach to hybrid adaptability, with community mobilization and a vision and/or program, allows change to occur. This is an important legacy and lesson from pandemic adaptability.

THE LEGACY OF POST-COVID ADAPTABILITY

As this book goes to press, "back to normal" and "forgetting about COVID-19" are the narrative claimed by national and local governments, despite a wave of new geopolitical and socioeconomic downturns affecting households, particularly the most vulnerable, around the world. This section isn't about predicting the future of urban adaptations (I will sketch some of those directions in chapter 8). However, I do want to examine what the pandemic did to the adaptability paradigm. I question the extent to which the lockdowns; and the changes in how people behaved, consumed, lived, and worked, really changed the approach to adaptability and temporary urbanisms. Work published during the pandemic called for important lessons to be drawn from such a dramatic episode, but much of this research drew conclusions out of extrapolations and hypotheses.[100] The reality of how cities have been moving forward is different. It reveals the complexity of critically "learning" from the pandemic and delivering transformative changes. There seems to be a lost opportunity to build on some of the pandemic transformations rather than just return to normal and to quite rigid thinking about urban making. There has been little attempt to learn from reactive adaptable processes and shift toward more proactive adaptable thinking. COVID-19 has become a banned word, and it is assumed that research and policy should move away from looking at this past event. Postpandemic urban adjustments have already occurred, however, with more surely to come, and most will be grounded in accelerations of previous trends (e.g. hybrid working).[101]

COVID-19 has had several significant impacts on the design and planning of cities. The pandemic put a renewed focus on streets for noncar use, which translated into various interpretations and legacies embedded in wider (postpandemic) agendas: active travel, behavioral changes, climate change. It also prompted people to question again the role of adaptability in urban development and elevated hybrid temporariness as an important feature of urban transformation strategies. This is partly because of the increase in hybrid modes of working across a wider range of sectors, with various immediate impacts on the

THE PANDEMIC AND POSTPANDEMIC ADAPTABLE CITY • 189

residential and office market (for example, WeWork filed for bankruptcy on November 7, 2023) and more to come over the medium and long terms.[102] The health crisis revealed existing intersectional inequalities that future pandemic and crisis preparedness cannot ignore.

The regulated/deregulated process that characterized the transformation of mobility spaces and transport strategies during the pandemic, although triggered by new health requirements, was nevertheless anchored in existing (and prepandemic) mobility strategies at both city and neighborhoods levels. The ciclovía initiatives, where roads are temporally closed, often during the weekend, for cycling didn't emerge, of course, in 2020. They were initiated in some cities, for example, Bogota, Columbia, in the 1970s.[103] The health crisis increased the number of these initiatives, with many new cities, for example, London, Paris, Milan, Berlin, New York, and Toronto, among many others), embracing pop-up bike lanes. These adaptations were in line with existing transport and climate change strategy.[104] The pandemic thus allowed us to accelerate the delivery of planned cycling lanes but also, with the pop-up lanes, to consider if others could be made permanent in controversial locations. As mentioned by a representative from Transport for London (TFL): "Experimental temporary schemes allowed us to see what works and what doesn't. In some areas, it was just a kind of temporary measure to help movement during the pandemic and then we've had to, kind of like, wind it back after that. For some . . . the negative impacts were too much. For me, that's okay, you know, as it allowed us to get to that point a lot quicker than you would have had after spending three or four years at the drawing board."[105] In London, several experimental cycling lanes sponsored by TFL failed and were removed; others are still under review. Failures are to be attributed to conflicts with other modes of transport (buses, taxi);

190 • THE PANDEMIC AND POSTPANDEMIC ADAPTABLE CITY

safety concerns; the car lobby; and, of course, political decisions. "The politicians there decided that it wasn't the right scheme for them at that time although it did massively increase cycling and safety during that period. So, you take a step back then, but overall these schemes put down important markers and increased visibility that help move the conversation on."[106]

In addition to testing the location of new lanes, pop-up cycling initiatives also allowed testing of new types of design. "The speed of implementation and the way those lanes were then sustained didn't relate to more speedy processes but also flexibility in how the lanes were physically created: all pop-up lanes were put in with very cheap materials. Before, we were using expensive materials. All those have been sustained—just minor tweaks were made."[107] There is a learning legacy here: "The pop-up cycling lanes went very well but we can't afford expensive stuff to separate the lanes. So, design wise, the use of semi-permanent or temporary cheaper materials has to be the way for the time being due to financial constraints. That's going to be the legacy of COVID."[108] Context matters incredibly here. The pop-up lanes referred to in this quote are located in Lambeth, a London borough that has been at the forefront of adaptable urban making because it supported meanwhile uses for over a decade.

This proactive use of adaptability in the delivery of transformative changes is based on very strong political support and leadership. As a legacy of the pandemic, additional strategies and programs, such as the Big Shift programme, are now developed with a focus on behavioral changes and hence sustainable forms of transport. This includes the introduction of community support grants to support different initiatives, including road closure:

> I don't think we did enough of it [using streets differently]. We don't really see much of that now, so we want to make sure that

if you have got a local group who wants to do something every Sunday, you know, for about two hours, they can; if they want to create a play area for kids we want to be able to accommodate. This is a hybrid to way to help businesses, and also to help local people, consolidate safe space and the road. But the important thing for us is making it very simple for them, you know we don't want to try to make this really bureaucratic. It needs to be a very, very simple thing.[109]

Lambeth's proactive engagement with adaptability is relatively unique and hasn't been initiated in all the boroughs in London, although others (for example, Hammersmith and Fulham) are catching up. Street closures (known as healthy school

FIGURE 6.8 Open street dining plans used during the COVID-19 pandemic made permanent on Charlotte Street, London.

Source: Lauren Andres.

streets and playstreets prior to the pandemic) didn't spread during the health emergency crisis to respond to community needs. To date, the legacy of pandemic-led adaptations in London is limited. A limited amount of open dining and outdoor seating areas have been sustained in high-profile streets in affluent areas. Adaptable urban making has mostly translated into pop-up mobility lanes being made permanent and school street closures being widely rolled over from 2022, with a sustained utilization of meanwhile use strategies for high-street recovery and local regeneration.

The legacy of adaptability in New York City is different because the city has historically been more proactive in encouraging walking and cycling and in using streets differently for community purposes. Such ambitions received strong political support from past and current mayors (Michael Bloomberg in partnership with Janette Sadik-Khan, his then commissioner of the New York City Department of Transportation, Bill de Blasio, and Eric Adams) along with a long-lasting legacy of strong community engagement (e.g., neighborhood groups) that thrived through tactical urbanism initiatives. Street closures were already implemented in the city prior to the pandemic (one example is the high-profile Times Square closure). Other small-scale initiatives, such as the weekend walks program or the summer streets program, were also already running.

Both open streets and open dining programs were sustained and made permanent but were effectively reduced in scale. The goal of reaching one hundred miles of open streets hasn't however been reached (the program peaked at eighty-three miles and coverage is dropping since then to concerning numbers).[110] Some of the more successful and active schemes remain though; key element of success has been the place-based governance of the program and how it has enabled community empowerment,

THE PANDEMIC AND POSTPANDEMIC ADAPTABLE CITY • 193

with residents able to "assert their interests" and take full ownership of the scheme.[111] The open dining program, once made permanent, faced two lawsuits, which reflected the discontent of some residents; they claimed about a lack of consultation and environmental assessment when the program was expanded in 2020, and its overall impact on specific areas in terms of noise nuisance and garbage disposal. The new rules published in February 2024 allow outdoor dining to be expanded citywide on sidewalks year-round and in roadways seasonally from April through November. These changes are leading to a drop of applications with small restaurants not being able to face the seasoning constraints.

The strengths of the open streets and open dining plans and also their primary weaknesses are its reliance on communities and local businesses and the hybrid partnership between residents, business owners and DOT. Each street closure and open dining site reflect the socioeconomic characteristics of the neighborhoods, including the types of residents and local businesses and other urban features, and the proportion of car owners along with the perception of the car. As noted by an open street advocate, "economically deprived neighborhoods tend to be more resistant to change and sensitive to anything that can impact their livelihood."[112] Removing space for parking is problematic in poorer neighborhoods because the car is the way that households access work and hence generate income. Similar fears are shared by local businesses in more deprived areas. "Small businesses that have a vehicle really feel like the vehicle access to their business is super important. Wherever you're talking about making changes that impact the vehicle network, particularly in low-income or underserved areas, these kinds of difficult conversations crop up. Locals don't agree with them and they believe it is going to impact them negatively. So we are really seeing a lot of pushback."[113] Additional challenges come from communities' awareness of the scheme, ability and time to develop a proposal and then run the scheme. "It requires the initiative to come from us, the citizen, which is harder when your citizens are under resourced. It's not surprising that you just don't see as much activity in some neighbourhoods as people may not have the resources or capacity to do it. Those are neighbourhoods where you have less institutional capacity and institutional activity and less individual capacity."[114] Such challenges testify to the difficulties in applying adaptable strategies at city level because, of course, context and locality matter.

As a result of the pandemic, however, hybrid temporary urbanisms spread as rapid and effective solutions to tackle urgent needs while also reactivating the willingness of residents and groups to be together in their neighborhood. Some of these community initiatives will certainly continue to fade away because of a general fatigue associated with a return to more standard living and working rhythms; others will stay, evidence of long-lasting but small-scale transformations inherited from the pandemic. What is clear, however, is the turn of adaptability toward local-based hybrid models of temporary urbanisms, particularly in the face of ongoing and new disruptions. "Local governments will have to retain some drive and keep promoting their local assets and community initiatives alongside supporting more localised economies of production and consumption if they are serious about recovery."[115] Hybrid adaptability resonates with many priorities characterizing postpandemic cities: well-being, high-street recovery, but also the push toward a more health-driven city.[116]

At the start of the pandemic, Remon Rooij et al. rightly hypothesized that the pandemic may have "actually amplified a debate that was started already: the scale of mixed-use, sustainable mobility and the meaning of public space."[117] This is true for adaptability too. Prior to 2020, adaptability was already resonating with the concepts of circular cities and economies, but it also became embedded in calls to push forward the implementation of 15 min types of cities and hence to rethink urban trends and models.[118] Adaptability became integrated into approaches promoting proximity, as it did in Paris. "The world has been amassed with innovative temporary urban infrastructures, which has helped to partially deal with some challenges presented by the pandemic. Such success highlights that the public wishes that urban managers will concentrate henceforth on investing in proximity-based needs rather than rolling out further investments in large infrastructural projects as a means of economic support through COVID-19 relief packages."[119] Proximity and temporary uses joined to serve different purposes: tackling food provision, providing access to play and green and open spaces (e.g., pocket parks), and also health services (e.g. temporary vaccination centers). This happened around the globe, for example, in the Teatro de Contêiner Mungunzá (discussed in chapter 4). The concept of the fifteen-minute city is based on rhythms and "chrono-urbanism" applied to the provision of services in urban areas, and it resonates fully with adaptability and temporary urbanisms.

Beyond the proximity discourse, principles of place-based adaptations and hybrid temporary urbanism translated into the pursuit of meanwhile strategies as ways to regenerate high streets and tackle economic decline. In England, the Local Government Association (LGA), while strategizing how to create resilient and revitalized high streets in the "new normal," argued that:

> Flexibility can be integrated into the high street through evidence-based strategy, policy amendments, and up-to-date awareness of community needs and demands. For example, allowing Meanwhile Use or pop-up organisations to operate can temporarily fill

vacant units and generate interest in the high street. Collaboration with community stakeholders is an important part of facilitating flexibility, considering change of use and integrating multipurpose spaces into the high street.[120]

This explains how adaptable urban making has been translated in recovery and resilience strategies and promoted as such by multinational professional services firms focusing on the built environment, for example, Arup:

> Affordability and flexibility of commercial space plays an important role in helping businesses get back on their feet and opening the door for SMEs [small and medium-sized enterprises] and start-ups. Local planning authorities, public landlords and licensing bodies play an important role in supporting meanwhile use. These strategies can allow temporary use of underused and vacant spaces by businesses (including SMEs and start-ups) and community organisations. Interventions can take many forms, from temporary community and recreational activities, to arts, culture and commercial uses. Using spaces in this way can optimise the use of assets by local communities, facilitating the human connections that build community resilience. Although the physical use of space is temporary, these activities can promote long-lasting economic and social benefits to local communities. Lively ground or businesses (shops, food and beverage, and leisure) and bustling commercial districts play a big part in developing sense of place and attracting investment.[121]

There is nothing new here: this quotation clearly reflects how top-down adaptability stimulated urban making extensively and strategically.

Such market-driven approaches to adaptability have been embedded in recovery strategies constructed on "live, work, play models" of urban development, particularly for central business districts aimed at providing urban experiential playgrounds as places of relaxation, socializing, and entertainment.[122] This takes us back to the role of cognitive-cultural capitalism in cities and how city centers have been transitioning away from places to purchase products to experiential spaces as playgrounds for conspicuous consumption based on hospitality, tourism, entertainment, and leisure.[123] In the United States, successful postpandemic office districts are envisaged as necessarily including outdoor spaces and entertainment activities.[124] While this strategy isn't new, clearly business models seem to be inclined to include more agility and flexibility. Reports exploring the future of London's Central Activities Zone (CAZ) have been arguing that strategies must "be agile, embrace experimentation, encourage temporary solutions and continue to move with the fast pace of change"; part of this includes embracing "the flexibility in timings offered by new ways of working to spread footfall around the clock, reducing crowds at certain times, and to make the CAZ more attractive for people after 6pm".[125] Such strategies are highly exclusive, socioeconomically speaking, because they target specific workers, consumers, and age groups. They are also spatially restrained because they are solely concerned with specific strategic areas (high streets and central business districts). A great risk hence remains in how the legacy of the pandemic will lead to a stronger perpetuation of intersectional misbalance, leading to a missed opportunity to learn, from such an exceptional crisis, about an inclusive and socially fair way. This risk is far higher in low- and middle-income countries where socioeconomic inequalities have dramatically increased as a result of the pandemic while everyday adaptability and survival-led improvisations have been further ignored and neglected.

Overall, the temporary adaptability window favored by the unprecedented health crisis quickly gave way to a prompt return to regulations, rigidity, and very limited proactive adaptable thinking. "In just a blip, you get back to normal. So, how do you take advantage of that to experiment and develop and test ideas and have strategies for them to stay if they work? I am a bit disappointed that actually London hasn't done more. The political rhetoric was clearly we'll get back to normal soon . . ."[126] The pandemic allowed us to see and use space differently but "the gift of space" that was provided here was ephemeral;[127] it didn't translate into a matter of policy priority to integrate adaptability proactively into crisis preparedness and a wider resilience strategy, contrary to what could have been expected. In other words, temporary hybrid urbanism and reactive adaptability matter, and still do, but the advances that could have been expected from adaptability seem relatively limited, particularly in regard to proactive anticipatory adaptable thinking because few lessons seem to have been learned from this dramatic event around the globe.

CONCLUSION

The COVID-19 pandemic had a significant impact on the interpretation of adaptability and how temporary urbanisms spread in various new hybrid forms around the world. It concerned both indoor and outdoor spaces and resulted from an unprecedented interpretation of creative urban making, reaction, disorder, and (in)stability based on emergency and rapid adaptations.

The pandemic led unfortunately to predictable and detrimental impacts on places and people, particularly those whose ordinary, everyday struggles and pressures were exacerbated further. The pandemic revealed that those who were the most at risk and the worst affected by COVID, while facing dramatic everyday living pressures, were also those who benefited the least from adaptable schemes (with some few exceptions, as illustrated earlier looking at the example of New York City). The most vulnerable, those living in poverty, were again excluded from political priorities. Many of these people work in low-skilled positions, where hybrid working wasn't possible. Many belong to ethnic minorities.[128] Race is a factor in understanding the impact of the pandemic and its legacy.

The rush to return to normal and to face new challenges and disruptions has led to the failure to reflect on what worked and what didn't work in efforts to adapt cities and allow communities to cope. Any lessons from the pandemic should be shaped with a proactive understanding of adaptability, not solely to tackle preparedness and resilience but also social justice and equity. Evidence that this is happening is limited.

7

KNOWLEDGE, SKILLS, AND THE DELIVERY OF THE ADAPTABLE CITY

This book has already demonstrated how adaptability is inextricably linked with knowledge and skills. More important, however, is how knowledge is connected to adaptability becoming a political matter. Knowledge is a fundamental lens for examining the transformation trajectories of temporary and adaptable processes. The expansion, diversification, and manifestation of how temporary uses have been sustained have been concomitant with a professionalization of adaptable urban making, including its monetarization as a profitable activity. Its recognition as a relevant policy tool has caused the activity to grow into an attractive market segment for both small and larger organizations.

Some temporary projects succeeded in the longer-term and were then raised as leading examples of successful transformations. Despite being set up as nonpermanent, these projects were thoroughly strategized and planned by highly experienced professionals. Experimental skills and knowledge also matter significantly for everyday coping in more informal and unplanned contexts. Knowledge and learning are different in these contexts and illustrate how individual and community skills can converge in transformative actions if there is support from international nongovernmental organizations (INGOs) and nongovernmental organizations (NGOs). In all cases, the diffusion of temporary models and ways of delivering adaptability and temporariness have been achieved through the transfer of ideas and the creation of what can be referred to as communities of practice, which are constructed thanks to organic or more structured relationships. This chapter navigates the dynamics and mechanisms behind such shared practices and skills and examines the likely directions toward knowledge and skills production in regard to the adaptability paradigm and the prospect of elevating it within the policy sphere.

FRAMING THE IMPORTANCE OF KNOWLEDGE FOR SHAPING AND DELIVERING THE ADAPTABLE CITY

Knowledge and skills are crucial in revealing the complexity and diversity of temporary uses and adaptable mechanisms. They are also essential in the trajectory that characterizes such processes. This relates to the ability of developing and running adaptable schemes of all forms (i.e., bottom-up, top-down, and hybrid) which are responses to specific needs and perceived rights by those leading such initiatives. It also concerns the ability to sustain such schemes from practical and financial perspectives but also from a political point of view. Two core issues show how the process of adaptability becomes a policy problem or a matter that would require policy attention, hence relying on the production of knowledge. They are related to processes of assembling knowledge but also skill sets that embrace to a greater extent the principle of unfinishedness. The work of Colin McFarlane on knowledge fragments offers an illuminating perspective, particularly on how knowledge is produced through adaptable grassroots mechanisms led by individuals, communities, or organizations.[1] The issue of knowledge production also relates to a poststructuralist approach to policy development and particularly how problems are shaped by different types of logic in order to reach the policy sphere and be implemented. These institutional logics shape a context of influence, drive policy formation, and thus determine implementation and outcomes.[2] They are important when questioning how temporary experimentations evolve and can be sustained; questioning how individuals, groups, and communities of practice get together to drive projects; and revealing the professionalization and the monetarization of temporary and adaptable urban making.

The concept of knowledge fragments is anchored in critical urbanism and inequalities debates along with assemblage theory.[3] The concept has been used by McFarlane to examine the complexity of the urban. Knowledge and skills about adaptability are extracted from individuals' innovative thoughts, ability to experiment, and ability to do things differently to fill gaps. These skills and the knowledge are highly specific and tailored to specific places and contexts. Knowledge fragments allow us to focus on the more ordinary and less common modes of constructing urban spaces. They "are a lure to ways of thinking about the urban and the city, often obscured or radically distinct from dominant and mainstream ways of knowing in policy, research and practice."[4] It can be argued that knowledge fragments, when transferred to the idea of adaptability, derive from social inequalities, everyday adaptations, and ways to cope and in some cases survive. They are also expressions and translations of "political and legal rights or economic opportunity."[5] Knowledge fragments are extremely complex and dynamic because they are associated with both permanent and temporary arrangements that characterize cities globally. In low- and middle-income countries, they

THE DELIVERY OF THE ADAPTABLE CITY • 203

are specifically embedded in the "visible and invisible realities" of the urban condition comprised of formal, informal, and blended dynamics.[6] In other contexts, and typically higher-income nations, they reveal the level of inequality and fragmentation that characterize cities globally.

The concept of fragments draws heavily from Henri Lefebvre's accounts of rights and rhythms in the production of cities. Lefebvre describes space as "homogenous yet at the same time broken up into fragments."[7] Such spatial fragments are products of capitalist production and are positioned as part of processes of fragmentation across the global capitalist space.[8] Fragments can be considered as both "material entity" and a "form of expression or a type of knowledge."[9] Applied to adaptable and temporary cities, the concept of knowledge fragments relates to the everyday living conditions of the poor. It characterizes knowledgeable responses to specific needs and gaps.

Key here is understanding how knowledge, and specifically knowledge of fragments, is constructed, passed over by whom and for what purpose. This differs from one project, place, and context to another. Such understanding cannot be disconnected from how knowledge is recognized and validated by those holding power. Knowledge fragments are difficult, however, to track. They tend to be put on the side "because of their position to or within a wider set of political, social, and cultural power-knowledge relations. Constructions of the urban whole involved a set of power relations that can exclude, subordinate or otherwise transform knowledge fragments."[10] Such a process constitutes a policy assemblage and hence resonates with the diverse institutional logics in place that shape policies and the production of space. Knowledge production, and specifically how knowledge of fragments do or do not feed into it, is embedded in the political nature of urban making; applied to adaptability and temporary urbanism, it refers to dynamics related to top-down and hybrid-driven initiatives.

The use of poststructuralist approaches to policy development and a focus on institutional logics have been applied to other urban matters but not to the temporary and adaptability research field.[11] Doing so allows us to surpass the process of assemblage and transfer of models and ideas from one place to another.[12] Poststructuralist approaches allow the questioning of how and why initiatives, strategies, and programs based on temporary and adaptable practices are being elevated into policy priorities and hence transferred to policy agendas. This process resonates with the discussion so far in this book and particularly with how some leading temporary initiatives (for example, La Friche de la Belle de Mai in Marseille, France) evolved from perceived alternative and nonpermanent projects to flagship initiatives. It goes beyond examining the construction of *lieux propres* and allows the examination of hybrid temporary practices. It is important to understand how such practices rely on knowledge being exchanged among different stakeholder groups but also how knowledge is used to construct temporary initiatives and then manage and possibly sustain them. Such processes are intrinsically connected to policy formulation and the constitution of communities of practice.

"Policy emerges from a process in which enactment might not meet intent. Logics are a fundamental component in this process of shaping interpretations and enactment of policy."[13] Such logics are defined as "socially constructed, historical patterns of cultural symbols and material practices, including assumptions, values and beliefs, by which individuals and organizations provide meaning to their daily activity, organize time and space, and reproduce their lives and experiences."[14] These are constructed by different institutions (here understood as groups able to

THE DELIVERY OF THE ADAPTABLE CITY • 205

construct practices, ideas, and knowledge) that can be involved in producing adaptable cities and hence different forms of temporary urbanisms. Such policy production relies on an interplay of scales, going beyond the local level to include a national and international dimension. This, of course, resonates with how policy, idea, and knowledge transfer has resulted in the rise of top-down and hybrid forms of adaptability. It also echoes other policy analysis frameworks and typically the policy mobility literature denoting the role that actors and institutions play in promoting, mobilizing, and adapting policy models, practices, and knowledge through processes of learning and knowledge exchange.[15] Institutional logics shape policy outcomes in two ways: by their convergence (i.e., agreement) but also their divergence. In both processes, the way knowledge is produced and mobilized is key.

Policy decisions and also decisions made by landowners and developers rely on being able to access relevant knowledge, information, and skills to make those decisions in line with other agenda or priorities. Poststructuralist approaches have emphasized that policy development is embedded within territorial and scalar assemblages of actors.[16] As a result, stakeholders mobilize and engage with notions of power, autonomy, strategy, and identity.[17] When those notions don't converge, divergence emerges as a result of tensions, disagreements, or the absence of interactions between organizations with competing institutional logics. This can result in failure to develop or implement policy but also in misinterpretations and changes of meaning given to some projects or initiatives. If applied to temporary projects, the temporary element is thus fully revisited and renegotiated. Convergence and divergence of institutional logics is influenced by knowledge and how it is connected to individuals and group of individuals, particularly their skills, abilities, educational background (i.e., training), networks, and previous experiences.

Institutional logics emerge within an institutional setting but are enacted and interpreted through individual actions, that is, by individual, groups, and communities of shared practice in the case of temporary urbanism, which is why knowledge and skills matter. While policy problems are based on several and often contradictory institutional logics,[18] not all acquire equal importance in the policy process. Policy priorities are negotiated through path dependency and trade-offs. They are also influenced by the allocation of limited resources and other urgent—at least politically perceived as such—needs. This resonates with whether the question of adaptability is perceived as a useful tool for urban policies and how this connects to knowledge about temporary uses, but also the nature of emerging communities of practice promoting and/or in charge of such processes of adaptability.

ADAPTABILITY AND RADICAL AND TACTICAL KNOWLEDGE

Returning first to unplanned settings is a good starting point to demonstrate how skills and knowledge from individuals and communities living in very dire situations play a fundamental role in allowing them to survive on an everyday basis, as demonstrated in chapter 4. While knowledge fragments are not necessarily tied to geography,[19] they are nevertheless linked to economic margins and hence to places where adaptations, improvisations, marginalization, and deprivation prevail. Such knowledge and skills thus derive from the need to alter the built environment to generate transformative changes; they are practical but also radical and tactical responses to address specific needs in situations where no one else will (particularly the state). If we return to Syrian refugees' living conditions in informal

THE DELIVERY OF THE ADAPTABLE CITY • 207

tented settlements (ITSs)[20] and their imposed temporary settlement status (see chapter 4), we can see that knowledge and skills acquired prior to being displaced are complementary to radical knowledge fragments guided by survival necessities. As shown by Paul Moawad, this includes being able to construct a shelter with nonpermanent materials; finding ways to grow, prepare, and cook food; and generating small incomes incrementally and informally—all outside any INGO, NGO, or state support and in a context of uncertainties and "protracted waiting."[21] The importance of knowledge and skills is also fundamental in other forms of unplanned settings, as in sub-Sahara African townships or Brazilian favellas. However, it deeply questions and challenges any attempt to plan or regulate those settlements and hence clashes with the policy process and divergent institutional logics.

Adaptability relies on knowledge being constructed, used, and shared. This process of sharing has two components. It is shared among individuals and community members in relation to everyday coping and adaptations, but it is also transferred as a spatial materialization to those in charge of overseeing, planning, and trying to navigate the complexity of informal settings. The realities of ITSs are extremely diverse and complex. They are subject to multiple dynamics, and many are often located on serviced sites where built units were purposely constructed by the government to address housing needs, as in South Africa.[22] Such housing developments were effectively planned with allocated land uses and parceling; however, these settlements have grown and expanded through informal occupations of land. The most common are backyard dwellings: extended informal units built to provide additional income or accommodate family extension space.[23] "The owner of a (typically subsidized) formal house rents a portion of his yard area to occupants who live in a dwelling constructed either by formal or informal methods, thus gaining access to the house's water and electricity connections and to an outside toilet."[24] Backyard dwellings are examples of how knowledge of fragments affect space and its regulatory nature. They do so as a radical response to survival in a (planning) system that isn't suited and doesn't account for everyday realities. The consequences of such adaptations can be dramatic in some cases, reflecting the limitations of knowledge fragments. Backyard dwellings significantly increase the risk of fire due to do-it-yourself (DIY) wiring systems and challenge access to water and sanitation (with effects on health) because networks aren't tailored to accommodate so many individuals.

For planners, understanding and accounting for the importance of knowledge fragments is challenging because knowledge fragments deeply question their own knowledge of informal settings and their ability to understand how knowledge fragments are materialized. "I think informal settlements are growing and the problem is that there's no long-term plan. So, I would say, the planning profession hasn't evolved, informal settlements are very, very dynamic and they evolve all the time, but it's the planning profession that's stuck behind."[25]

"Being stuck" is related to how knowledge is constructed and whether it informs policy agenda. Knowledge, particularly knowledge informing decision making on urban questions, is dominated by "particular actors and their ways of seeing and narrativizing the world."[26] Recognizing that informality is part of formal settings would mean that the state recognizes its failure and hence its inability to respond to all individuals' needs.[27] For planners, understanding knowledge fragments is therefore tricky. The latest are formed within a shadowed, radical, and informal community of practice where the planners do not belong and hence don't have full insight. This is where the problem sits. Educating planners about informality is an extremely

THE DELIVERY OF THE ADAPTABLE CITY • 209

complex task because general planning knowledge is constrained by the highly rigid nature of the planning system, which does not allow many crossovers. Of course, this adds to the complexity and dynamic nature of informal settings, as do the constraints of limited financial resources and the resources of local and planning authorities. As a public sector planner revealed during an interview: "We don't know how to plan with more flexible standards. The designing schemes have not been amended to take account of informality."[28] Another planner commented: "So, government gets swamped by the enormity of the problem that is identified . . . And then tries to do everything by the book and doesn't get anywhere, you know, and then wonders why."[29]

Such difficulties are also linked to divergent institutional logics and hence policy priorities reflecting very unbalanced distributions of power. Knowledge fragments belong to the economic margins, to those whose voices are heard often and those who tend to be more invisible.[30] Adaptations and temporary improvisations triggered by knowledge fragments, when they are successful, represent organic forms of empowerment. These were explicit in the case of the DIY water system in Marikana, outside Potchefstroom in the northwest province of South Africa (see chapter 4). This is a remarkable example of how a knowledge fragment responded to the failure of the system and hence shaped communities' radical way to have their needs and rights addressed. This highlights the revolutionary component of knowledge fragments that penetrate mainstream thinking and become part of "acceptable" solutions.[31] All sides then acknowledge that the system is broken, and adaptability is a way to overturn the policy process. This case is exceptional, however, and the general pattern usually reflects a clear schism between knowledge fragments and the common knowledge that is also the dominant and politically correct.

Such radical and tactical knowledge isn't specific to dire informal settings; it can also apply to bottom-up and hybrid forms of adaptability found in all types of urban contexts. Knowledge and skills are essential for launching and implementing temporary initiatives and then sustaining them. In this configuration, however, a knowledge fragment differs from the one mobilized in informal settings; it tends to be very strategically constructed and articulated, and associated with individuals, communities, and organizations with specific skills and levels of education, as well as means and networks. These resources allow them to shape projects and narratives strategically; ensure that their voices, views, and claimed needs are heard; and advocate for specific rights on the grounds of perceived opportunities, dysfunction, or injustice. Such dynamics are explicit in how tactical initiatives spread in North American cities, as Gordon Douglas demonstrated.[32]

Tactical urbanism results from intertwining tactical and radical knowledge gained through education, and primarily higher education. Most DIY urbanists identified by Douglas in his work, are young, progressive urban thinkers who are often trained within the built environment disciplines and attuned to past and ongoing critical urban debates (typically David Harvey's work).[33] This is complemented by their creativity and desire to experiment and engage with urban dysfunctions and inequalities. This combination fosters the emergence of a knowledge fragment. "It is the formal knowledge and skills that come first, followed by an inspiration to act informally."[34] The inspiration to act informally is linked with the ability to dedicate time to informal activities and have enough flexibility in life versus work balance to do so. It also goes back, of course, to interest and care, particularly a dedication to shaping cities and tackling urban inequalities and dysfunctions. Douglas's observation resonates greatly with the profile of built environment experts interested in adaptability and temporary urbanism whom I encountered in Europe and around the globe.[35] This is illustrated by the following quote from a built environment expert in the United Kingdom: "With my town planning background, I just always thought we were taught the wrong things and we were making terrible city environments. The best cities are the ones where there is freedom for experimentation, and I think people will pay for that and the standard approach to regeneration is still where they think they are not going to make this place better until we get Westfield or a stadium."[36]

These built environment professionals all share similar socioeconomic profiles. "The typical DIY urban designer—the vast majority of those I [Gordon Douglas] spoke to or learned about—is white, middle class, adult, male and possessing of some degree of familiarity with professional or scholarly urbanism."[37] Aside from gender distribution, I concur again with Douglas's point that radical and tactical knowledge is constructed, shared, and used within a relatively small and elitist community of practitioners. Here a knowledge fragment isn't given to anyone. The exclusive nature of adaptable and temporary knowledge requires diligent attention and, as discussed previously in chapter 6, can lead to significant spatial inequalities. As noted by a member from the Open Streets Program in Brooklyn, New York: "Who has time to go out and, you know, volunteer? Who is at home during the pandemic? It's young people like me, right, who could just walk down the street and take a break from Zoom meetings. A lot of people in New York didn't have that luxury and won't have that luxury in the future."[38] Such professional skills and knowledge are therefore a core factor to explain the transformation of key temporary initiatives, particularly the differences between those that managed to secure widespread attention, and hence political visibility, and those that didn't and faded away.

I illustrate this point by returning to my first example, La Friche de la Belle de Mai in Marseille.

As stressed in chapter 3, La Friche emerged out of a three-way negotiation between the *Société d'exploitation industrielle des tabacs et des allumettes* (SEITA, owner), local decision makers, and two experienced artists/cultural professionals (Philippe Foulquié and Fabrice Lextrait) in a context of laissez-faire and economic crisis.[39] Nothing was spontaneous or fully organic in the setup of the project, despite its elevation as one of the leading examples of an alternative bottom-up, cultural brownfield and its being sustained as such. The consortium leading to the creation of La Friche was intrinsically hybrid, although at the time, it was an entirely unique and innovative model of urban transformation. Knowledge about cultural management and public policy along with a knowledge fragment were completely intertwined and then translated into complementary, newly framed institutional logics.

It started with an existing relationship between Philippe Foulquié and the deputy leader in charge of cultural policy in the municipality, Christian Poitevin. Poitevin (alias Julien Blaine) was also a poet who frequently visited places of alternative cultural production, for example, Melweg in Amsterdam[40].[41] With the full support of Gaston Deferre, mayor of Marseille at that time, Poitevin set up the program based on the nomadic use of spaces for alternative forms of culture in order to reactivate a city in desperate need of revival. Nomadism here was informed by grounded knowledge, creativity, and experience. It was also highly politicized because of the status and role of Poitevin in the local governance of the city. The narrative of nomadic uses was quickly translated into a municipal institutional logic. To implement his vision, Poitevin contacted Foulquié, who already had a very strong local and national reputation in the cultural

THE DELIVERY OF THE ADAPTABLE CITY • 213

field; he had directed several cultural companies in the Paris region prior to returning to the south of France to work for the *Direction régionale des Affaires culturelles* (DRAC; in English, Regional Directorate of Cultural Affairs, a service of the French Ministry of Culture). Foulquié and his artistic company first settled in a vacant unit in the north of Marseille (very quickly deemed as inappropriate as too small and not flexible enough), prior to turning their attention to the former tobacco manufacturing plant (see chapter 3).

Foulquié almost immediately sought the help of a master of science graduate in cultural management and local development, Fabrice Lextrait, who was already deeply involved in the city and local cultural and artistic community and networks; together, they started negotiating with SEITA, with the full political and financial support of the municipality.[41] These negotiations were deemed successful because they were anchored in the trust between the different parties; this trust was related, of course, to knowledge, skills, but also reputation. Once settled in the factory, this initial duo was joined by a team of professionals who structured the project further. "The Friche is a very institutional agency, drive by an administrative entity—*Système friche théatre* (SFT)—that is managing who is coming in (both vertically and horizontally). There is no process of democratic engagement and an open-process of consultation was never what we had in mind."[42] This very rigorous process allowed La Friche to establish its own institutional logic that matched the municipality's nomadism one.

The synergy of both the institutional logic along with the materialization of a knowledge fragment used to shape the identity and image of the place led to its rapid visibility and recognition at local, national, and international levels. "From 1994, we told ourselves that if we wanted to survive, we had to change scale."[43] This included being very active on the alternative cultural scene (for instance, the international network Trans Europe Halles) but also positioning La Friche within the built environment community of practice and some of its most visible figures. To achieve this, the architect Jean Nouvel was contacted and named president of La Friche in 1994. "We needed a notorious president, an artist, who was working on cities and was talented. We wanted someone determined, who never quits, a militant. He is an amazing architect, but also a great urbanist."[44]

The convergence and juxtaposition of knowledge, skills, networks, and expertise, and also the merging of distinct communities of practice and institutional logic, were vital to consolidating the project, and also to shaping its reputation within the cultural, built environment and policy spheres, leading to its inclusion as a flagship entity for the regeneration scheme Euroméditerranée (see chapter 3). More important, it fed into a wider transfer of knowledge and skills about ways of using cultural projects to reactivate spaces. La Friche was elevated to the forefront of a national program of the *Nouveaux territoires de l'art* (NTAs; in English, New Territory of Arts) that Lextrait was commissioned to lead. La Friche "was considered as a model. It has an anteriority, a gigantism, teams in the ground, an architecture, a site, key political support behind it. It was gathering almost all the conditions to be a model, or at least—as our goal wasn't to identify models, a symbol of success."[45] This success relied on a unique configuration that excluded those outside the convergent institutional logics and communities of practice. This explains in part the strong animosity that spread among members of the community and other, smaller cultural organizations, creating implicit but clear boundaries that took years to overcome between La Friche, the neighborhood of the Belle de Mai, and other local cultural institutions. Despite the local criticisms, the

THE DELIVERY OF THE ADAPTABLE CITY • 215

legacy of La Friche went beyond its local, national, and international success and recognition and ultimately played a role in professionalizing transient urbanism in France. The professionalization of adaptable and temporary urbanism reflects the latest trend commonly found in most countries around the world, but particularly in North America, Europe, and Australia.[46]

TOWARD A PROFESSIONALIZATION OF ADAPTABLE AND TEMPORARY URBANISM

The professionalization of tactical, temporary, or transient forms of urbanism started over a decade ago with the inclusion of top-down temporary practices in the policy and urban process (see chapter 5). This professionalization demonstrates, on the one hand, the trajectory through which the nonpermanent has been part of the planning and the built environment practice more and more often. It also shows how it emerged as an attractive market segment in a neoliberal planning context. This professionalization was progressive and displayed different mechanisms and opportunities from one country to another.

"Temporariness in city making—or rather, a specific construct of temporariness—is indeed here to stay, both as a practice and as an object of knowledge (and research) about forms of acting in the city."[47] The purpose and use of the "temporary" and related forms of adaptability have fed into the discourses of built environment experts and, more important, policymakers around the world.[48] The professionalization of temporary urban making has been related here to the convergence of three core institutional logics supported by policymakers, developers, and/or landowners and built environment experts. The latest has played a key role in assembling knowledge, initially incrementally and then later by feeding into the development of the large and international community of practices sharing experiences and ways of delivering transformative temporary initiatives.

In the United Kingdom, the spread of temporary uses, and particularly meanwhile uses, as politically validated solutions was indeed related to the economic crisis that hit the country at the end of the 2000s. This crisis largely questioned the delivery of both urban renaissance and urban regeneration. In this context, meanwhile strategies became practical but also financially acceptable solutions for the problematic management of dereliction and the future of declining local high streets. The "meanwhile" community of practice emerged through the confluence of regeneration, architecture, and urban design knowledge and skills; these converged into a reinterrogation of how to deliver change and transformations at community levels and within contexts where the prospects of improvements and recovery are long term. It led to the creation of a few small organizations and firms by urban regeneration and design professionals who led the sector for the first ten years. These companies, for example, Meanwhile Space Inc., created new, regenerative transformation strategies, through temporary leases and experimentation, on behalf of boroughs or large companies—for example, Network Rail, which owned a portfolio of small properties largely underused or unoccupied.

As it did in Marseille, France, the meanwhile community of practice emerged through a limited number of professionals with very strong networks in place. Emerging meanwhile professionals originally joined forces with the Development Trusts Association in 2009 and received support from the then Ministry of Housing, Communities & Local Government, here again reflecting a convergence of knowledge, visions, and institutional logics in time of crisis.[49] The collaboration led, in less than a year, to over thirty talks, presentations, and workshops expanding the scope and visibility of the meanwhile community of practice within the public and private built environment sector, which connected it to the relevant policymaking spheres, particularly in the Greater London area.[50] Besides leading to a consolidation of the purposes of meanwhile spaces as policy solutions, it also elevated the activity as a niche market segment targeting various spaces and purposes: rundown neighborhoods, empty commercial units, temporary landscaping, temporary reuse for media and filming purposes, and so on.

The pandemic and the latest economic downturns led to an expansion of the sector of activity with large international groups (for example, Arup) embracing it within the consultancy portfolio. Arup typically led the London City Resilience Strategy for meanwhile spaces in 2020 for the Greater London Authority (GLA) while working with numerous London boroughs to support the revival and transformation of their declining high streets. In the 2022 postpandemic context, the company started shifting their discourse from meanwhile uses toward tactical urbanism, thus further expanding their portfolio of services to include temporary interventions on public spaces and streets (with clear reference to tactical urbanism in North America).

In North America, the market, and hence professionalization process, for the temporary has been directed for over a decade toward public and outdoor spaces (including streets) under the label of "tactical urbanism." Similar to the meanwhile community in the United Kingdom, the movement was officially created in 2010; it was built on a long tradition of DIY narratives but also embedded in the new urbanism movement.[51] Its roots are therefore not within the urban regeneration field but in an influential movement promoting new forms of urban development shaped around human-scale urban design.[52] It is thus situated within an expanded and recognized community of practice with its own institutional logic.[53] Knowledge and skills building about tactical urbanism was supported by key publications that reached both the academic and practice communities and shaped urban narratives. Key principles at the micro level were also translated into detailed strategies and guides offering micro-level technical explanations on how to implement specific interventions and the types of material, design, budget, and location.[54] These written documents were disseminated widely and made available via open access, which has allowed tactical urbanists to configure a niche but very active community of practice strongly embedded in key cities, for example New York City; Los Angeles; San Francisco; Portland, Oregon; and Miami. Its connection to the new urbanism movement has allowed tactical design to feed into higher education and curriculum debates while informing wider urban and policy priorities at the city and national levels. These priorities typically include livability, well-being, walkability and cycling.

As a recognized community of practice, tactical urbanism and its principles have reached the relevant spheres of policymaking and informed larger interventions founded on temporary urban interventions (for example, the Open Streets Program in New York City). This has been achieved by an implicit recognition of the importance of convergent institutional logics but also interest in allowing the support of innovation in the project delivery process.[55] Successful delivery of tactical projects has been achieved by ensuring that all core actors are on board and share similar goals. These actors comprise "community, agency leader (civil group organisations, city transport and planning departments for example) and political support, at higher level (i.e. mayor) for example in Los Angeles (People St program) and New York City (Open Streets), both programs being fully politically supported and led by the respective department of

THE DELIVERY OF THE ADAPTABLE CITY • 219

transportation."[56] In other words, this is about making certain that knowledge is used to guarantee "buy-in from everyone who is impacted by the new processes or materials being introduced."[57] To do so, the tactical urbanism community of practice has been sustaining their action by constantly negotiating, communicating, and using the relevant participatory methods to engage with communities.[58] This again is using skills to ensure the spread of such practice across U.S. cities, at the project and city levels. This knowledge is not given to everyone, however, as in the discussion in chapter 6 about the spread of the Open Streets Program in New York City; this also resonates with La Friche de la Belle de Mai in Marseille but, more important, with how, in France, the so-called transient urbanism community of practice has emerged and grown steadily.

Compared to the United Kingdom and the United States, adaptable urban making in France is not grounded in the traditional approach to urban development (new urbanism), ways of reclaiming open spaces, urban regeneration, meanwhile uses, and high-street renewal. It was originally situated in alternative and creative approaches to urban transformation using art and culture as leverage (i.e., the NTA movement). Transient urbanism includes two complementary policy agendas: the development of cultural and creative economies along with community and social enterprises development (*économie solidaire* in French). It progressively became elevated as a powerful urban development tool for very large companies to manage their real estate portfolio. SNCF Immobilier has played a significant role here, as Juliette Pinard revealed, again reflecting the role of narrow and very networked-based communities of practice.[59]

SNCF Immobilier embraced transient urbanism as an alternative strategy to manage a large but diverse portfolio of assets, including many empty and underused sites. The choice made by the company was linked to the vision of one of its senior executives, who had previously "worked on the development of cultural projects in non-traditional spaces, through the hosting of artistic events and exhibitions, and the creation of partnerships with major cultural institutions."[60] This individual knew NTAs well and how they had been used by some cities to foster significant transformations. His acquaintance with such alternative forms of urban making was crucial to the push for such an innovative approach to real estate management. The mobilization of the group then converged with the action of other built environment professionals, which led to the constitution of a new community of practice comprising both "external influences (experiments carried out by others, exchanges of good practices) and internal influences (past internal experiences, professional trajectories of certain members)."[61] This allowed for strategic and technical knowledge to be shared at higher levels within the group and then for the strategy to be applied starting in 2015. In parallel, the practice of transient urbanism spread in key cities in France and was led by both private and public organizations.

Transience as a mode of urban (re)development and management of land assets was tested at first on a couple of sites prior to being institutionalized across the company's portfolio, starting in the Paris region and then beyond. The Paris municipality embraced it to reframe its narrative around new ways of producing and renewing the city. Clear convergence of institutional logics demonstrating subsequent political support merged further into the "formation of a new epistemic community" leading to a new momentum in ways to produce the city differently.[62] "This community, of which SNCF Immobilier is part, is made up of architects, local authorities, non-profit associations, new transient urbanism professionals, researchers, town planners and a few developers, all of whom are advocates for the development of these uses."[63] These advocates participated in key international events (for example, the Venice Biennale of Architecture) with the goal of elevating transient urbanism as a "'common doctrine."[64] In 2019, SNCF Immobilier and Plateau Urbain, a social enterprise firm specializing in temporary urbanism, held a special session on transient urbanism at the leading international property market fair in Cannes, *Le marché international des professionnels de l'immobilier* (MIPIM), and invited representatives from other temporary movements, for example, Meanwhile Space. The structure, internationalization, and professionalization of the movement energized practices across France and influenced major transformation projects, for example, in Nantes (see chapter 5).[65]

From the start, transient urbanism immerged from path-dependent political recognition at both the local and national levels, but it has acquired further recognition more recently by being considered complementary to other priorities, such as the proximity and circularity discourses translated into the fifteen-minute narratives in Paris.[66] Transient urbanism is put forward as a means of responding to contemporary crises in cities, be they economic, humanitarian, ecological, social, and so on. The importance of acquiring the right knowledge and skills converged into the singular development of dedicated academic courses, Continuing Professional Development (CPD) types of offer and also master programs.[67] This recognition is now changing how urbanism is approached as a discipline, with most schools recognizing in their master's programs the importance for students to be trained in alternative and transient forms of urban making. This is an important step for the adaptable paradigm, and it reflects the distinct French approach to the urbanism discipline (see chapter 2).

CONCLUSION

Knowledge, knowledge fragments, and the convergence of complementary institutional logics led in many countries to the spread of singular communities of practice, gathering temporary, tactical, transient, and meanwhile urbanists. Those communities of practice have grown and become professionalized, and temporary urbanism has also become a recognized sector of activity, building on its high potential for experimentation, activation, and the transformation of underused but valuable assets.

Such dynamics have been widely criticized, particularly because they have resulted in incentivizing precarity or shifting municipal services away from the state to individuals or organizations, who then became complicit in neoliberalism.[68] While those criticisms are relevant and deserve significant attention, it is also crucial to look beyond them when questioning the role of knowledge and its diffusion and materialization.

Meanwhile, tactical, transient, and other forms of temporary urbanisms do have, of course, a dark side embedded in neoliberal planning processes; however, they are also responses to dysfunction and crises. While serving clear economic needs, many still provide significant community benefits that cannot be ignored and need to be accounted for and recognized. A wider issue remains: the elitist and exclusive nature of adaptable and temporary knowledge that often reinforces both spatial and socioeconomic inequalities.

8

THE FUTURE OF ADAPTABLE CITIES AND TEMPORARY URBANISMS

A t this point, it is important to take a step back and reflect on two key questions and also set up future research directions. First, what is the future of adaptable and temporary urbanisms? Second, what does it tell us about key paradoxes impinging on the work of built environment experts and urban scholars when dealing with the constant tensions between permanence and impermanence but also certainty and uncertainty? In effect, these paradoxes share the commonality of embracing and interrogating how places, people, and policies are tuned to relying on eminently complex and diverse adaptative processes. As argued all along in this book, this requires different and complementary theoretical intakes but also insights that cross over disciplines through three correlated processes: researching, shaping, and implementing, which feed into the policy process.

A RETURN TO THE FOUR ARGUMENTS OUTLINED IN CHAPTER 1

One way to start those reflections is to return to the four arguments that shaped this book. Argument 1 refers to *how adaptation and temporariness are constitutive of diverse urban conditions, have very diverse rhythms and keep evolving over time.* Throughout the chapters, I have explored how adaptability and temporariness have shaped cities over time but, more important, have allowed communities and places to adapt, cope, and transform in the face of everyday disruptions or more significant crises. This has emphasized the unfinished nature of urban environments. A distinction is to be made here between adaptability and forms of adaptability. Whereas adaptability has remained a constant feature of the process of urban making, the dynamics of adaptability have significantly evolved and diverged toward tangential extremities inherent to the neoliberal production of the city and the everyday realities of urban dwellers. They serve informal urban making and an urbanism of fragments while being also used as a process of valorization of assets, often triggering gentrification. The adaptable city has also become the temporary figure of the pandemic city. A question emerges then: have adaptation and temporariness reached their limits in the way they can manifest differently and in how they have and should be used in cities? Probably not. While adaptation and temporariness are essential mechanisms in dealing with unaddressed needs, everyday pressures, and minor or major disruptions, it can also be assumed that new forms of adaptable and temporary use of spaces will emerge. How they will be molded and implemented and by whom is still to be revealed and investigated, pushing the geographical and disciplinary frontiers further. Standardization of practices may indeed characterize many planned forms of adaptability and temporariness. However, the spread of hybrid approaches and an overall lack of resources dedicated to urban making and community support (including financial means but also institutional capacities) means that landowners and local authorities will rely more on local, low-cost, grassroots informed

THE FUTURE OF ADAPTABLE CITIES • 225

efforts to tackle new challenges, for example, the impact of climate change and rising socioeconomic inequalities. Key to this is how the accumulation and acceleration of changes combined with the multiplication of intersectional inequalities will ultimately keep positioning adaptability as a crucial way of thinking about and addressing uncertainty, disruption, shocks, and cumulative crises. I will come back to this point later in this chapter.

Argument 2 emphasises *the importance of adaptability in ensuring sustainability, resilience, informality and survival and how it is directly embedded within governance arrangements, power and governmental responses.* These refer to two important elements: the political nature of adaptable and temporary urbanisms but also the power of bricolage, adjustments, improvisation, and experimentation to counter, interfere with, or influence policy agenda. The nature of local contexts matters, particularly the extent to which acceptance of the need for adaptability includes informality and hence an acknowledgment that the state (and all forms of government bodies) is not able to respond to the needs and rights of many. As a result, adaptability and temporariness are extremely contentious and can be rejected by those holding power, although they can still be partly or fully supported by planners, nongovernmental organizations (NGOs), and international nongovernmental organization (INGOs) in the field. The connection between immediate and long-term sustained existence is questioned, and the forms of regulatory, financial, practical, and more grassroots arrangements emerge out of these processes. Tensions are far less acute in contexts where informality is less prevalent and adaptability is unrolled thanks to the support of strategies, negotiations, tactics, and networks but also knowledge and skills—all influence the development of institutional logics and ultimately the decision- and policymaking process. Cities will continue to be at the center of everyday disruptions, shocks, and both sudden and longer-term structural and cyclical crises leading to failing places and neighborhoods. These disruptions will likely increase, multiply, and amplify, and further tensions and conflicts will likely emerge about how adaptable cities can be governed, transformed, but also regulated, in a soft way, to promote *livable* spaces for all.

Argument 3 brings together the question of *governmentality, power and the political nature of adaptability as a policy and a (non) policy problem.* Temporary urbanisms and modes of approaching adaptability have evolved, deeply diversified, and diverged over time. These processes of adaptability have stimulated various fields of decision making and communities of practice. They also reflect how adaptability has continued to inform more tactical ways of claiming ownership and producing the city, here incentivized by the unprecedented COVID-19 pandemic. In times of crisis, adaptability has distanced itself from the regulatory and procedural planning process to push boundaries and deliver transformative and urgent changes. In many contexts, when adaptability is viewed as an acceptable practice, it is no longer a cause for concern and hence is not a political problem (and instead a political solution). There is a key tension here, however, and this constitutes a fundamental paradox: while localized and relying on community effort, successful recent adaptable and temporary urbanisms have thrived because standard participatory practices were set aside in a context of emergency. In other words, in forums, often the most vocal and less hidden voices—which are rarely the most representative and those fundamentally in need of adaptability—were given less of a role. This raises significant questions about the process needed to foster prompt and proactive adaptability. Expressions of agility and experimentation contrast greatly with the lengthy procedural and sometimes controversial participatory planning (and policy) process that urban making depends on.

THE FUTURE OF ADAPTABLE CITIES • 227

Argument 4 finally insists on the crucial role of *a set of abilities, knowledge and skills in the (re)imagining of the adaptable city, and how these influence where adaptability can spatially and socioeconomically occur or not.* The rise of adaptable cities is linked with the ability of individuals to gather, assemble, and develop new skills, but it is also linked with the formation of a community of practice. Both are linked to socioeconomic backgrounds and hence the advantages that come from educational background, professional networks, and job occupations. They reveal the wider harsh realities that characterize cities' deep inequalities grounded in several deadlocks, including gender and race. Individuals, community groups, INGOs, and NGOs, but also built environment experts (particularly planners) must remain committed to delivering transformative changes; through their actions, they can challenge and counter any dominant economic and political rationales where certain rights are ignored. It is ultimately a question of values and ethos for those who, through traditional education or more informal learning, have been given the skills and hence power to activate and support change. There is indeed a strong humanist credo in this statement based on the view (or hope) that a better future is possible. Some countries and built environment communities of practice are more advanced: they are at the forefront of setting up clear crossovers between tactical practices and the regulatory urbanism field. Tensions between regulatory permanence and fuzzily regulated impermanence remain and will still need to be overcome.

URBAN MAKING, UNCERTAINTIES, AND COMPLEXITY

Adaptability and temporariness are universal conditions. As explained in this book, they constitute a shared commonality within their extreme diversity that allows disparate urban contexts characterizing low-, middle-, and high-income countries to be brought together. In effect, adaptability, temporariness, and accepting that cities are unfinished works are lenses to investigate urban transformations and how urban dwellers live, produce, cope, and survive in cities. They bring together thematic lines of inquiry that are relevant to what so-called development studies would call "North and South"[1] issues that have long been shared around the world as a result of "restructuring the state; poverty reduction and livelihood; political development and governance; gender inequality; social capital; agency and participation . . . the list goes on—and of course includes social exclusion."[2] In line with Rory Horner's call for the development of a new paradigm of global development, adaptable and temporary urbanisms are types of urban making that manifest in various ways but characterize cities globally. They are an integral part of "global development" as a process but also as a field of study, with their relevance to and interconnectedness with a range of other global issues: sustainability, resilience and climate change, globalization and finalization, health and livability, and extreme poverty and socioeconomic inequalities.[3]

This is where the term "urban making" is crucial in the interpretation of adaptable and temporary urbanisms. Urban making stands outside academic disciplines. It is more than a planning, geography, architectural, sociological, or urban studies term. It highlights the realities of the meanings, framings, and relational processes of permanent and nonpermanent transformations that characterize places globally and are initiated and used by an extremely diverse group of individuals, groups of stakeholders, and communities of practice; this illustrates the complexity of the production and governance of adaptable urban places. The process of *making* allows reiterating the importance of crafting, experimenting, and improvising that is intrinsic to adaptability

THE FUTURE OF ADAPTABLE CITIES • 229

practices. Adaptable and temporary forms of urban making and their wider implications for planning, developing, and transforming cities constantly address and challenge tensions between permanence and impermanence but also certainty and uncertainty. They have an impact on the built environment and also resonate with wider paradoxes concerning all societies. Such paradoxes are complex in addition to being contradictory. In other words, adaptable and temporary forms of urban making need to be framed within a body of antithetical principles that, on the one hand, align with transformative changes but, on the other hand, often have detrimental repercussions. This is how, as scientists, we engage with complex problems and have done so for decades. "We face opposite tendencies that indicate an inbuilt dynamic, if not a race, between the increase of complexity and its reduction."[4]

Adaptable and temporary urbanisms are fundamentally fostered by two distinct but related processes: crisis and emergency (reactionary responses) and value and income generation (at various scales but through similar neoliberal and globalized narratives). Both share a common area of concern: uncertainty and how to account and deal with uncertainty. This isn't unique to the built environment field and is a dominant concept in the social sciences, in all scientific fields. Scholars, including David Peat and Helga Nowotny, have thoroughly deconstructed how science has approached certainty and uncertainty in the face of complexity.[5] Both share a positivist view of how complex uncertainties that characterize all societies have been driving scientific enquiry. Chaos effectively leads to action because disruptions are ways to shake the way places function and hence how adaptability can be exercised. Peat argues that:

the move from certainty to uncertainty that characterized the twentieth century has brought with it a great responsibility. Each of us today realized our connection to the society in which we live through countless feedback loops. Each of us helps to generate and sustain the meaning by which that society functions. What's more, chaos is no longer something to be afraid of; it is an expression of the deep richness that lies within the order of the cosmos and our very lives.[6]

Within uncertainty is where the key paradoxes of adaptability and temporariness are anchored and where the agenda for future scholarship can be set up.

AN AGENDA FOR FUTURE SCHOLARSHIP: THE KEY PARADOXES OF ADAPTABILITY AND TEMPORARINESS

Agility with Permanence as a Form of Preparedness

If we were to dissect cities and see them as layers of systems, they would be characterized by both hard and soft strata. Hard strata would include infrastructure networks, from water, electricity, and broadband to roads and railways, along with the overall urban morphology of cities. While not entirely sealed, they are the prevalent manifestation of rigidity and permanence in the production of cities, impinging on cities' overall structure, form, and modes of functioning. Agility thus can occur only in softer infrastructures, in other words, buildings, public spaces, and also streets or pavements, as illustrated throughout this book. Of course, this agility is also highly regulated by the nature of the planning and regulatory processes. Both hard and soft infrastructures are viewed as part of a pragmatic vision that rely on

THE FUTURE OF ADAPTABLE CITIES • 231

certainty and rationality. The prospect of sustainability has exacerbated this to a greater extent by perpetuating and improving existing systems deeply tied to the principle of permanence and survival. While this point relates to policy and overall strategic visions, it also concerns science as a whole.

Science is founded on the principle of seeking certainty, but it is constructed on uncertainties, experimentations, and hypotheses. "Rationality and reason were championed as the signposts to safeguard and assure a double-anchored future. One route was through the epistemological foundations of the certainly of knowledge gained through experimentation and proof. The other route was through the practical applications of the new knowledge which were the result of such efforts."[7] These routes apply to adaptability and temporariness in urban making. Certainties are a way to navigate among the complexities of transformations, shifts, and accelerations that characterize cities; they are a way to engage more fully with uncertainties that emerge out of shocks and disruptions, and hence with the willingness to rethink the urban-making process creatively. After numerous experiments and tests, new knowledge is created: local knowledge, which is useful for communities' everyday lives, and practical knowledge that can be mobilized by built environment experts and shape communities of practice and trusted knowledge—as a form of power—that can then feed into the policy process and academic debates. Nowotny says, "Knowledge generated when confronted with uncertainty has proven to be the most powerful means developed in our cultural evolutionary trajectory so far to assure survival and striving for continuous improvements in material living standards and wellbeing."[8] Knowledge here leads to innovation and innovations and, of course, connects with advancements.

The duality between certainty and uncertainly seems to constitute a basic principle. However, the preference given to certainty compared to uncertainty, and to permanence versus adaptability, has fundamentally misled how places have been preparing themselves for various types of disruptions and crises (the COVID-19 pandemic was unfortunately just one example). The craving for certainty that has characterized the most contemporary interpretations of urban making, but also how cities have been developed and politicized over time, has materialized in processes of foresights and forecasting. At the core of this is the role of data and modeling, the identification of general patterns that tend to discard more subjective assumptions and localized insights. The development of such general trends generally contradicts what local places and local communities need every day.

Prevention, of course, entails preparation. It relies on immediate coping responses along with wider lessons that allow foresight and anticipation. A shift to proactive forms of adaptability, as explored in this book, should be understood as a way to break through the tensions between (and fears about) certainty and uncertainly and thus foster change. However, proactive adaptability is still an emergency field in academia, policy, and practice. More work needs to be done on the extent to which proactive forms of adaptability can become mainstream tools in the production of cities. "Uncertainty is not seen as an enemy, but can be welcomed as a friend or ally."[9] This takes us back to the adaptability framework constructed on creative urban making, reaction, disorder, and (in)stability. Uncertainty does, however, question the relationship between time and duration, leading to tensions between latency and stasis versus impatience and predictions. All interfere with the process of urban making and with the political nature of the planning and development process.

Latency and Creative Stasis Versus Impatience and Predictions

Predictions and foresight struggle to engage with adaptability because they aim to render uncertainties more manageable. Societies have always had to deal with uncertainties. Uncertainties and the acceptance of adaptability therefore rely on the prospect of an end point that can be reached through a process of transition; the most successful examples of initially temporary projects have been shaped and sustained along these lines, as have the principles of meanwhile uses and transient urbanisms, among other forms of temporary urban making, have thrived. An issue here (and this goes back to how adaptability as a form of coping and survival tends to be rejected) is that uncertainties can be long-lasting and so can the stage of temporariness and the need for adaptable urbanisms (typically in more informal settings). This resonates with the difficulty of accepting latency and stasis. Such impatience finds its roots not only in social movements and ways to claim basic rights but also in the inability of long-term uncertainties to be fully accounted for in political agenda (the short time frame of political cycles requires rapid success) and economic viability calculations. Navigating among uncertainties and forms of temporary adaptations is inherently chaotic and introduces various forms of repetitions, routines, or more ad hoc scenarios aligned with forms of experimentation and improvisation.[10] These are the processes of bricolage alluded to in chapters 3, 4 and 6. They form the pillars of how science and ideas have been constructed over the twentieth and twenty-first centuries but also shape the directions for research in the adaptability field.

234 • THE FUTURE OF ADAPTABLE CITIES

Uncertainties are here linked to creativity but also doubt, as Peat narrated in his *Story of Science and Ideas in the Twentieth Century*:

> The ways we represent the world, in everything from language to art and science, deeply influence the ways we structure our world and understand ourselves. During the twentieth century many of these means of representation underwent a change from certainty to uncertainty, and today our world is more tentative and open to doubt and uncertainty. This lack of fixed strategies means that there are more ways to explore the world and that we must therefore exercise a deeper sense of the responsibility that goes along with this freedom.[11]

Creativity in periods of stasis and latency is thus fundamental and can have different purposes: from being a way to experiment, innovate, and generate new knowledge to serving specific basic but crucial needs. From a psychological perspective, creativity can also serve as a leverage to support mental well-being, healing, and hope. Adaptations as part of preparations and coping follow similar patterns to those shaping predictions and the search for certainty. All share a way to tackle uncertainties. Adaptations are path dependent to contexts and to localized changing circumstances, even in situations of global crisis. Additional continuous research is needed to recognize the conditions for diverse forms of creativity leading to adaptations and how these shape complex forms of (mostly hybrid) temporary urbanisms.

Professional futurists and other analysts will continue to make technological forecasts, even if the list of past predictions that turned out to be wrong is almost as long as the list of major developments that they missed. The reason for this failure is simple: successful innovations must meet a human need, however latent

THE FUTURE OF ADAPTABLE CITIES • 235

it may be. Knowledge must be captured by human ingenuity to find a use for ideas and things in a vast space of possible uses.[12] Nowotny's point is important regarding the relationship with science and innovation and how similar processes are to be pushed forward in scientific enquiries but also in practice and shaping policy. Boundaries—both visible and invisible—have to be pushed and broken to challenge and shake existing modes of thinking and hence urban making along with adaptability.

Permanence, Comfort Zones, and Breaking Boundaries to Tackle Endless Crises

The way temporary and adaptable urbanisms manifest today but also how adaptable processes have evolved and shaped cities over time are the result of the efforts made to challenge common standards and visions. They demonstrate an ability to dispute commonly accepted—and often politically incorrect—assumptions. There is an element of risk in this process, which illustrates the ability of a range of actors to lead change, defend ideas and rights, and also demonstrate the validity (and viability) of experimentations, as discussed in this book. This process involves breaking and/or stretching boundaries in various fields of academic and practical expertise, and influencing debates and policymaking. It isn't about shocking the system, however, but shaking up general trends and assumptions. This is where the scholars can contribute and where future agendas for research need to find root and inspiration, specifically in line with the more innovative hybrid forms of adaptability that will continue to emerge in the future.

This goes back to the nature of scientific enquiry and the fact that any models developed to tackle complexity—with the view of untangling uncertainties—rely on some kind of bricolage.[13] Those tensions aren't new, nor are they specific to urban making and global development. They have characterized how different scientific fields have been shaped and have evolved over time. "The interplay between overcoming uncertainty and striving for certainty underpins the wish to know in order to be able to influence present and future. It is as old as humanity. It is rooted in the deep-seated desire for security, the material, technological and social protection necessary for survival, comfort, and well-being."[14]

Security, well-being, survival, desire, and the need for protection, as well as ways to express and defend rights, bring together certainty and uncertainty as well as permanence and adaptability. What constitutes an anchoring point is the notion of risk and the process of risk taking as a form of experimentation and a way of reacting to disruptions but also of prevention. Here, risk is related to knowledge but also to path dependency and intersectionality in the ability to describe risks by their constitutive factors and forms of overcoming. This takes us back to power and how preventive measures can shape empowerment. "Prevention empowers one to act in full awareness of one's status as a potential patient who is at risk . . . Unintended consequences enter when the balance between risk and precaution tilts towards over-cautiousness. Then, the space for action shrinks and risk taking may be stifled, even when it is a reasonable option."[15] This point resonates with the difficulties encountered in attempts to shift reactionary adaptability to proactive adaptability. Again, much more work is needed not only to fill gaps in the scholarly literature but also, most important, to inform policy and practice.

Accounting and preventing risks can challenge standard practice and norms. This is about distinguishing between transformative visions only and transformative visions and actions

THE FUTURE OF ADAPTABLE CITIES • 237

with demonstrable outcomes. Such outcomes are expressions of power. They are tools for reaching political arenas, which are shaped by priorities and framed by selected crises that take two forms: universal crises as structural events affecting places and people, either locally and internationally, and politically shaped crises (i.e., crises identified as political). There is a very subtle game between how crises become policy matters and the role of media and social media. Although this book doesn't address this further, it does raise the issue of what and who are given priority in times of crisis.[16] This resonates with the governance of uncertainty and how this has fed into the governmentalization of resilience in the past two decades.[17] The governance of adaptability should be at the core of academic debates in the future.

Adaptable and temporary urbanisms are a crucial field of enquiry for all disciplines focusing on the urban and are central to practice and policy. It is still a field *en devenir* that will continue to evolve in a context of endless and rising socioeconomic, political, and environmental crises that are both global, national, and local. In September 2023, a team of international scientists provided a detailed outline of planetary resilience by mapping all nine boundary processes that define a safe operating space for humanity.[18] They demonstrated that six of the nine boundaries have been transgressed, suggesting that Earth is now well outside the safe operating space for humanity.[19] Adaptable and temporary urbanisms apply to all scales where interventions are and will be needed. An ultimate research agenda is thus to call for new ways of thinking about the future of places because the shaping of this future may not be about sustainability or resiliency but about constant rapid adaptations in the light of the climate emergency. Those are fundamental uncertainties that, of course, trigger dramatic concerns and fear, particularly for those who will still be at the core of shaping livable places in the decades to come.

238 • THE FUTURE OF ADAPTABLE CITIES

This thought contrasts with the rather optimistic stand adopted in the conclusion to this book. I don't want to end on this point, so I would like to return to Helga Nowotny's epilogue and particularly her final paragraph, where she states:

> Embracing uncertainty and entering into collusion with its cunning remains an open-ended process. Uncertainty is not to be confused with insecurity. Material and intangible means are the building blocks and preconditions for the always unfinished and highly unequally distributed securitization of human existence. Uncertainty is the dynamic balance between what we know and do not yet know about the world and about ourselves. Recognizing its cunning and entering into collusion with it enables us to exploit the dynamic balance in favour of moving on. It opens the cracks in the wall to let the new in. Unwrapping the gifts we receive from randomness, thriving on the cusp of uncertainty and knowing when is the right moment to act, delay or forgo action are different ways of embracing uncertainty.[20]

Her words take me back to the start of my book and why adaptability and temporariness matter. Embracing uncertainty and adaptability is about embracing difference and fostering forms of care and support in urban making. While the prospect of creating fairer and more just cities seems like a very distant utopia, accommodating daily and more long-term needs in the face of disruptions and dysfunctions—through adaptability—is key and a fundamental pillar of livable and less unequal places. Achieving this includes shaping and understanding adaptable and temporary cities, and this is what urban scholars should continue pursuing, where future scholarship enquiries should begin. Key is the articulation of micro, macro, and meso levels for reading, understanding, and producing cities. It is also about accepting the richness of unfinishedness as a liberating process for reframing forms of urban making. Embracing uncertainty and adaptability relies on adopting a holistic approach to thinking about the urban. Uncertainty and adaptability are a result of waiting and the betweenness that favors creativity and experimentation. The shaping of better futures is thus based on large-scale visions and efforts but also on a multitude of small steps forward and liminal forces that allow transformative changes while converging. We, as urban scholars working in the adaptability field, are the leading contributors in driving those changes forward.

NOTES

1. WHAT IS THE ADAPTABLE AND TEMPORARY CITY?

1. Peter Hall, *Cities of Tomorrow: An Intellectual History of Urban Planning and Design in the Twentieth Century* (Oxford: Blackwell, 1988).

2. Peter Bishop and Lesley Williams, *The Temporary City* (London: Routledge, 2012).

3. Editorial, "Time to Revise the Sustainable Development Goals," *Nature* 583, no. 14 (July 2020): 331–332, https://www.nature.com/articles/d41586-020-02002-3; Ethan Freedman, "'Systemic Greenwash': Scientists Call on UN to Ditch Sustainability Goals," *Independent*, May 26, 2022, https://www.independent.co.uk/climate-change/news/un-sustainable-development-failure-b2088465.html.

4. Lauren Andres and Peter Kraftl, "New Directions in the Theorisation of Temporary Urbanisms: Adaptability, Activation and Trajectory," *Progress in Human Geography* 45, no. 5 (October 2021): 1237–1253, https://doi.org/10.1177/0309132520985321.

5. Lars Lerup, *Building the Unfinished: Architecture and Human Action* (Thousand Oaks, CA: Sage, 1977).

6. Jonathan Reades and Martin Crookston, *Why Face-to-Face Still Matters: The Persistent Power of Cities in the Post-Pandemic Era* (Bristol, UK: Bristol University Press, 2021).

7. Pablo Sendra and Richard Sennett, *Designing Disorder: Experiments and Disruptions in the City* (London: Verso, 2020).

242 • I. WHAT IS THE ADAPTABLE AND TEMPORARY CITY?

8. Rachel Rodrigues Malta, *Refaire la ville au temps présent* (Grenoble: Université Pierre Mendes France, 2005).

9. Colin McFarlane, "Assemblage and Critical Urbanism," *City: Analysis of Urban Trends, Culture, Theory, Policy, Action* 15, no. 2 (June 2011): 204–224, https://doi.org/10.1080/13604813.2011.568715.

10. Bishop and Williams, *The Temporary City*; Ali Madanipour, *Cities in Time: Temporary Urbanism and the Future of the City* (London: Bloomsbury, 2017).

11. Andres and Kraftl, "New Directions in the Theorisation of Temporary Urbanisms."

12. Jacqueline Groth and Eric Corijn, "Reclaiming Urbanity: Indeterminate Spaces, Informal Actors and Urban Agenda Setting," *Urban Studies* 42, no. 3 (March 2005): 503–526, https://www.jstor.org/stable/43198269; Philipp Oswalt et al., *The Power of Temporary* (Berlin: DOM Publishers, 2017); Robert Temel and Florian Haydn, eds., *Temporary Urban Spaces: Concepts for the Use of City Spaces* (Basel: Birkhauser, 2006).

13. Ella Harris, "Navigating Pop-Up Geographies: Urban Space–Times of Flexibility, Interstitially and Immersion," *Geography Compass* 9, no. 11 (November 2015): 592–603, https://doi.org/10.1111/gec3.12248; Panu Lehtovuori and Sampo Ruoppila, "Temporary Uses Producing Difference in Contemporary Urbanism," in *Transience and Permanence in Urban Development*, ed. John Henneberry (Chichester: Wiley, 2017), 47–63; Olly Mould, "Tactical Urbanism: The New Vernacular of the Creative City," *Geography Compass* 8, no. 8 (August 2014): 529–539, https://doi.org/10.1111 /gec3.12146; Armelle Tardiveau and Daniel Mallo, "Unpacking and Challenging Habitus: An Approach to Temporary Urbanism as a Socially Engaged Practice," *Journal of Urban Design* 19, no. 4 (June 2014): 456–472, https://doi.org/10.1080/13574809.2014.923743; Fran Tonkiss, "Austerity Urbanism and the Makeshift City," *City* 17, no. 3 (June 2013): 312–324, https://doi.org/10.1080/13604813.2013.795332.

14. Kurt Iveson, "Cities Within the City: Do-It-Yourself Urbanism and the Right to the City," *International Journal of Urban and Regional Research* 37, no. 3 (April 2013): 941–956, https://doi.org/10.1111/1468-2427.12053; Mould, "Tactical Urbanism;" Gordon Douglas, *The Help-Yourself City: Legitimacy and Inequality in DIY Urbanism* (New York: Oxford University Press, 2019).

2. THE FLEXIBLE AND INFLEXIBLE CITY • 243

15. See the various chapters in Lauren Andres and Amy Zhang, eds., *Transforming Cities Through Temporary Urbanism—A Comparative Overview* (Dordrecht: Springer, 2020); and Lauren Andres et al., "Planning, Temporary Urbanism and Citizen-Led Alternative-Substitute Place-Making in the Global South," *Regional Studies* 55, no. 1 (2021): 29–39, https://doi.org/10.1080/00343404.2019.1665645.

16. Douglas, *The Help-Yourself City*; Mara Ferreri, *The Permanence of Temporary Urbanism: Normalising Precarity in Austerity London* (Amsterdam: Amsterdam University Press, 2021); Quentin Stevens and Kim Dovey, *Temporary and Tactical Urbanism: (Re)Assembling Urban Space* (New York: Routledge, 2022).

17. Andres and Kraftl, "New Directions in the Theorisation of Temporary Urbanisms."

18. Andres et al., "Planning, Temporary Urbanism."

19. Paul Moawad, "Temporary Forms of Urbanism in Contested Urban Spaces in Lebanon: The Case of Dbayeh Camp," in *Transforming Cities Through Temporary Urbanism—A Comparative Overview*, ed. Lauren Andres and Amy Zhang (Dordrecht: Springer, 2020), 73–87.

20. Andres and Zhang, *Transforming Cities Through Temporary Urbanism.*

21. Faranak Miraftab, "Insurgent Planning: Situating Radical Planning in the Global South," *Planning Theory* 8, no. 1 (February 2009): 32–50, https://doi.org/10.1177/1473095208099297.

22. John F. C. Turner, *Housing by People: Towards Autonomy in Building Environments* (London: Marion Boyars, 1976); John F. C. Turner, "Issues in Self-Help and Self-Managed Housing," in *Self-Help Housing: A Critique*, ed. Peter M. Ward (London: Mansell, 1982), 93–113.

23. Mara Ferreri and Alexander Vasudevan, "Vacancy at the Edges of the Precarious City," *Geoforum* 101 (May 2019): 165–173, https://doi.org/10.1016/j.geoforum.2019.03.009.

24. Colin McFarlane, *Fragments of the City. Making and Remaking Urban Worlds* (Berkeley: University of California Press, 2021).

2. THE FLEXIBLE AND INFLEXIBLE CITY

1. Lauren Andres and Peter Kraftl, "New Directions in the Theorisation of Temporary Urbanisms: Adaptability, Activation and Trajectory,"

244 • 2. THE FLEXIBLE AND INFLEXIBLE CITY

Progress in Human Geography 45, no. 5 (October 2021): 1237–1253, https://doi.org/10.1177/0309132520985321.

2. Peter Bishop and Lesley Williams, *The Temporary City* (London: Routledge, 2012); Ali Madanipour, *Cities in Time: Temporary Urbanism and the Future of the City* (London: Bloomsbury, 2017); Quentin Stevens and Kim Dovey, *Temporary and Tactical Urbanism: (Re)Assembling Urban Space* (London: Routledge, 2022); Gordon Douglas, *The Help-Yourself City: Legitimacy and Inequality in DIY Urbanism* (New York: Oxford University Press, 2019); Mara Ferreri, *The Permanence of Temporary Urbanism: Normalising Precarity in Austerity London* (Amsterdam: Amsterdam University Press, 2021).

3. Patsy Healey, *Collaborative Planning: Shaping Places in Fragmented Societies* (London: Red Globe Press London, 1997).

4. Gordon E. Cherry, *Cities and Plans: Shaping of Urban Britain in the Nineteenth and Twentieth Centuries* (London: Edward Arnold, 1988).

5. Peter Hall, *Cities of Tomorrow: An Intellectual History of Urban Planning and Design in the Twentieth Century* (Oxford: Blackwell, 1988).

6. Stephen Ward, *Planning and Urban Change* (London: Sage, 2004).

7. Douglas, *The Help-Yourself City*, 77.

8. Robert Temel and Florian Haydn, eds., *Temporary Urban Spaces: Concepts for the Use of City Spaces* (Basel: Birkhauser, 2006), 29.

9. Mario Reimer et al., eds., *Spatial Planning Systems and Practices in Europe: A Comparative Perspective on Continuity and Changes* (London: Routledge, 2014); Vincent Nadin and Dominic Stead, "European Spatial Planning Systems, Social Models and Learning," *disP* 172, no. 1 (November 2012): 35–47, https://doi.org/10.1080/02513625.2008.10557001.

10. Commission of the European Communities (CEC), "The EU Compendium of Spatial Planning Systems and Policies," *Regional Development Studies* 28 (Luxembourg: CEC, 1997).

11. Rachel Rodrigues Malta, *Refaire la Ville au Temps Présent* (Grenoble: Université Pierre Mendes France, 2005).

12. Jane Jacobs, *The Death and Life of Great American Cities* (New York: Random House, 1961); Aldo Rossi, *L'Architettura Della Città*, 4th ed. (Torino: CittàStudi, 2006 [1966]); Giancarlo Cataldi, "Saverio Muratori: il Debito e l'Eredità," in *Saverio Muratori Architetto (Modena 1910–Roma 1973): A Cento Anni Dalla Nascita: Atti del Convegno Itinerante*, ed. Giancarlo Cataldi (Firenze: Aión, 2013).

2. THE FLEXIBLE AND INFLEXIBLE CITY • 245

13. Rodrigues Malta, *Refaire la Ville*.

14. Michel Lussault, "Temps et Récit des Politiques Urbaines," in *Le Quotidien Urbain: Essais sur les Temps des Villes*, ed. Thierry Pacquot, 145–167 (Paris: La découverte, 2001).

15. Ariella Masboungi, "Du Bon Usage de la Chronotopie," in *Le Quotidien Urbain: Essais sur les Temps des Villes*, ed. Thierry Pacquot, 167–179 (Paris: La découverte, 2001).

16. Hall, *Cities of Tomorrow*.

17. Ferreri, *The Permanence of Temporary Urbanism*; Lauren Andres, *La ville mutable. Mutabilité et référentiels urbains: Les cas de Bouchayer-Viallet, de la Belle de Mai et du Flon* (Grenoble: Université Pierre Mendes France, 2008).

18. Madanipour, *Cities in Time*.

19. Madanipour, *Cities in Time*.

20. Amy Frearson, "United States Pavilion at the Venice Architecture Biennale 2012," *DeZeen* (September 1, 2012), https://www.dezeen.com/2012 /09/01/united-states-pavilion-at-the-venice-architecture-biennale-2012/.

21. Hall, *Cities of Tomorrow*.

22. Richard Sennett, *The Uses of Disorder: Personal Identity and City Life* (New Haven, CT: Yale University Press, 1970).

23. Pablo Sendra and Richard Sennett, *Designing Disorder: Experiments and Disruptions in the City* (London: Verso, 2020), 6.

24. Richard Sennett, "The Open City," *Urban Age* (November 2006), https://urbanage.lsecities.net/essays/the-open-city.

25. Sendra and Sennett, *Designing Disorder*, 23.

26. Mike Raco and Sonia Freire Trigo, "Urban Governance: Re-thinking Top-down and Bottom-up Power Relations in the Wake of Neo-liberalisation," in *Handbook of Urban Geography*, ed. Tim Schwanen and Ronald van Kempen, 383–395 (Northampton, MA: Edward Elgar, 2019); Lauren Andres et al., "Urban Value Chains and Re-framing Agglomeration-centric Conceptions of Urban Theory," *Urban Geography* 44, no. 8 (2023): 1701–1722, https://doi.org/10.1080/02723638.2022.2125665.

27. Luke Tipene, "Openings of Uncertainty: Critiques of Modernity in the Drawings of Lars Lerup and Gunnar Asplund," *Journal of Architecture* 25, no. 6 (October 2020): 759–786, https://doi.org/10.1080/13602365.2020 .1806337.

28. Nigel Thrift, "Afterwords," *Environment and Planning D: Society and Space* 18, no. 2 (April 2000): 213–255, https://doi.org/10.1068/d214t; Peter

Kraftl, "Architectural Movements, Utopian Moments: (In)coherent Renderings of the Hundertwasser-Haus, Vienna," *Geografiska Annaler: Series B, Human Geography* 92, no. 4 (December 2010): 327–345, https://www.jstor.org/stable/40981002; Peter Kraftl, "Liveability and Urban Architectures: Mol(ecul)ar Biopower and the 'Becoming Lively' of Sustainable Communities," *Environment and Planning D: Society and Space* 32, no. 2 (January 2014): 274–292, https://doi.org/10.1068/d21012; Kim Kullman, "Politics of Dissensus in Geographies of Architecture: Testing Equality at Ed Roberts Campus, Berkeley," *Transactions of the Institute of British Geographers* 44, no. 2 (December 2019): 284–298, https://doi.org/10.1111/tran.12276.

29. Kraftl, "Architectural Movements, Utopian Moments."
30. Andres and Kraftl, "New Directions in the Theorisation of Temporary Urbanisms."
31. Centre for Cities, *Cities Outlook 2021* (London: Centre for Cities, 2021).
32. Andres and Kraftl, "New Directions in the Theorisation of Temporary Urbanisms."
33. Bishop and Williams, *The Temporary City.*
34. Leonardo Benevolo, *The European City* (Oxford: Blackwell, 1993).
35. Yvonne Rydin et al., "Shaping Cities for Health: Complexity and the Planning of Urban Environments in the 21st Century," *Lancet* 379, no. 9831 (May 2012): 2079–2108, https://doi.org/10.1016/S0140-6736(12)60435-8; Andres et al., "Urban Value Chains," 1701–1722.
36. Jean-Luc Pinol, *Histoire de l'Europe Urbaine, T1: De l'Antiquité au 18ème siècle* (Paris: le Seuil, 2003).
37. Benevolo, *The European City.*
38. Bishop and Williams, *The Temporary City.*
39. Georges Duby, *Histoire de la France Urbaine: La Ville Médiévale* (Paris: Le Seuil, 1980).
40. Sennett, *The Uses of Disorder.*
41. Andres, *La ville mutable.*
42. Jean-Luc Pinol, *Histoire de l'Europe Urbaine, T2: De l'Ancien Régime à Nos Jours* (Paris: Seuil, 2003); Andres, *La ville mutable.*
43. Hall, *Cities of Tomorrow*; Charles Delfante, *Grande Histoire de la Ville de la Mésopotamie aux Etats-Unis* (Paris: Armand Colin, 1997).
44. Benevolo, *The European City.*

2. THE FLEXIBLE AND INFLEXIBLE CITY • 247

45. Andres, *La ville mutable*.

46. Hall, *Cities of Tomorrow*.

47. John Henneberry, ed., *Transience and Permanence in Urban Development* (Chichester: Wiley, 2017).

48. Bishop and Williams, *The Temporary City*.

49. Neil Brenner, "Debating Planetary Urbanisation: Towards an Engaged Pluralism," *Environment and Planning D: Society and Space* 36, no. 3 (February 2018): 570–590, https://doi.org/10.1177/0263775818757510; Neil Brenner, *New Urban Spaces: Urban Theory and the Scale Question* (Oxford: Oxford University Press, 2019).

50. Lauren Andres et al., "Temporary Urbanisms as Policy Alternatives to Enhance Health and Well-Being in the Post-Pandemic City," *Current Environmental Health Reports* 8, no. 2 (2021): 167–176, https://doi .org/10.1007/s40572-021-00314-8.

51. Lauren Andres and Amy Zhang, eds., *Transforming Cities Through Temporary Urbanism—A Comparative Overview* (Dordrecht: Springer, 2020).

52. Ferreri, *The Permanence of Temporary Urbanism*.

53. Alex Vasudevan, *The Autonomous City: A History of Urban Squatting* (London: Verso, 2017).

54. Alex Vasudevan, "The Makeshift City: Towards a Global Geography of Squatting," *Progress in Human Geography* 39, no. 3 (June 2015): 338–359, https://doi.org/10.1177/0309132514531471.

55. Elsa Vivant, *Le rôle des pratiques culturelles "off" dans les dynamiques urbaines* (Paris: Université Paris 8 Vincennes-Saint-Denis, 2006).

56. Lauren Andres and Oleg Golubchikov, "The Limits to Artist-Led Regeneration: Creative Brownfields in the Cities of High Culture," *International Journal of Urban and Regional Research* 40, no. 4 (July 2016): 757–775, https://doi.org/10.1111/1468-2427.12412.

57. Douglas, *The Help-Yourself City*.

58. Andres and Zhang, *Transforming Cities Through Temporary Urbanism*.

59. Philipp Oswalt et al., *The Power of Temporary* (Berlin, DOM Publishers, 2017); Temel and Haydn, *Temporary Urban Spaces*.

60. Urban Pioneers, *Temporary Use and Urban Development in Berlin* (Berlin: Jovis, 2007).

61. Fran Tonkiss, "Austerity Urbanism and the Makeshift City," *City* 17, no. 3 (June 2013): 312–324, https://doi.org/10.1080/13604813.2013.795332.

62. Jenny Pickerill and Paul Chatterton, "Notes Towards Autonomous Geographies: Creation, Resistance and Self-Management as Survival Tactics," *Progress in Human Geography* 30, no. 6 (December 2006): 1–17, https://doi.org/10.1177/0309132506071516; Jeffrey Hou, ed., *Insurgent Public Space: Guerrilla Urbanism and the Remaking of Contemporary Cities* (London: Routledge, 2010).

63. Pickerill and Chatterton, "Notes Towards Autonomous Geographies," 1–17.

64. Bishop and Williams, *The Temporary City*.

65. Frank Van Der Beuken et al., *The Shadow City: Freezones in Brussels and Rotterdam* (Rotterdam: Urban Unlimited, 2004).

66. Madanipour, *Cities in Time*.

67. Peter Bishop, "From the Subversive to the Serious," *Counterpoint* 235, no. 3 (April 2015): 136–141, https://doi.org/10.1002/ad.1913; Peter Bishop, "Urban Design in the Fragmented City," in *Contemporary Urban Design Thinking: The Australian Approach*, ed. Rob Roggema, 71–93 (Dordrecht: Springer, 2019).

68. Andres and Zhang, *Transforming Cities Through Temporary Urbanism*.

69. Michael Storper and Anthony J. Venables, "Buzz: Face-to-Face Contact and the Urban Economy," *Journal of Economic Geography* 4, no. 4 (August 2004): 351–370, https://doi.org/10.1093/jnlecg/lbh027; Joseph Pine and James H. Gilmore, *The Experience Economy* (Boston: Harvard Business Press, 2011); Richard Florida, *Cities and the Creative Class* (New York: Routledge, 2005).

70. Jeroen Beekmans and Joop de Boer, *Pop-Up City: City-Making in a Fluid World* (London: Laurence King, 2014).

71. Madanipour, *Cities in Time*.

72. Andres et al., "Temporary Urbanisms as Policy Alternatives," 167–176.

73. Douglas, *The Help-Yourself City*.

74. Ferreri, *The Permanence of Temporary Urbanism*.

3. ADAPTABILITY, ACTIVATION, AND WEAK PLANNING

1. Lauren Andres, "Differential Spaces, Power Hierarchy and Collaborative Planning: A Critique of the Role of Temporary Uses in Shaping and Making Places," *Urban Studies* 50, no. 4 (2013): 759–75, https://doi.org/10.1177/0042098012455719.

3. ADAPTABILITY, ACTIVATION, AND WEAK PLANNING • 249

2. Claire Colomb, "Pushing the Urban Frontier: Temporary Uses of Space, City Marketing, and the Creative City Discourse in 2000s Berlin," *Journal of Urban Affairs* 34, no. 2 (May 2012): 131–152, https://doi.org/10.1111/j.1467-9906.2012.00607.x; Mara Ferreri, *The Permanence of Temporary Urbanism: Normalising Precarity in Austerity London* (Amsterdam: Amsterdam University Press, 2021); Panu Lehtovuori and Sampo Ruoppila, "Temporary Uses Producing Difference in Contemporary Urbanism," in *Transience and Permanence in Urban Development*, ed. John. Henneberry, 47–63 (Chichester: Wiley, 2017).

3. Eduardo Mendieta, "The Production of Urban Space in the Age of Transnational Mega-Urbes," *City* 12, no. 2 (August 2008): 148–153, https://doi.org/10.1080/13604810802259320.

4. Ali Madanipour, *Cities in Time: Temporary Urbanism and the Future of the City* (London: Bloomsbury, 2017), 144.

5. Françoise Balibar et al., "Moment, Instant, Occasion," in *Vocabulaire Européen des Philosophies. Dictionnaire des Intraduisibles*, ed. Barbara Cassin, 813–818 (Paris: Seuil, 2004); Madanipour, *Cities in Time.*

6. Helge Jordheim, "Conceptual History Between Chronos and Kairos—The Case of 'Empire,'" *Redescriptions* 11, no. 1 (2007): 127, https://doi.org/10.7227/R.11.1.8.

7. Henri Lefebvre and Catherine Régulier, "The Rythmanalytical Project," *Rethinking Marxism* 11, no. 1 (Spring 1995): 6.

8. Liz Crump, "Reimagining Urban Planning: From Institution to Innovation—A Comparative Exploration of Temporary Urbanism and the Future of City-Making," in *Transforming Cities Through Temporary Urbanism—A Comparative Overview*, ed. Lauren Andres and Amy Zhang, 107–125 (Dordrecht: Springer, 2020).

9. Jacqueline Groth and Eric Corijn, "Reclaiming Urbanity: Indeterminate Spaces, Informal Actors and Urban Agenda Setting," *Urban Studies* 42, no. 3 (March 2005): 503–526, https://www.jstor.org/stable/43198269.

10. Lehtovuori and Ruoppila, "Temporary Uses Producing Difference."

11. Lauren Andres and Peter Kraftl, "New Directions in the Theorisation of Temporary Urbanisms: Adaptability, Activation and Trajectory," *Progress in Human Geography* 45, no. 5 (October 2021): 1237–1253, https://doi.org/10.1177/0309132520985321.

12. Henri Lefebvre, *The Production of Space* (Oxford: Blackwell, 1991); Henri Lefebvre *Rhythmanalysis: Space, Time and Everyday Life* (London: Continuum, 2004).

250 • 3. ADAPTABILITY, ACTIVATION, AND WEAK PLANNING

13. Lefebvre and Régulier, "The Rythmanalytical Project," 1–13.
14. David Harvey, *Rebel Cities: From the Right to the City to the Urban Revolution* (London: Verso, 2012).
15. Lehtovuori and Ruoppila, "Temporary Uses Producing Difference."
16. Harvey, *Rebel Cities*, 4.
17. Lehtovuori and Ruoppila, "Temporary Uses Producing Difference."
18. Gordon Douglas, *The Help-Yourself City: Legitimacy and Inequality in DIY Urbanism* (New York: Oxford University Press, 2019).
19. Lefebvre, *Rhythmanalysis.*
20. Andres and Kraftl, "New Directions in the Theorisation of Temporary Urbanisms."
21. Lehtovuori and Ruoppila, "Temporary Uses Producing Difference."
22. Andres and Kraftl, "New Directions in the Theorisation of Temporary Urbanisms."
23. Lefebvre and Régulier, "The Rythmanalytical Project," 5.
24. Lefebvre, *Rhythmanalysis.*
25. Douglas, *The Help-Yourself City.*
26. Lefebvre, *Rhythmanalysis.*
27. Andres and Kraftl, "New Directions in the Theorisation of Temporary Urbanisms."
28. Lefebvre and Régulier, "The Rythmanalytical Project," 5.
29. Lefebvre, *Rhythmanalysis.*
30. Lefebvre and Régulier, "The Rythmanalytical Project," 5–6.
31. Groth and Corijn, "Reclaiming Urbanity."
32. Lehtovuori and Ruoppila, "Temporary Uses Producing Difference."
33. Lefebvre and Régulier, "The Rythmanalytical Project," 8.
34. Ferreri, *The Permanence of Temporary Urbanism.*
35. Interview with one of the creators of the Friche de la Belle de Mai, March 23, 2006 (Marseille).
36. Interview with a public-sector urban planner/designer, October 4, 2016 (Greater London).
37. Peter Bishop and Lesley Williams, *The Temporary City* (London: Routledge, 2012), 4.
38. Madanipour, *Cities in Time*, 58.
39. Madanipour, *Cities in Time*, 58.
40. Madanipour, *Cities in Time*, 58.

3. ADAPTABILITY, ACTIVATION, AND WEAK PLANNING • 251

41. Douglas, *The Help-Yourself City*; Nicole Blumner, *Planning for the Unplanned: Tools and Techniques for Interim Use in Germany and the United States, Occasional Papers* (Berlin: Deutshes Institut für Urbanistik, 2006), http://www.difu.de/english/occasional/.

42. Robert Temel and Florian Haydn, eds., *Temporary Urban Spaces: Concepts for the Use of City Spaces* (Basel: Birkhauser, 2006), 39.

43. Michael Ziehl et al., *Second Hand Spaces: Recycling Sites Undergoing Urban Transformation* (Berlin: JOVIS Verlag, 2012).

44. John Henneberry, ed., *Transience and Permanence in Urban Development* (Chichester: Wiley, 2017); Blumner, *Planning for the Unplanned*; Colomb, "Pushing the Urban Frontier."

45. Bishop and Williams, *The Temporary City*; Ziehl et al., *Second Hand Spaces*; Blumner, *Planning for the Unplanned*; Colomb, "Pushing the Urban Frontier"; Andres, "Differential Spaces, Power Hierarchy and Collaborative Planning."

46. Andres and Kraftl, "New Directions in the Theorisation of Temporary Urbanisms."

47. John R. Bryson, "Obsolescence and the Process of Creative Reconstruction," *Urban Studies* 34, no. 9 (August 1997): 1439–1458, https://www.jstor.org/stable/43083989.

48. Andres and Kraftl, "New Directions in the Theorisation of Temporary Urbanisms."

49. Andres and Kraftl, "New Directions in the Theorisation of Temporary Urbanisms."

50. Danny MacKinnon et al., "Rethinking Path Creation: A Geographical Political Economy Approach," *Economic Geography* 95, no. 2 (January 2019): 113–135, https://doi.org/10.1080/00130095.2018.1498294.

51. Luís Carvalho and Mário Vale, "Biotech by Bricolage? Agency, Institutions and New Path Development in Peripheral Regions," *Cambridge Journal of Regions, Economy and Society* 11, no. 2 (July 2018): 275–295, https://doi.org/10.1093/cjres/rsy009.

52. Andres and Kraftl, "New Directions in the Theorisation of Temporary Urbanisms."

53. Juliette Pinard, *L'urbanisme transitoire, entre renouvellement des modalités de fabrique de la ville et évolution de ses acteurs: Une immersion ethnographique au sein de SNCF Immobilier* (Paris: Université Paris Est, 2021).

252 • 3. ADAPTABILITY, ACTIVATION, AND WEAK PLANNING

54. Juliette Pinard, "Developing 'Transient Urbanism' as a New Urban and Real Estate Strategy: The Case of the French National Railway Company (SNCF)," in *Transforming Cities Through Temporary Urbanism—A Comparative Overview*, ed. Lauren Andres and Amy Zhang, 141 (Dordrecht: Springer, 2020).

55. Michel Peraldi and Michel Samson, *Gouverner Marseille: Enquête sur les mondes politiques Marseillais* (Paris: La découverte, 2005).

56. Interview with a public-sector built environment expert, May 5, 2006 (Marseille).

57. Lauren Andres, "Alternative Initiatives, Cultural Intermediaries and Urban Regeneration: The Case of La Friche (Marseille)," *European Planning Studies* 19, no. 5 (May 2011): 795–811, https://doi.org/10.1080/0 9654313.2011.561037.

58. Lauren Andres and Boris Grésillon, "Cultural Brownfields in European Cities: A New Mainstream Object for Cultural and Urban Policies," *International Journal of Cultural Policy* 19, no. 1 (October 2011): 40–62, https://doi.org/10.1080/10286632.2011.625416.

59. Peraldi and Samson, *Gouverner Marseille*.

60. Andres, "Alternative Initiatives."

61. Lauren Andres, *La ville mutable. Mutabilité et référentiels urbains: Les cas de Bouchayer-Viallet, de la Belle de Mai et du Flon* (Grenoble: Université Pierre Mendes France, 2008).

62. Euroméditerranée is one of the few program in France labeled "of national interest" (Opération d'intérêt National). In other words, it is a program that, from a planning perspective, has the benefit of a specific legal, regulatory, and funding status where the state (and the organization created to operate on its behalf), not the municipality per se, holds the power of shaping the transformation of a specific area of significant interest.

63. Urban Catalyst, *Strategies for Temporary Uses: Potential for Development of Urban Residual Areas in European Metropolises* (Berlin: Studio Urban Catalyst, 2003).

64. Ferreri, *The Permanence of Temporary Urbanism*.

65. Lefebvre, *The Production of Space*.

66. Ali Madanipour, "Urban Design and Dilemmas of Space," *Environment and Planning D: Society and Space* 14, no. 3 (June 1996): 331–355, https://doi.org/10.1068/d140331.

3. ADAPTABILITY, ACTIVATION, AND WEAK PLANNING • 253

67. Donovan Finn, "DIY Urbanism: Implications for Cities," *Journal of Urbanism* 7, no. 4 (March 2014): 381–398, https://doi.org/10.1080/17549175.2014.891149.

68. Colomb, "Pushing the Urban Frontier."

69. Andres and Grésillon, "Cultural Brownfields in European Cities."

70. Claire Colomb, "The Trajectory of Berlin's 'Interim Spaces': Tensions and Conflicts in the Mobilisation of 'Temporary Uses' of Urban Space in Local Economic Development," in *Transience and Permanence in Urban Development*, ed. John. Henneberry, 131–149 (Chichester: Wiley, 2017).

71. Jean Paul Deridder, *Stadt Der Kinder, Berlin, City of Transience* (Berlin: Hatje Cantz, 2008); Temel and Haydn, *Temporary Urban Spaces*; Philipp Oswalt et al., *The Power of Temporary* (Berlin, DOM Publishers, 2017); Urban Pioneers, *Temporary Use and Urban Development in Berlin* (Berlin: Jovis, 2007).

72. Andres, "Differential Spaces, Power Hierarchy and Collaborative Planning."

73. Temel and Haydn, *Temporary Urban Spaces*, 25.

74. Madanipour, *Cities in Time.*

75. Madanipour, *Cities in Time.*

76. Ferreri, *The Permanence of Temporary Urbanism.*

77. Patsey Healey, "Building Institutional Capacity Through Collaborative Approaches to Urban Planning," *Environmental Planning A* 30, no. 9 (September 1998): 1546, https://doi.org/10.1068/a301531.

78. Lehtovuori and Ruoppila, "Temporary Uses Producing Difference."

79. Andres, "Differential Spaces, Power Hierarchy and Collaborative Planning."

80. Michel de Certeau, *The Practice of Everyday Life*, trans. Steven Rendall (Berkeley: University of California Press, 1984); Michel de Certeau, "Walking in the City," in *The Cultural Studies Reader*, ed. Simon During, 126–133 (London: Routledge, 1993); John Round et al., "Everyday Tactics and Spaces of Power: The Role of Informal Economies in Post-Soviet Ukraine," *Social & Cultural Geography* 9, no. 2 (May 2008): 171–185, https://doi.org/10.1080/14649360701856110.

81. de Certeau, *The Practice of Everyday Life*, 38.

82. de Certeau, *The Practice of Everyday Life*, 36.

83. Andres, "Differential Spaces, Power Hierarchy and Collaborative Planning."

84. Lehtovuori and Ruoppila, "Temporary Uses Producing Difference."

254 • 3. ADAPTABILITY, ACTIVATION, AND WEAK PLANNING

85. Michel de Certeau, "Actions culturelles et stratégie politique: Sortir du cercle," *La Revue Nouvelle* (April 1974): 351–360.

86. Lauren Andres et al., "Negotiating Polyvocal Strategies: Re-reading de Certeau Through the Lens of Urban Planning in South Africa," *Urban Studies* 57, no. 12 (September 2020): 2440–2455, https://doi.org/10.1177/0042098019875423.

87. Ferreri, *The Permanence of Temporary Urbanism.*

88. Interview with one of the creators of the Friche de la Belle de Mai, April 6, 2006 (Marseille).

89. Andres et al., "Negotiating Polyvocal Strategies."

90. Andres, *La ville mutable.*

91. In Switzerland, under a certain threshold of citizen opposition, a local referendum can be called to validate or reject a decision. This can be used to resolve key tensions between the owner and the local municipality that has blocked progression of a new master plan.

92. Andres, "Differential Spaces, Power Hierarchy and Collaborative Planning."

93. Interview with a tenant who settled in the district in 1989, January 12, 2006 (Lausanne).

94. Andres, *La ville mutable.*

95. Interview with one the temporary users, tenants of a restaurant, January 5, 2008 (Lausanne).

96. Jean-Claude Peclet, "Lausanne, le Flon: Une victoire à courte vue," *L'hebdo* (September 15, 1994).

97. Andres, " Differential Spaces, Power Hierarchy and Collaborative Planning."

98. Groupe LO, *L'avenir du Flon* (Lausanne: Groupe LO Holding, 1998), 2.

99. Interview with a representative from the landowner company, June 16, 2007 (Lausanne).

100. Interview with a tenant who settled in the district in the 1990s, February 6, 2006 (Lausanne).

4. EVERYDAY ADAPTABILITY, COPING, AND RESILIENCE

1. Henri Lefebvre, *The Production of Space* (Oxford: Blackwell, 1991); Henri Lefebvre, *Rhythmanalysis: Space, Time and Everyday Life* (London:

4. EVERYDAY ADAPTABILITY, COPING, AND RESILIENCE • 255

Continuum, 2004); Henri Lefebvre and Catherine Régulier, "The Rythmanalytical Project," *Rethinking Marxism* 11, no. 1 (Spring 1995): 1–13.

2. Lawrence J. Vale and Thomas J. Campanella, eds., *The Resilient City: How Modern Cities Recover from Disaster* (New York: Oxford University Press, 2005).

3. Siambabala Bernard Manyena, "The Concept of Resilience Revisited," *Disasters* 30, no. 4 (December 2006): 433–450, https://doi.org/10.1111/j.0361-3666.2006.00331.x.

4. Azad M. Madni and Scott Jackson, "Towards a Conceptual Framework for Resilience Engineering," *IEEE Systems Journal* 3, no. 2 (2009): 181–191, https://doi.org/10.1109/JSYST.2009.2017397.

5. Andy Pike, Stuart Dawley, and John Tomaney, "Resilience, Adaptation and Adaptability," *Cambridge Journal of Regions, Economy and Society* 3, no. 1 (March 2010): 60, https://doi.org/10.1093/cjres/rsq001.

6. Fikret Berkes and Dyanna Jolly, "Adapting to Climate Change: Social–Ecological Resilience in a Canadian Western Arctic Community," *Conservation Ecology* 5, no. 2 (2001): 514–532, http://www.consecol.org/vol5/iss2/art18/; W Neil Adger et al., "Social–Ecological Resilience to Coastal Disasters," *Science* 309, no. 5757 (August 12, 2005): 1036–1039, https://doi.org/10.1126/science.1112122.

7. Pike, Dawley, and Tomaney, "Resilience, Adaptation and Adaptability," 62.

8. Ron Martin, "Regional Economic Resilience, Hysteresis and Recessionary Shocks," *Journal of Economic Geography* 12, no. 1 (January 2012): 1–32, https://doi.org/10.1093/jeg/lbr019; Jon Coaffee et al., *The Everyday Resilience of the City: How Cities Respond to Terrorism and Disaster* (London: Palgrave Macmillan, 2008); Lauren Andres and John Round, "The Role of 'Persistent Resilience' Within Everyday Life and Polity: Households Coping with Marginality Within the 'Big Society,'" *Environment and Planning A: Economy and Space* 47, no. 3 (2015): 676–690, https://doi.org/10.1068/a46299.

9. Vale and Campanella, *The Resilient City*.

10. Coaffee et al., *The Everyday Resilience of the City*; Andres and Round, "The Role of 'Persistent Resilience;'" Ioannis Chinis, Georgia Pozoukidou, and Theodora Istoriou, "Renegotiating Spatial Planning Practices: The Role of Collective Initiatives and Informal Networks," *European Planning Studies* (March 22, 2021), https://doi.org/10.1080/09654313.2021.1903400.

256 • 4. EVERYDAY ADAPTABILITY, COPING, AND RESILIENCE

11. Coaffee et al., *The Everyday Resilience of the City*.
12. Pike, Dawley, and Tomaney, "Resilience, Adaptation and Adaptability," 62.
13. Simin Davoudi et al., "Evolutionary Resilience and Strategies for Climate Adaptation," *Planning Practice & Research* 28, no. 3 (April 2013): 307–332, https://doi.org/10.1080/02697459.2013.787695.
14. Simin Davoudi, "Resilience, Uncertainty, and Adaptive Planning," *Journal of the Western Balkan Network on Territorial Governance* 1 (2019): 120–128, https://doi.org/10.32034/CP-TGWBAR-I01-10.
15. Andres and Round, "The Role of 'Persistent Resilience.'"
16. Andres and Round, "The Role of 'Persistent Resilience.'"
17. Michel de Certeau, *The Practice of Everyday Life*, trans. Steven Rendall (Berkeley: University of California Press, 1984).
18. Faranak Miraftab, "Insurgent Planning: Situating Radical Planning in the Global South," *Planning Theory* 8, no. 1 (February 2009): 32–50, https://doi.org/10.1177/1473095208099297; Alexandre Apsan Frediani and Camila Cociña, "'Participation *as* Planning': Strategies from the South to Challenge the Limits of Planning," *Built Environment* 45, no. 2 (Summer 2019), https://doi.org/10.2148/benv.45.2.143.
19. Lauren Andres et al., "Planning, Temporary Urbanism and Citizen-Led Alternative-Substitute Place-making in the Global South," *Regional Studies* 55, no. 1 (2021): 29–39, https://doi.org/10.1080/00343404.2019.1665645.
20. This case study was examined within the "Re-Inhabiting the City: Bringing New Life to City Centres of Emerging Economies in a Changing Climate" funded by Engineering and Physical Sciences Research Council/São Paulo Research Foundation (EPSRC/FAPESP) and which run between 2018–19 (Principal investigators—Prof. Lucelia Rodrigues [UoN], and Dr. Joana Soares Gonçalves [University of Sao Paulo]). This project explored the issue of "Re-Inhabiting the City" and questioned the reuse/redesign of vacant spaces in Sao Paulo's vacant urban core.
21. Alex Daniels, "São Paulo in Poverty: Improving Life in the Slums," *Buzz* (January 21, 2021), https://buzz.bournemouth.ac.uk/2021/01/nearly-20-of-residents-in-sao-paulo-live-in-poverty/; Lucelia Rodrigues et al., "Exploring Urban Regeneration Through Temporary Uses in Central São Paulo, Brazil," in *Transforming Cities Through Temporary Urbanism—A Comparative Overview*, ed. Lauren Andres and Amy Zhang, 199–213 (Dordrecht: Springer, 2020).

4. EVERYDAY ADAPTABILITY, COPING, AND RESILIENCE • 257

22. Rodrigues et al., "Exploring Urban Regeneration."

23. Fieldwork visit, Sao Paulo, May 2023.

24. Rodrigues et al., "Exploring Urban Regeneration."

25. Ali Madanipour, *Cities in Time: Temporary Urbanism and the Future of the City* (London: Bloomsbury, 2017), 99.

26. Lauren Andres et al., "Planning for Sustainable Urban Livelihoods in Africa," in *The Routledge Handbook on Livelihoods in the Global South*, ed. Fiona Nunan et al., 335–344 (London: Routledge, 2023).

27. Views of South African planners were collected as part of the Economic Social Research Council (ESRC) and National Research Foundation (NRF) project "The appropriateness, usefulness, and impact of the current urban planning curriculum in South African Higher Education (ES/P00198X/1)". It ran between 2016 and 2019 (PI Prof. Lauren Andres and Dr. Denoon-Stevens). This research focused on the needs and challenges faced by planning practitioners in South Africa, where urban planning is considered a scarce skill but plays a crucial role in tackling spatial and social segregation, inherited from apartheid, while addressing other challenges (e.g., housing provision, health, and wellbeing); Interview with a private-sector planner, February 8, 2018 (Cape Town, South Africa).

28. Miraftab, "Insurgent Planning;" Richard de Satgé and Vanessa Watson, *Urban Planning in the Global South: Conflicting Rationalities in Contested Urban Space* (Cham: Springer, 2018); Phil Harrison et al., *Planning and Transformation: Learning from the Post-Apartheid Experience* (London: Routledge, 2007).

29. Andres et al., "Planning, Temporary Urbanism."

30. Lauren Andres et al., "Negotiating Polyvocal Strategies: Re-reading de Certeau Through the Lens of Urban Planning in South Africa," *Urban Studies* 57, no. 12 (September 2020): 2440–2455, https://doi.org /10.1177/0042098019875423.

31. Madanipour, *Cities in Time*, 148.

32. Interview with a public-sector planner, April 11, 2018 (Pretoria, South Africa).

33. Andres et al., "Planning, Temporary Urbanism."

34. Interview with a public-sector planner, March 16, 2018 (Cape Town, South Africa).

35. Interview with a private-sector planner, February 8, 2018 (Cape Town, South Africa).

36. Andres et al., "Planning for Sustainable Urban Livelihoods."

37. Jan K. Brueckner et al., "Backyarding: Theory and Evidence for South Africa," *Regional Science and Urban Economics* 79 (November 2019), https://doi.org/10.1016/j.regsciurbeco.2019.103486.

38. Charlotte Lemanski, "Augmented Informality: South Africa's Backyard Dwellings as a By-Product of Formal Housing Policies," *Habitat International* 33, no. 4 (October 2009): 472–484, https://doi.org/10.1016/j.habitatint.2009.03.002; Thashlin Govender et al., "The Impact of Densification by Means of Informal Shacks in the Backyards of Low-Cost Houses on the Environment and Service Delivery in Cape Town, South Africa," *Environmental Health Insights* 5 (May 2011): 23–52, https://doi.org/10.4137/ehi.s7112.

39. Interview with a public-sector planner, March 16, 2018 (Cape Town, South Africa).

40. Global Water.org, "'The Rise of SkyWater'—Challenges of an Aerial Water Distribution System" (March 2020), https://www.globalwaters.org/us-global-water-strategy-stories/rise-skywater-challenges-aerial-water-distribution-system.

41. Interview with a public-sector planner, April 6, 2018 (Potchefstroom, South Africa).

42. Hestia Victor, "'There Is Life in This Place': 'DIY Formalisation', Buoyant Life and Citizenship in Marikana Informal Settlement, Potchefstroom, South Africa," *Anthropology Southern Africa* 42, no. 4 (December 2019): 302–315, https://doi.org/10.1080/23323256.2019.1639522.

43. Interview with a public-sector planner, December 2, 2018 (Cape Town, South Africa).

44. Paul Moawad, *Deconstructing the Lebanese-Syrian Borderscape Through Modalities of 'Waiting' and Spatio-Temporality: An Investigative Study on Informal Tented Settlements in Lebanon Along the Borderline* (London: University College London, 2022).

45. Paul Moawad and Lauren Andres, "Tackling COVID-19 in Informal Tented Settlements (Lebanon): An Assessment of Preparedness and Response Plans and Their Impact on the Health Vulnerabilities of Syrian Refugees," *Journal of Migration and Health* 1–2 (2020), https://doi.org/10.1016/j.jmh.2020.100011.

4. EVERYDAY ADAPTABILITY, COPING, AND RESILIENCE • 259

46. Paul Moawad and Lauren Andres, "Decoding Syrian Refugees' Covid-19 Vulnerability in Informal Tented Settlements: A Community/Refugee-Led Approach to Mitigate a Pandemic Outbreak," *Town Planning Review* 92, no. 1 (January 2021), https://doi.org/10.3828/tpr.2020.55.

47. International Federation of Red Cross and Red Crescent Societies (IFRC), *Emergency Plan of Action (EPoA) Lebanon: Population Movement* (Disaster Response Emergency Fund (DREF) Operation no. MDRLB007 2019).

48. Moawad, *Deconstructing the Lebanese-Syrian Borderscape.*

49. Moawad, *Deconstructing the Lebanese-Syrian Borderscape.*

50. Moawad, *Deconstructing the Lebanese-Syrian Borderscape.*

51. Andres et al., "Planning, Temporary Urbanism.".

52. Gordon Douglas, *The Help-Yourself City: Legitimacy and Inequality in DIY Urbanism* (New York: Oxford University Press, 2019).

53. Douglas, *The Help-Yourself City.*

54. Douglas, *The Help-Yourself City*; Panu Lehtovuori and Sampo Ruoppila, "Temporary Uses Producing Difference in Contemporary Urbanism," in *Transience and Permanence in Urban Development*, ed. John. Henneberry, 47–63 (Chichester: Wiley, 2017).

55. Douglas Kelbaugh, "Three Paradigms: New Urbanism, Everyday Urbanism, Post Urbanism—An Excerpt from the Essential COMMON PLACE," *Bulletin of Science, Technology & Society* 20, no. 4 (August 2000): 285–289, https://doi.org/10.1177/027046760002000406.

56. Douglas Kelbaugh, "Toward an Integrated Paradigm: Further Thoughts on the Three Urbanisms," *Places* 19, no. 2 (2007): 15.

57. David Crouch, "Reinventing Allotments for the Twenty-First Century: The UK Experience," *Acta Hortic* 523 (2000): 135–142, https://doi.org/10.17660/ActaHortic.2000.523.18.

58. Loughborough Farm: A Patchwork of Community Growing Spaces, https://www.loughboroughfarm.org/about-loughborough-farm.

59. Ella Harris, *Rebranding Precarity. Pop-Up Culture as the Seductive New Normal* (London: Bloomsbury 2020).

60. Mara Ferreri, *The Permanence of Temporary Urbanism: Normalising Precarity in Austerity London* (Amsterdam: Amsterdam University Press, 2021).

61. Harris, *Rebranding Precarity.*

62. Ferreri, *The Permanence of Temporary Urbanism.*

63. Peter Bishop and Lesley Williams, *The Temporary City* (London: Routledge, 2012), 37.

64. Harris, *Rebranding Precarity.*

65. Interview with a meanwhile tenant, November 7, 2016 (London).

66. This initial time frame has not been respected, with the project still being on the same site as of 2023. The pandemic significantly slowed down its removal; Rogers Stirk Harbour + Partners (RSHP), "PLACE/Ladywell," https://rshp.com/projects/residential/place-ladywell/.

67. Harris, *Rebranding Precarity.*

68. Harris, *Rebranding Precarity*; Ferreri, *The Permanence of Temporary Urbanism.*

5. ADAPTABILITY AND THE "COOL" ARTIFICIAL CITY

1. Richard Florida, *Cities and the Creative Class* (New York: Routledge, 2005); Charles Landry and Franco Bianchini, *The Creative City, A Toolkit for Urban Innovators* (London: Demos, 1995).

2. Richard Lloyd, *Neo-Bohemia: Art and Commerce in the Post-Industrial City* (London: Routledge, 2005).

3. Elizabeth Currid, "Bohemia as Subculture: Bohemia as Industry Art, Culture, and Economic Development," *Journal of Planning Literature* 23, no. 4 (May 2009): 368–382, https://doi.org/10.1177/0885412209335727.

4. Lauren Andres and Oleg Golubchikov, "The Limits to Artist-Led Regeneration: Creative Brownfields in the Cities of High Culture," *International Journal of Urban and Regional Research* 40, no. 4 (July 2016): 757–775, https://doi.org/10.1111/1468-2427.12412.

5. Justin O'Connor and Kate Shaw, "What Next for the Creative City?," *City, Culture and Society* 5, no. 3 (September 2014), 165–170, https://doi.org/10.1016/j.ccs.2014.05.010.

6. Joseph Pine and James H. Gilmore, *The Experience Economy* (Boston: Harvard Business Press, 2011).

7. Mara Ferreri, *The Permanence of Temporary Urbanism: Normalising Precarity in Austerity London* (Amsterdam: Amsterdam University Press, 2021).

8. Interview with a representative from the Greater London Authority, November 14, 2016 (London).

5. ADAPTABILITY AND THE "COOL" ARTIFICIAL CITY • 261

9. Sharon Zukin, *The Cultures of Cities* (Oxford: Blackwell: 1995); Lilly Kong, "Culture, Economy, Policy: Trends and Developments," *Geoforum* 31, no. 4 (November 2000): 385–390, https://doi.org/10.1016/S0016-7185(00)00004-X.

10. Charles Landry, *The Creative City: A Toolkit for Urban Innovators* (London: Earthscan, 2000).

11. Ann Markusen and David King, *The Artistic Dividend: The Arts' Hidden Contributions to Regional Development. Project on Regional and Industrial Economics* (Minneapolis: University of Minnesota, 2003).

12. Cian O'Callaghan and Philip Lawton, "Temporary Solutions? Vacant Space Policy and Strategies for Re-use in Dublin," *Irish Geography* 48, no. 1 (February 2015): 69–87, http://nbn-resolving.de/urn:irg:ie:0000-igj.v48i1.5260.

13. Gordon Douglas, *The Help-Yourself City: Legitimacy and Inequality in DIY Urbanism* (New York: Oxford University Press, 2019).

14. Douglas, *The Help-Yourself City*.

15. Nicholas Karachalis, "Temporary Use as a Participatory Placemaking Tool to Support Cultural Initiatives and Its Connection to City Marketing Strategies—The Case of Athens," *Sustainability* 13, no. 4 (February 2021), https://doi.org/10.3390/su13041652.

16. Karachalis, "Temporary Use"; Constantine E. Kontokosta et al., "Up-and-Coming or Down-and-Out? Social Media Popularity as an Indicator of Neighborhood Change," *Journal of Planning Education and Research* (March 23, 2021), https://doi.org/10.1177/0739456X21998445.

17. John Henneberry, ed., *Transience and Permanence in Urban Development* (Chichester: Wiley, 2017).

18. Ella Harris, *Rebranding Precarity: Pop-Up Culture as the Seductive New Normal* (London: Bloomsbury, 2020).

19. Jonathan Reades and Martin Crookston, *Why Face-to-Face Still Matters: The Persistent Power of Cities in the Post-Pandemic Era* (Bristol: Bristol University Press, 2021), 220.

20. London School of Economics and Political Science (LSE) et al., *The Economic Future of the Central Activity Zone (CAZ) Phase 2 Final Report: Scenario Development, Model Findings and Policy Recommendations. Report to the Greater London Authority* (GLA) (London: LSE, 2021).

21. Ferreri, *The Permanence of Temporary Urbanism*.

22. Lauren Andres and Boris Grésillon, "Cultural Brownfields in European Cities: A New Mainstream Object for Cultural and Urban Policies," *International Journal of Cultural Policy* 19, no. 1 (October 2011): 40–62, https://doi.org/10.1080/10286632.2011.625416.

23. Claire Colomb, "The Trajectory of Berlin's 'Interim Spaces': Tensions and Conflicts in the Mobilisation of 'Temporary Uses' of Urban Space in Local Economic Development," in *Transience and Permanence in Urban Development*, ed. John Henneberry, 131–149 (Chichester, Wiley, 2017).

24. Urban Pioneers, *Temporary Use and Urban Development in Berlin* (Berlin: Jovis, 2007).

25. Colomb, "The Trajectory of Berlin's 'Interim Spaces.'"

26. Andrej Holm and Armin Kuhn, "Squatting and Urban Renewal: The Interaction of Squatter Movements and Strategies of Urban Restructuring in Berlin," *International Journal of Urban and Regional Research* 35, no. 3 (December 2011): 644–658, https://doi.org/10.1111/j.1468-2427.2010.001009.x. This isn't unique to Berlin. A similar strategy was used in London when meanwhile strategies were explicitly disconnected to any references to anarchist roots (see Ferreri, *The Permanence of Temporary Urbanism*).

27. Colomb, "The Trajectory of Berlin's 'Interim Spaces.'"

28. Colomb, "The Trajectory of Berlin's 'Interim Spaces.'"

29. Panu Lehtovuori and Sampo Ruoppila, "Temporary Uses Producing Difference in Contemporary Urbanism," in *Transience and Permanence in Urban Development*, ed. John Henneberry, 47–63 (Chichester: Wiley, 2017); Claire Colomb, "Pushing the Urban Frontier: Temporary Uses of Space, City Marketing, and the Creative City Discourse in 2000s Berlin," *Journal of Urban Affairs* 34, no. 2 (May 2012): 131–152, https://doi.org/10.1111/j.1467-9906.2012.00607.x.

30. Harris, *Rebranding Precarity*; Fran Tonkiss, "Austerity Urbanism and the Makeshift City," *City* 17, no. 3 (June 2013): 312–324, https://doi.org/10.1080/13604813.2013.795332.

31. Ferreri, *The Permanence of Temporary Urbanism*.

32. Eduardo Mendieta, "The Production of Urban Space in the Age of Transnational Mega-Urbes," *City* 12, no. 2 (August 2008): 148–153, https://doi.org/10.1080/13604810802259320.

5. ADAPTABILITY AND THE "COOL" ARTIFICIAL CITY • 263

33. Karachalis, "Temporary Use."

34. Interview with a representative from the London Borough of Lambeth, November 15, 2016 (London).

35. Malcom Sawyer, "What Is Financialization?," *International Journal of Political Economy* 42, no. 4 (December 2014): 5–18, https://doi.org/10.2753/IJP0891-1916420401.

36. Louis Moreno, "The Urban Process Under Financialised Capitalism" *City* 18, no. 3 (June 2014), 244–268, https://doi.org/10.1080/13604813.2014.927099.

37. David Harvey, *Social Justice and the City* (Athens: University of Georgia Press, 1973).

38. Brett Christophers, "The Limits to Financialization," *Dialogues in Human Geography* 5, no. 2 (July 2015): 183–200, https://doi.org/10.1177/2043820615588153.

39. Andrew Leyshon and Nigel Thrift, "The Capitalization of Almost Everything: The Future of Finance and Capitalism," *Theory, Culture and Society* 24, no. 7–8 (December 2007): 97–115, https://doi.org/10.1177/0263276407084699.

40. Rodrigo Fernandez and Reijer Hendrikse, "Offshore Finance," in *The Routledge International Handbook of Financialization*, ed. Philip Mader et al., 224–237 (London: Routledge, 2020); Desiree Fields, Constructing a New Asset Class: Property-Led Financial Accumulation After the Crisis, *Economic Geography* 94, no. 2 (2018): 118–140, https://doi.org/10.1080/00130095.2017.1397492.

41. Calum Ward and Erik Swyngedouw, "Neoliberalisation from the Ground Up: Insurgent Capital, Regional Struggle, and the Assetisation of Land," *Antipode* 50, no. 4 (February 2018): 1077–1097, https://doi.org/10.1111/anti.12387.

42. Kean Birch and Calum Ward, "Assetization and the 'New Asset Geographies,'" *Dialogues in Human Geography* (November 8, 2022): 122, https://doi.org/10.1177/20438206221130807.

43. Ferreri, *The Permanence of Temporary Urbanism.*

44. Federico Savini and Manuel Aalbers, "The Decontextualisation of Land-Use Planning through Financialisation: Urban Redevelopment in Milan," *European Urban and Regional Studies* 23, no. 4 (October 2016): 878–894, https://doi.org/10.1177/0969776415585887.

45. Rachel Weber, "Extracting Value from the City: Neoliberalism and Urban Redevelopment," *Antipode* 34, no. 3 (July 2002): 519–540, https://doi.org/10.1111/1467-8330.00253.

46. Weber, "Extracting Value from the City."

47. Joseph Schumpeter, *Capitalism, Socialism, and Democracy* (New York: Harper and Row, 1942).

48. Weber, "Extracting Value from the City," 519–40.

49. Moreno, "The Urban Process."

50. Moreno, "The Urban Process."

51. Harris, *Rebranding Precarity*; David Harvey, *The Condition of Postmodernity: An Enquiry into the Origins of Cultural Change* (Cambridge: Wiley-Blackwell, 1990).

52. Harris, *Rebranding Precarity*, 25.

53. Moreno, "The Urban Process."

54. Calum Ward, "Land Financialisation, Planning Informalisation and Gentrification as Statecraft in Antwerp," *Urban Studies* 59, no. 9 (2022): 1837–1854, https://doi.org/10.1177/00420980211028235.

55. Ward, "Land Financialisation."

56. Bethan Alexander et al., "The Growing Permanence of Pop-Up Outlets Within the International Location Strategies of Fashion Retailers," *International Journal of Retail & Distribution Management* 46, no. 5 (2018): 487–506, https://doi.org/10.1108/IJRDM-09-2017-0217.

57. Peter Bishop and Lesley Williams, *The Temporary City* (London: Routledge, 2012).

58. Juliana Taube and Gary Warnaby, "How Brand Interaction in Pop-Up Shops Influences Consumers' Perceptions of Luxury Fashion Retailers," *Journal of Fashion Marketing and Management* 21 (2017): 385–399, https://doi.org/10.1108/JFMM-08-2016-0074.

59. Alexander et al., "The Growing Permanence of Pop-Up Outlets."

60. Micaela Surchi, "The Temporary Store: A New Marketing Tool for Fashion Brands," *Journal of Fashion Marketing and Management* 15, 2 (2011): 257–270, https://doi.org/10.1108/13612021111132672.

61. Liz Crump, "Reimagining Urban Planning: From Institution to Innovation—A Comparative Exploration of Temporary Urbanism and the Future of City-Making," in *Transforming Cities Through Temporary Urbanism—A Comparative Overview*, ed. Lauren Andres and Amy Zhang, 107–125 (Dordrecht: Springer, 2020).

5. ADAPTABILITY AND THE "COOL" ARTIFICIAL CITY • 265

62. Bishop and Williams, *The Temporary City.*
63. Interview with a private developer, November 21, 2016 (London).
64. Fabrique urbaine & creative de l'ile de Nantes, *Fabriquer la ville autrement* (2023) https://www.iledenantes.com.
65. Cécile Diguet et al., *Temporary Urbanism: Planning Differently. Note Rapide no. 10* (Paris: Paris Region Development and Urban Planning Institute, 2017).
66. Juliette Pinard, "Developing 'Transient Urbanism' as a New Urban and Real Estate Strategy: The Case of the French National Railway Company (SNCF)," in *Transforming Cities Through Temporary Urbanism—A Comparative Overview*, ed. Lauren Andres and Amy Zhang, 141–154 (Dordrecht: Springer, 2020).
67. Pinard, "Developing 'Transient Urbanism.'"
68. Juliette Pinard, "L'urbanisme transitoire, outil de patrimonialisation et de mise en scène en amont du projet urbain? L'exemple de SNCF Immobilier et de ses emprises ferroviaires à Paris," *Territoire en Mouvement Revue de Géographie et Aménagement* 56 (July) 2022), https://doi .org/10.4000/tem.8744.
69. L'agence nationale pour la rénovation urbaine (ANRU), *L'urbanisme transitoire dans les quartiers en renouvellement urbain: Boîte à outils pour la mise en œuvre de projets d'occupation temporaire* (Paris: ANRU, 2021).
70. Ferreri, *The Permanence of Temporary Urbanism*; Harris, *Rebranding Precarity.*
71. Henri Lefebvre, *Rhythmanalysis: Space, Time and Everyday Life* (London: Continuum, 2004).
72. Lefebvre, *Rhythmanalysis.*
73. Phil Jones and Saskia Warren, "Time, Rhythm and the Creative Economy," *Transactions of the Institute of British Geographers* 41, 3 (2016): 286–296, https://www.jstor.org/stable/45147039.
74. Douglas, *The Help-Yourself City*, building on Karl Marx, Antonio Gramsci, Theodor Adorno, Max Horheimer, David Harvey, and Edward Purcell.
75. Peter Bishop, "Urban Design in the Fragmented City," in *Contemporary Urban Design Thinking: The Australian Approach*, ed. Rob Roggema, 71–93 (Dordrecht: Springer, 2019).
76. Peter Bishop, "From the Subversive to the Serious," *Counterpoint* 235, no. 3 (April 2015): 136–141, https://doi.org/10.1002/ad.1913.

266 • 5. ADAPTABILITY AND THE "COOL" ARTIFICIAL CITY

77. Adam Kasaa et al., *Designing Politics: The Limits of Design* (London: Theatrum Mundi, LSECities, Fondation Maison des Sciences de L'Homme, 2016), http://eprints.lse.ac.uk/68075/1/Designing-Politics-The -limits-of-design.pdf.

78. Interview with a developer representative, December 3, 2016 (Wembley, London).

79. Harris, *Rebranding Precarity.*

80. Bishop, "From the Subversive to the Serious."

81. Florida, *Cities and the Creative Class.*

82. Lauren Andres, "Alternative Initiatives, Cultural Intermediaries and Urban Regeneration: The Case of La Friche (Marseille)," *European Planning Studies* 19, no. 5 (May 2011): 795–811, https://doi.org/10.1080 /09654313.2011.561037.

83. Douglas, *The Help-Yourself City.*

84. Thomas Honeck, "From Squatters to Creatives: An Innovation Perspective on Temporary Use in Planning," *Planning Theory & Practice* 18, 2 (April 2017): 268–287, https://doi.org/10.1080/14649357.2017.1303536.

85. Douglas, *The Help-Yourself City.*

86. Andres and Grésillon, "Cultural Brownfields in European Cities."

87. O'Callaghan and Lawton, "Temporary Solutions?"

88. Bishop, "From the Subversive to the Serious," 136–41.

89. Harris, *Rebranding Precarity.*

90. Harris, *Rebranding Precarity.*

91. Harris, *Rebranding Precarity.*

92. Mara Ferreri and Alexander Vasudevan, "Vacancy at the Edges of the Precarious City," *Geoforum* 101 (May 2019): 165–173, https://doi.org /10.1016/j.geoforum.2019.03.009.

93. Tonkiss, "Austerity Urbanism."

94. Harris, *Rebranding Precarity.*

6. THE PANDEMIC AND POSTPANDEMIC ADAPTABLE CITY

1. Lauren Andres, "Fragmented Recoveries and Proactive Adaptability: New Paradigm Shifts, and Theoretical Directions to Unpacking Recovery Processes and Behavioural Change," in *Pandemic Recovery?*

6. THE PANDEMIC AND POSTPANDEMIC ADAPTABLE CITY • 267

Reframing and Rescaling Societal Challenges, ed. Lauren Andres et al., 359–381 (Cheltenham: Edward Elgar, 2024).

2. Jennifer Robinson, "Global and World Cities: A View from off the Map," *International. Journal of Urban and Regional Research* 26, no. 3 (September 2002): 531–554, https://doi.org/10.1111/1468-2427.00397.

3. John R. Bryson et al., "Ordinary Cities, Extraordinary Geographies: Parallax Dimensions, Interpolations and the Scale Question," in *Ordinary Cities, Extraordinary Geographies: People, Place and Space*, ed. John R. Bryson, 1–22 (Cheltenham: Edward Elgar, 2021).

4. Bryson et al., "Ordinary Cities, Extraordinary Geographies."

5. Doreen Massey, *For Space* (London: Sage, 2005), 9; Georges Perec, *Species of Spaces and Other Places* (London: Penguin, 1999 [1973]).

6. Bryson et al., "Ordinary Cities, Extraordinary Geographies," 12.

7. Olena Hankivsky and Anuj Kapilashrami, *Beyond Sex and Gender Analysis: An Intersectional View of the COVID-19 Pandemic Outbreak and Response* (Victoria, Australia: Melbourne School of Populations and Global Health, 2020), https://www.qmul.ac.uk/gpi/media/global-policy-institute/Policy-brief-COVID-19-and-intersectionality.pdf; Elaine Lynn-Ee Ho and Avril Maddrell, "Intolerable Intersectional Burdens: A COVID-19 Research Agenda for Social and Cultural Geographies," *Social & Cultural Geography* 22, no. 1 (2021): 1–10, https://doi.org/10.1080/14649365.2020.1837215.

8. Francesca Sartorio et al., "Towards an Antifragile Urban Form: A Research Agenda for Advancing Resilience in the Built Environment," *Urban Design International* 26, (2021): 135–158, https://doi.org/10.1057/s41289-021-00157-7.

9. Lauren Andres et al., "Learning from COVID-19 and Planning Post-Pandemic Cities to Reduce Pathogen Transmission Pathways," *Town Planning Review* 94, no. 1 (2022), https://doi.org/10.3828/tpr.2022.5.

10. Zaheer Allam and David S. Jones, "Pandemic Stricken Cities on Lockdown: Where Are Our Planning and Design Professionals [Now, Then and into the Future]?," *Land Use Policy* 97 (September 2020), https://doi.org/10.1016/j.landusepol.2020.104805; Yvonne Rydin et al., "Shaping Cities for Health: Complexity and the Planning of Urban Environments in the 21st Century," *Lancet* 379, no. 9831 (May 2012): 2079–2108, https://doi.org/10.1016/S0140-6736(12)60435-8.

11. Rydin et al., "Shaping Cities for Health."

12. Chris Webster, "How High Can We Go? Urban Density, Infectious Versus Chronic Disease, and the Adaptive Resilience of Cities," *Town Planning Review* 92, no. 1 (2021): 123–130.

13. Philip Hubbard et al., "Housing: Shrinking Homes, COVID-19 and the Challenge of Homeworking," *Town Planning Review* 92, no. 1 (2021): 3–10, https://doi.org/10.3828/tpr.2020.46.

14. Negar Ahmadpoor and Sina Shahab, "Urban Form. Realising the Value of Green Space: A Planners' Perspective on the COVID-19 Pandemic," *Town Planning Review* 92, no. 1 (2021): 49–55, https://doi.org/10.3828/tpr.2020.37.

15. Helen Pineo, *Healthy Urbanism: Designing and Planning Equitable, Sustainable and Inclusive Places* (London: Palgrave Macmillan, 2022), 236.

16. Pineo, *Healthy Urbanism*.

17. Paul Moawad and Lauren Andres, "Refugees in Abject Spaces, Protracted 'Waiting' and Spatialities of Abjection During the COVID-19 Pandemic," *Social and Cultural Geography* 24, no. 3–4 (2023): 467–483, https://doi.org/10.1080/14649365.2022.2121980;Kabengele Munanga, "Desenvolvimento, Construção da Democracia e da Nacionalidade nos Países Africanos: Desafio para o Milênio," *Cadernos CERU* 27, no. 2 (2016): 45–56, https://doi.org/10.11606/issn.2595-2536.v27i2p45-56.

18. Ambe J. Njoh, "Urban Planning as a Tool of Power and Social Control in Colonial Africa," *Planning Perspectives* 24, no. 3 (June 2009): 311, https://doi.org/10.1080/02665430902933960.

19. Susan Parnell, "Creating Racial Privilege: The Origins of South African Public Health and Town Planning Legislation," *Journal of Southern African Studies* 19, no. 3 (1993): 488, https://doi.org/10.1080/03057079308708370.

20. Vanessa Watson, "Seeing from the South: Refocusing Urban Planning on the Globe's Central Urban Issues," *Urban Studies* 46, no. 11 (2009): 2259–2275, https://www.jstor.org/stable/43198476; Phil Jones et al., "Planning Out Abjection? The Role of the Planning Profession in Post-Apartheid South Africa," *Planning Theory* 21, no. 1 (April 29, 2021, doi.org/10.1177/14730952211012429.

21. Lauren Andres et al., *International Overview of the Impact of COVID-19 on Education, Food and Play/Leisure and Related Adaptations—PANEX-Youth WP2 Full Report*, (London: University College London, 2023).

6. THE PANDEMIC AND POSTPANDEMIC ADAPTABLE CITY • 269

22. Moawad and Andres, "Refugees in Abject Spaces."

23. Abraham R. Matamanda et al., "Broken Bridges over Troubled Waters: COVID-19 and the Urban Poor Residing in Dinaweng Informal Settlement, Bloemfontein, South Africa," *South African Geographical Journal* 104, no. 3 (January 2022), 309–327, https://doi.org/10.1080/03736245.2022.2028669.

24. Jane Flanagan, "Townships in Lockdown—But Poor South Africans Fear Hunger More Than Covid 19," *The Times*, April 17, 2020, https://www.thetimes.co.uk/article/townships-in-lockdown-but-poor-south-africans-fear-hunger-more-than-covid-19-cgd8xv2xz.

25. Andres et al., *International Overview of the Impact of COVID-19.*

26. Hesam Kamalipour and Nastaran Peimani, "Informal Urbanism in the State of Uncertainty: Forms of Informality and Urban Health Emergencies," *Urban Design International* 26 (2021): 122–134, https://doi.org/10.1057/s41289-020-00145-3.

27. Gordon Douglas, *The Help-Yourself City: Legitimacy and Inequality in DIY Urbanism* (New York: Oxford University Press, 2019).

28. Douglas, *The Help-Yourself City.*

29. Interview with a private urban planner/urban designer, June 28, 2023 (New York City).

30. Interview with a private urban planner, June 7, 2023 (New York City).

31. Interview with a public urban planner, July 14, 2023 (London).

32. Interview with a public urban planner, June 22, 2023 (London).

33. Richard Florida et al., "Cities in a Post-COVID World," *Urban Studies* 60, no. 8 (2021), https://doi.org/10.1177/0042098021101807².

34. Quentin Stevens and Kim Dovey, *Temporary and Tactical Urbanism: (Re)Assembling Urban Space* (London: Routledge, 2022), 168.

35. Gary Warnaby and Dominic Medway, "Productive Possibilities? Valorising Urban Space Through Pop-up?," *Qualitative Market Research: An International Journal* 25, no. 5 (2022): 557–569, https://doi.org/10.1108/QMR-12-2021-0145.

36. Andres et al., "Learning from COVID-19."

37. Nathaniel Lichfield & Partners, *COVID-19 Implications for Law and Policy in England* (London: Nathaniel Lichfield & Partners, 2020), https://lichfields.uk/business-as-un-usual/changes-to-law-policy/guidance-on-planning-policy-and-law-england/#:~:text=From%20

270 • 6. THE PANDEMIC AND POSTPANDEMIC ADAPTABLE CITY

the%20beginning%20of%20lockdown,will%20have%20faced%20 implementing%20permissions.

38. Nathaniel Lichfield & Partners, *COVID-19 Implications.*

39. Laura Sharman, "Government Announces £250m Emergency Active Travel Fund," Local Gov.com, May 11, 2020, https://www.localgov.co.uk /Government-announces-250m-emergency-active-travel-fund/50445.

40. Iain Deas et al., "Temporary Urban Uses in Response to COVID-19: Bolstering Resilience via Short-term Experimental Solutions," *Town Planning Review* 92, no. 1 (2020), 81–89, https://doi.org/10.3828/tpr .2020.45; Stevens and Dovey, *Temporary and Tactical Urbanism.*

41. William Booth et al., "Vast Coronavirus 'Field Hospitals' Fill Spaces That Hosted Wedding Expos and Dog Shows," *Washington Post*, March 31, 2020, https://www.washingtonpost.com/world/europe/coronavirus -field-hospitals/2020/03/31/3a05ba28-6f0f-11ea-a156-0048b62cdb51 _story.html.

42. Nicholas Pleace et al., *European Homelessness and COVID-19* (Brussels: European Observatory on Homelessness, 2021).

43. Jordi Honey-Rosés et al., "The Impact of COVID-19 on Public Space: An Early Review of the Emerging Questions—Design, Perceptions and Inequities," *Cities & Health* 5, no. 1 (2021): 263–279, https://doi.org /10.1080/23748834.2020.1780074.

44. Deas et al., "Temporary Urban Uses."

45. Peter Beech, "This Hospital Built from a Shipping Container Could be a COVID-19 Game-Changer," *World Economic Forum COVID Action Platform* (April 30, 2020), https://www.weforum.org/agenda/2020/04 /inside-the-covid-19-hospital-made-from-shipping-containers/.

46. Lauren Andres et al., "Temporary Urbanisms as Policy Alternatives to Enhance Health and Well-Being in the Post-Pandemic City," *Current Environmental Health Reports* 8, no. 2 (2021): 167–176, https://doi .org/10.1007/s40572-021-00314-8.

47. Laura Laker, "World Cities Turn Their Streets Over to Walkers and Cyclists," *The Guardian*, April 11, 2020, https://www.theguardian .com/world/2020/apr/11/world-cities-turn-their-streets-over-to-walkers -and-cyclists.

48. Warnaby and Medway, "Productive Possibilities?"

49. Warnaby and Medway, "Productive Possibilities?"

6. THE PANDEMIC AND POSTPANDEMIC ADAPTABLE CITY • 271

50. Lauren Andres et al., "Urban Value Chains and Re-Framing Agglomeration-Centric Conceptions of Urban Theory," *Urban Geography* 44, no. 8 (2023): 1701–1722, https://doi.org/10.1080/02723638.2022.2125665.

51. Moawad and Andres, "Refugees in Abject Spaces."

52. Cathrine Brun et al., "Displaced Citizens and Abject Living: The Categorical Discomfort with Subjects Out of Place," *Norsk Geografisk Tidsskrift (Norwegian Journal of Geography)* 71, no. 4 (2017): 220–232, https://doi.org/10.1080/00291951.2017.1369458.

53. Paul Moawad and Lauren Andres, "Tackling COVID-19 in Informal Tented Settlements (Lebanon): An Assessment of Preparedness and Response Plans and Their Impact on the Health Vulnerabilities of Syrian Refugees," *Journal of Migration and Health* 1–2 (2020), https://doi.org/10.1016/j.jmh.2020.100011.

54. Matamanda, et al., "Broken Bridges over Troubled Waters."

55. Paul Jones "Too Many Left Behind: The Failing of COVID-19 Prevention Measures in Informal Settlements and Slums," *The Conversation*, May 4, 2020, https://theconversation.com/too-many-left-behind-the-failing-of-covid-19-prevention-measures-in-informal-settlements-and-slums-137288.

56. Matthew French et al., "Informal Settlements in a COVID-19 World: Moving Beyond Upgrading and Envisioning Revitalisation," *Cities & Health* 5, no. 1 (2021), https://doi.org/10.1080/23748834.2020.1812331.

57. Matamanda, et al., "Broken Bridges over Troubled Waters."

58. Andres et al., *International Overview of the Impact of COVID-19.*

59. Andres et al., *International Overview of the Impact of COVID-19.*

60. Moawad and Andres, "Tackling COVID-19 in Informal Tented Settlements."

61. Moawad and Andres, "Refugees in Abject Spaces."

62. Andres et al., *International Overview of the Impact of COVID-19.*

63. Kamalipour and Peimani, "Informal Urbanism in the State of Uncertainty."

64. Caroline Skinner and Vanessa Watson, "Planning and Informal Food Traders Under COVID-19: The South African Case," *Town Planning Review* 92, no. 3 (January 2021), https://doi.org/10.3828/tpr.2020.38.

65. Kamalipour and Peimani, "Informal Urbanism in the State of Uncertainty"; Sigrid Wertheim-Heck, "The Impact of the COVID-19

272 • 6. THE PANDEMIC AND POSTPANDEMIC ADAPTABLE CITY

Lockdown on the Diets of Hanoi's Urban Poor," *International Institute for Environment and Development* (blog), April 8, 2020, https://www.iied.org/impact-covid-19-lockdown-diets-hanois-urban-poor.

66. Michael Taylor and Rina Chandran, "Asia's Street Food Hawkers Struggle During Coronavirus Lockdowns," *Reuters*, March 25, 2020, https://www.reuters.com/article/health-coronavirus-asia-idUSL4N2BH2ZA.

67. Andres, "Fragmented Recoveries and Proactive Adaptability."

68. Stuart Paul Denoon-Stevens and Katrina du Toit, "The Job–Food–Health Nexus in South African Townships and the Impact of COVID-19," in *Living with Pandemics: Places, People, Policy and Rapid Mitigation and Adaptation to Covid-19*, ed. John R. Bryson, Lauren Andres, Aksel Ersoy, and Louise Reardon, 69–78 (Northampton, MA: Edward Elgar, 2021); Andres et al., *International Overview of the Impact of COVID-19*; Matamanda et al., "Broken Bridges over Troubled Waters"; Mukhlid Yousif et al., "Measles Incidence in South Africa: A Six-Year Review, 2015–2020," *BMC Public Health* 22, no. 1647 (August 2022): 1647, https://doi.org/10.1186/s12889-022-14069-w.

69. Skinner and Watson, "Planning and Informal Food Traders."

70. Skinner and Watson, "Planning and Informal Food Traders."

71. Andres et al., *International Overview of the Impact of COVID-19*.

72. Deas et al., "Temporary Urban Uses."

73. Andreas Wesener, "Temporary Urbanism and Urban Sustainability After a Natural Disaster: Transitional Community-Initiated Open Spaces in Christchurch, New Zealand," *Journal of Urbanism* 8, no. 4 (July 2015), 406–422, https://doi.org/10.1080/17549175.2015.1061040.

74. Deas et al., "Temporary Urban Uses."

75. Arup, *Meanwhile Use London: A Research Report for the Greater London Authority* (London: Arup, 2020), https://www.london.gov.uk/sites/default/files/meanwhile_use_for_london_final.pdf.

76. Interview with a meanwhile use representative, June 28, 2022 (London).

77. Interview with a meanwhile use representative, June 28, 2022 (London).

78. Interview with a meanwhile use representative, June 28, 2022 (London).

79. Interview with a community member from the Green Project, July 14, 2022 (London).

80. Interview with a community member from the Green Project, July 14, 2022 (London).

81. Please refer to the 82nd Street Partnership and its homepage, https://82ndstreet.org.

6. THE PANDEMIC AND POSTPANDEMIC ADAPTABLE CITY • 273

82. Interview with a member of the 82nd Street Partnership, May 20, 2022 (Queens, New York).

83. Interview with a member of the 82nd Street Partnership, May 20, 2022 (Queens, New York).

84. Interview with a public urban planner, July 14, 2023 (London).

85. Interview with a representative from the Department of Transportation (DOT), June 20, 2022 (New York City).

86. Interview with a representative from the Department of Transportation (DOT), June 20, 2022 (New York City).

87. Please refer to the Prospect Heights Neighborhood Development Council (PHNDC) and the Vanderbilt Avenue page: https://prospectheightsplaces .com/vanderbilt-avenue/.

88. Please refer to the Fort Greene Open Streets Coalition website: https:// fortgreeneopenstreets.org.

89. Interview with a community member from the Vanderbilt Open Street, March 20, 2022 (New York City).

90. Interview with a community member from the Vanderbilt Open Street, 20 March 2022 (New York City).

91. Please refer to the 34th Avenue Open Streets Coalition Website: https:// www.34aveopenstreets.com.

92. Michael Kimmelman, "Jackson Heights, Global Town Square," *New York Times*, August 27, 2020, https://www.nytimes.com/interactive/2020/08/27 /arts/design/jackson-heights-queens-virtual-walk-tour.html.

93. Interview with a community member from the Vanderbilt Open Street, February 28, 2022 (New York City).

94. Interview with a community member from the Vanderbilt Open Street, February 28, 2022 (New York City).

95. Interview with a community member from the Vanderbilt Open Street, February 28, 2022 (New York City).

96. Interview with a community member from the Caldwell Enrichment Program Inc., June 6, 2022 (New York City).

97. Interview with a community member from the Caldwell Enrichment Program Inc., June 6, 2022 (New York City).

98. Interview with a community member from the Caldwell Enrichment Program Inc., June 6, 2022 (New York City).

99. Caislin L. Firth et al., "Not Quite a Block Party: COVID-19 Street Reallocation Programs in Seattle, WA and Vancouver, BC," *SSM—Population Health 14* (June 2021), https://doi.org/10.1016/j.ssmph.2021.100769.

274 • 6. THE PANDEMIC AND POSTPANDEMIC ADAPTABLE CITY

100. Andres, "Fragmented Recoveries and Proactive Adaptability."

101. Andres et al., "Urban Value Chains."

102. Jonny Gifford, "Remote Working: Unprecedented Increase and a Developing Research Agenda," *Human Resource Development International* 25, no. 2 (2022): 105–113, https://doi.org/10.1080/13678868.2022.2049108.

103. Sergio Montero, "Worlding Bogotá's Ciclovía: From Urban Experiment to International 'Best Practice,'" *Latin American Perspectives* 44, no. 2 (2017): 111–131, https://doi.org/10.1177/0094582X16668310.

104. Jonas De Vos, "The Effect of COVID-19 and Subsequent Social Distancing on Travel Behavior," *Transportation Research Interdisciplinary Perspectives* 5 (May 2020), https://doi.org/10.1016/j.trip.2020.100121; Carlos Moreno et al., "Introducing the '15-Minute City': Sustainability, Resilience and Place Identity in Future Post-Pandemic Cities," *Smart Cities* 4, no. 1 (January 2021): 93–111, https://doi.org/10.3390/smartcities4010006.

105. Interview with a representative from Transport for London (TFL), July 25, 2023 (London).

106. Interview with a representative from Transport for London (TFL), July 25, 2023 (London).

107. Interview with a public urban planner, June 22, 2023 (Lambeth, UK).

108. Interview with a public urban planner, June 22, 2023 (Lambeth, UK).

109. Interview with a public urban planner, June 22, 2023 (Lambeth, UK).

110. Winnie Hu, "How New York City Lost 63 Miles of Pedestrian-Friendly 'Open Streets,'" *New York Times*, August 11, 2022, https://www.nytimes.com/2022/08/11/nyregion/open-streets-nyc.html.

111. Interview with planner/urban designer from nonprofit organization, June 7, 2022 (New York City).

112. Interview with planner/urban designer from nonprofit organization, June 7, 2022 (New York City).

113. Interview with a representative from the Department of Transportation (DOT), June 20, 2022 (New York City).

114. Interview with planner/urban designer from nonprofit organization, June 7, 2022 (New York City).

115. Sartorio. et al., "Towards an Antifragile Urban Form."

116. Pineo, *Healthy Urbanism.*

117. Remon Rooij et al., "Education for the Resilient City—Teaching and Learning Urban Design and Planning in COVID-19 Times,"

Proceedings of the Institution of Civil Engineers—Urban Design and Planning 173, no. 4 (August 2020): 119–124, https://doi.org/10.1680/jurdp.20.00052;Adrian V. Hill, *Foundries of the Future: A Guide to 21st Century Cities of Making* (Deflt: TU Delft Open, 2020); Peter Newman et al., "Create Sustainable Mobility Systems," in *Resilient Cities: Overcoming Fossil Fuel Dependence*, ed. Peter Newman, Timothy Beatley, Heather Boyer, 53–87 (Washington DC, Island Press/Center for Resource Economics, 2017); Matthew Carmona, "Re-Theorising Contemporary Public Space: A New Narrative and a New Normative," *Journal of Urbanism: International Research on Placemaking and Urban Sustainability* 8, no. 4 (2015): 373–405, https://doi.org/10.1080/17549175.2014.909518.

118. Jo Williams, *Circular Cities. A Revolution in Urban Sustainability* (London: Routledge, 2021); Moreno et al., "Introducing the '15-Minute City.'"

119. Moreno et al., "Introducing the '15-Minute City.'"

120. Local Government Association (LGA), *Creating Resilient and Revitalised High Streets in the 'New Normal'* (London: LGA, 2022).

121. Arup, *Ten Ideas for Local Authorities to Help Re-build Economies After COVID-19* (PDF) (London: Arup, 2021), https://www.arup.com/perspectives/publications/research/section/10-ideas-for-local-authorities-to-help-rebuild-economies-after-covid-19.

122. World Economic Forum, *A Framework for the Future of Real Estate* (Geneva: WEF, 2021), https://www.weforum.org/publications/a-framework-for-the-future-of-real-estate/.; Andres et al., "Urban Value Chains."

123. London School of Economics and Political Science (LSE) et al., *The Economic Future of the Central Activity Zone (CAZ) Phase 2 Final Report: Scenario Development, Model Findings and Policy Recommendations. Report to the Greater London Authority* (GLA) (London: LSE, 2021).

124. Florida et al., "Cities in a Post-COVID World."

125. LSE et al., *The Economic Future of Central Activity Zone.*

126. Interview with a meanwhile use representative, June 28, 2022 (London).

127. Interview with a private transport/active travel consultant, July 8, 2022 (London).

128. Thomas M Selden and Terceira A Berdahl, "COVID-19 and Racial/Ethnic Disparities in Health Risk, Employment, and Household Composition," *Health Affairs* 39, no. 9 (September 2020): 1624–1632, https://doi.org/10.1377/hlthaff.2020.00897.

7. KNOWLEDGE, SKILLS, AND THE DELIVERY OF THE ADAPTABLE CITY

1. Colin McFarlane, "Fragment Urbanism: Politics at the Margins of the City," *Environment and Planning D: Society and Space* 36, no. 6 (May 2018): 1007–1025, https://doi.org/10.1177/0263775818877749; Colin McFarlane, *Fragments of the City: Making and Remaking Urban Worlds* (Berkeley: University of California Press, 2021).

2. Lauren Andres et al., "Institutional Logics and Regional Policy Failure: Air Pollution as a Wicked Problem in East African Cities," *Environment and Planning C: Politics and Space* 41, no. 2 (March 2023): 313–332, https://doi.org/10.1177/23996544221136698.

3. McFarlane, *Fragments of the City.*

4. McFarlane, *Fragments of the City.*

5. McFarlane, "Fragment Urbanism."

6. AbdouMaliq Simone, "The Surfacing of Urban Life," *City* 15, no. 3–4 (August 2011): 356, https://doi.org/10.1080/13604813.2011.595108.

7. Henri Lefebvre, *The Production of Space* (Oxford: Blackwell, 1991), 342.

8. Lefebvre, *The Production of Space*, 37.

9. McFarlane, *Fragments of the City.*

10. McFarlane, *Fragments of the City.*

11. Andres et al., "Institutional Logics and Regional Policy Failure."

12. John Allen and Allan Cochrane, "Beyond the Territorial Fix: Regional Assemblages, Politics and Power," *Regional Studies* 41, no. 9 (2007): 1161–1175, https://doi.org/10.1080/00343400701543348.

13. Andres et al., "Institutional Logics and Regional Policy Failure."

14. Patricia H. Thornton et al., *The Institutional Logics Perspective: A New Approach to Culture, Structure and Process* (Oxford: Oxford University Press, 2012), 2.

15. Jamie Peck and Nik Theodore, "Mobilizing Policy: Models, Methods, and Mutations," *Geoforum* 41, no. 2 (March 2010): 169–174, https://doi.org/10.1016/j.geoforum.2010.01.002; Cristina Temenos and Eugene McCann, "The Local Politics of Policy Mobility: Learning, Persuasion, and the Production of a Municipal Sustainability Fix," *Environment and Planning A* 44, no. 6 (2012): 1389–1406, https://doi.org/10.1068/a44314.

16. Andres et al., "Institutional Logics and Regional Policy Failure."

7. THE DELIVERY OF THE ADAPTABLE CITY • 277

17. Rhys Jones et al., "Devolution, State Personnel, and the Production of New Territories of Governance in the United Kingdom," *Environment and Planning A: Economy and Space* 36, no. 1 (2004): 89–109, https://doi.org/10.1068/a3685/.
18. Andres et al., "Institutional Logics and Regional Policy Failure."
19. McFarlane, *Fragments of the City.*
20. Paul Moawad, *Deconstructing the Lebanese-Syrian Borderscape Through Modalities of 'Waiting' and Spatio-Temporality: An Investigative Study on Informal Tented Settlements in Lebanon Along the Borderline* (London: University College London, 2022).
21. Moawad, *Deconstructing the Lebanese-Syrian Borderscape*; Paul Moawad and Lauren Andres, "Refugees in Abject Spaces, Protracted 'Waiting' and Spatialities of Abjection During the COVID-19 Pandemic," *Social and Cultural Geography* 24, no. 3–4 (2023), https://doi.org/10.1080/14649365.2022.2121980.
22. Lauren Andres et al., "Planners, Blended (In)formality and a Public Interest of Fragments," *Planning Practice and Research* (August 28, 2023), https://www.tandfonline.com/doi/full/10.1080/02697459.2023.2247249.
23. Jan K Brueckner et al., "Backyarding: Theory and Evidence for South Africa," *Regional Science and Urban Economics* 79 (November 2019), https://doi.org/10.1016/j.regsciurbeco.2019.103486.
24. Brueckner et al., "Backyarding."
25. Interview with a public-sector planner, March 16, 2018 (Cape Town, South Africa).
26. McFarlane, *Fragments of the City*, 78.
27. Andres et al., "Planners, Blended (In)formality and a Public Interest of Fragments."
28. Interview with a public-sector planner, March 16, 2018 (Cape Town, South Africa).
29. Interview with private-sector planer, February 8, 2018.
30. Patsy Healey, *Collaborative Planning: Shaping Places in Fragmented Societies* (London: Red Globe Press London, 1997).
31. McFarlane, "Fragment Urbanism."
32. Gordon Douglas, *The Help-Yourself City: Legitimacy and Inequality in DIY Urbanism* (New York: Oxford University Press, 2019).

278 • 7. THE DELIVERY OF THE ADAPTABLE CITY

33. Douglas, *The Help-Yourself City.*
34. Douglas, *The Help-Yourself City.*
35. Douglas, *The Help-Yourself City.*
36. Interview with a public-sector urban planner/designer, October 4, 2016 (Greater London).
37. Douglas, *The Help-Yourself City.*
38. Interview with a private urban planner/urban designer, June 28, 2023 (New York City).
39. Names are important here, and the story of La Friche has been widely told for the past two decades in public arenas. The names of those who originated the project are public; see, for example, La Friche website: https://www.lafriche.org/la-friche-in-english/our-story/
40. Lauren Andres, *La ville mutable. Mutabilité et référentiels urbains: Les cas de Bouchayer-Viallet, de la Belle de Mai et du Flon* (Grenoble: Université Pierre Mendes France, 2008).
41. Andres, *La ville mutable.*
42. Interview with one of the creators of La Friche de la Belle de Mai, March 23, 2006 (Marseille).
43. Interview with one of the creators of La Friche de la Belle de Mai, March 23, 2006.
44. Interview with one of the creators of La Friche de la Belle de Mai, April 6, 2006.
45. Interview with a former cabinet director for the Ministry of Culture, July 4, 2006 (France).
46. Quentin Stevens and Kim Dovey, *Temporary and Tactical Urbanism: (Re)Assembling Urban Space* (London: Routledge, 2022); Douglas, *The Help-Yourself City.*
47. Mara Ferreri, *The Permanence of Temporary Urbanism: Normalising Precarity in Austerity London* (Amsterdam: Amsterdam University Press, 2021).
48. Stevens and Dovey, *Temporary and Tactical Urbanism.*
49. Ferreri, *The Permanence of Temporary Urbanism.*
50. Ferreri, *The Permanence of Temporary Urbanism.*
51. Mike Lydon and Anthony Garcia, *Tactical Urbanism: Short-Term Action for Long-Term Change* (Washington, DC: Island Press, 2015).
52. Congress for the New Urbanism (CNU), "What Is New Urbanism?," (CNU: Washington, DC, n.d.), https://www.cnu.org/resources/what -new-urbanism.

7. THE DELIVERY OF THE ADAPTABLE CITY • 279

53. Mike Lydon et al., *Tactical Urbanism 1: Short-Term Action, Long-Term Change* (Miami: Next Generation of New Urbanists, 2011); Mike Lydon et al., *Tactical Urbanism 2: Short-Term Action, Long-Term Change* (Miami: Next Generation of New Urbanists, 2012); Lydon and Garcia, *Tactical Urbanism*.

54. Lydon and Garcia, *Tactical Urbanism*; The Street Plan Collective, *Tactical Urbanist's Guide to Materials* (Miami: Street Plan, 2016).

55. The Street Plan Collective, *Tactical Urbanist's Guide*.

56. The Street Plan Collective, *Tactical Urbanist's Guide*.

57. The Street Plan Collective, *Tactical Urbanist's Guide*.

58. Douglas, *The Help-Yourself City*.

59. Juliette Pinard, "L'urbanisme transitoire, entre renouvellement des modalités de fabrique de la ville et évolution de ses acteurs: une immersion ethnographique au sein de SNCF immobilier" (PhD diss, Université Paris Est, 2021).

60. Juliette Pinard, "Developing 'Transient Urbanism' as a New Urban and Real Estate Strategy: The Case of the French National Railway Company (SNCF)," in *Transforming Cities Through Temporary Urbanism—A Comparative Overview*, ed. Lauren Andres and Amy Zhang, 141–154 (Dordrecht: Springer, 2020).

61. Pinard, "L'urbanisme transitoire."

62. Pinard, "L'urbanisme transitoire."

63. Pinard, "L'urbanisme transitoire."

64. Pinard, "L'urbanisme transitoire."

65. Francesca Bragaglia and Cristiana Rossignolo, "Temporary Urbanism as a New Policy Strategy: A Contemporary Panacea or a Trojan Horse?," *International Planning Studies* 26, no. 4 (2021): 370–386, https://doi.org/10.1080/13563475.2021.1882963.

66. Carlos Moreno et al., "Introducing the '15-Minute City': Sustainability, Resilience and Place Identity in Future Post-Pandemic Cities," *Smart Cities* 4, no. 1 (January 2021): 93–111, https://doi.org/10.3390/smartcities4010006.

67. Typically the Master 2 programme (AUDE-EP—Alternatives urbaines démarches expérimentales et espaces publics) urban alternative, experimental processes and public spaces offered at the Paris School of Planning.

68. Ferreri, *The Permanence of Temporary Urbanism*; Olly Mould, "Tactical Urbanism: The New Vernacular of the Creative City," *Geography Compass* 8, no. 8 (August 2014): 529–539, https://doi.org/10.1111/gec3.12146.

8. THE FUTURE OF ADAPTABLE CITIES AND TEMPORARY URBANISMS

1. Rory Horner, "Towards a New Paradigm of Global Development? Beyond the Limits of International Development," *Progress in Human Geography* 44, no. 3 (June 2020): 415–436, https://doi.org/10.1177/0309132519836158.

2. Simon Maxwell, "Comparisons, Convergence and Connections: Development Studies in North and South," *IDS Bulletin* 29, no. 1 (January 1998): 20–31, https://doi.org/10.1111/j.1759-5436.1998.mp29001003.x.

3. Horner, "Towards a New Paradigm."

4. Lars Löfgren, "Complexity of Systems," in *Systems and Control Encyclopedia: Theory, Technology, Applications*, ed. Madan G. Singh, 704–709 (Oxford: Pergamon Press, 1987).

5. David Peat, *From Certainty to Uncertainty. The Story of Science and Ideas in the Twentieth Century* (Washington, DC: John Henry Press, 2002); Helga Nowotny, *The Cunning of Uncertainty* (Cambridge: Polity Press, 2016); Helga Nowotny, "The Increase of Complexity and Its Reduction: Emergent Interfaces Between the Natural Sciences, Humanities and Social Sciences," *Theory, Culture & Society* 22, no. 5 (2005): 15–31, https://doi.org/10.1177/0263276405057189; Helga Nowotny, "The Radical Openness of Science and Innovation," *EMBO Reports* 16, no. 12 (December 2015): 1601–1604, https://doi.org/10.15252/embr.201541546.

6. Peat, *From Certainty to Uncertainty*, 153.

7. Nowotny, *The Cunning of Uncertainty*.

8. Nowotny, *The Cunning of Uncertainty*.

9. Nowotny, *The Cunning of Uncertainty*.

10. Nowotny, *The Cunning of Uncertainty*.

11. Peat, *From Certainty to Uncertainty*, 97.

12. Nowotny, "The Radical Openness of Science and Innovation."

13. Donald Mackenzie, "An Equation and Its Worlds: Bricolage, Exemplars, Disunity and Performativity," *Social Studies of Science* 33, no. 6 (December 2003): 831–868, https://doi.org/10.1177/0306312703336002.

14. Nowotny, *The Cunning of Uncertainty*.

15. Nowotny, *The Cunning of Uncertainty*.

16. The example here is how children and young people have been left out of COVID-19 policy because they are not considered a priority group,

8. THE FUTURE OF ADAPTABLE CITIES • 281

with detrimental consequences. See the list of resources provided by Panex Youth at https://panexyouth.com/home-2/resources/.

17. Marc Welsh, "Resilience and Responsibility: Governing Uncertainty in a Complex world," *Geographical Journal* 180, no. 1 (March 2014): 15–26, https://doi.org/10.1111/geoj.12012.

18. Stockholm Resilience Centre, Planetary Boundaries, https://www.stockholmresilience.org/research/planetary-boundaries.html#:~:text=In%20January%202022%2C%2014%20scientists,%E2%80%9Cnovel%20entities%E2%80%9D%20including%20plastics.

19. Katherine Richardson et al., "Earth Beyond Six of Nine Planetary Boundaries," *Science Advances* 9, no. 37 (September 2023), https://doi.org/10.1126/sciadv.adh2458.

20. Nowotny, *The Cunning of Uncertainty*, 172.

BIBLIOGRAPHY

Adger, W. Neil, Terry P. Hughes, Carl Folke, Stephen R. Carpenter, and Johan Rockström. "Social–Ecological Resilience to Coastal Disasters." *Science* 309, no. 5757 (August 12, 2005): 1036–1039. https://doi.org/10.1126/science.1112122.

Ahmadpoor, Negar, and Sina Shahab. "Urban Form. Realising the Value of Green Space: A Planners' Perspective on the COVID-19 Pandemic." *Town Planning Review* 92, no. 1 (2021): 49–55. https://doi.org/10.3828/tpr.2020.37.

Allam, Zaheer, and David S. Jones. "Pandemic Stricken Cities on Lockdown: Where Are Our Planning and Design Professionals [Now, Then and into the Future]?" *Land Use Policy* 97. https://doi.org/10.1016/j.landusepol.2020.104805.

Allen, John, and Allan Cochrane. "Beyond the Territorial Fix: Regional Assemblages, Politics and Power." *Regional Studies* 41, no. 9 (2007): 1161–1175. https://doi.org/10.1080/00343400701543348.

Andres, Lauren. "Alternative Initiatives, Cultural Intermediaries and Urban Regeneration: The Case of La Friche (Marseille)." *European Planning Studies* 19, no. 5 (May 2011): 795–811. https://doi.org/10.1080/09654313.2011.561037.

Andres, Lauren. "Differential Spaces, Power Hierarchy and Collaborative Planning: A Critique of the Role of Temporary Uses in Shaping and Making Places." *Urban Studies* 50, no. 4 (2013): 759–775. https://doi.org/10.1177/0042098012455719.

Andres, Lauren. "Fragmented Recoveries and Proactive Adaptability: New Paradigm Shifts, and Theoretical Directions to Unpacking Recovery Processes and Behavioural Change." In *Pandemic Recovery? Reframing and*

Rescaling Societal Challenges, ed. Lauren Andres, John R. Bryson, Aksel Ersoy, and Louise Reardon, 359–381. Cheltenham: Edward Elgar, 2024.

Andres, Lauren. *La ville mutable. Mutabilité et référentiels urbains: Les cas de Bouchayer-Viallet, de la Belle de Mai et du Flon.* Grenoble: Université Pierre Mendes France, 2008.

Andres, Lauren, Hakeem Bakare, John R. Bryson, Winnie Khaemba, Lorena Melgaço, and George R. Mwaniki. "Planning, Temporary Urbanism and Citizen-led Alternative-Substitute Place-Making in the Global South." *Regional Studies* 55, no. 1 (2021): 29–39. https://doi.org/10.1080/00343404 .2019.1665645.

Andres, Lauren, John R. Bryson, Aksel Ersoy and Louise Reardon, eds. *Pandemic Recovery? Reframing and Rescaling Societal Challenges.* Cheltenham: Edward Elgar, 2024.

Andres, Lauren, John R. Bryson, William Graves, and Barney Warf. "Urban Value Chains and Re-framing Agglomeration-centric Conceptions of Urban Theory." *Urban Geography* 44, no. 8 (2023). https://doi.org/10.1080 /02723638.2022.2125665.

Andres, Lauren, John R. Bryson, Hisham Mehanna, and Paul Moawad. "Learning from COVID-19 and Planning Post-Pandemic Cities to Reduce Pathogen Transmission Pathways." *Town Planning Review* 94, no. 1 (November 2022). https://doi.org/10.3828/tpr.2022.5.

Andres, Lauren, John R. Bryson, and Paul Moawad. "Temporary Urbanisms as Policy Alternatives to Enhance Health and Well-Being in the Post-Pandemic City." *Current Environmental Health Reports* 8, no. 2 (2021): 167–176. https://doi.org/10.1007/s40572-021-00314-8.

Andres, Lauren, Stuart Paul Denoon-Stevens, John R. Bryson, Hakeem Bakare, and Lorena Melgaço. "Planning for Sustainable Urban Livelihoods in Africa." In *The Routledge Handbook on Livelihoods in the Global South*, ed. Fiona Nunan, Clare Barnes, and Sukanya Krishnamurthy, 335–344. London: Routledge, 2023.

Andres, Lauren, Stuart Denoon-Stevens, and Phil Jones. "Planners, Blended (In)formality and a Public Interest of Fragments." *Planning Practice and Research* (August 28, 2023). https://doi.org/10.1080/02697459.2023 .2247249.

Andres, Lauren, and Oleg Golubchikov. "The Limits to Artist-Led Regeneration: Creative Brownfields in the Cities of High Culture." *International Journal of Urban and Regional Research* 40, no. 4 (July 2016): 757–775. https://doi.org/10.1111/1468-2427.12412.

BIBLIOGRAPHY • 285

Andres, Lauren, and Boris Grésillon. "Cultural Brownfields in European Cities: A New Mainstream Object for Cultural and Urban Policies." *International Journal of Cultural Policy* 19, no. 1 (October 2011): 40–62. https://doi.org/10.1080/10286632.2011.625416.

Andres, Lauren, Phil Jones, Stuart Paul Denoon-Stevens, and Melgaço Lorena. "Negotiating Polyvocal Strategies: Re-reading de Certeau Through the Lens of Urban Planning in South Africa." *Urban Studies* 57, no. 12 (September 2020): 2440–2455. https://doi.org/10.1177/0042098019875423.

Andres, Lauren, and Peter Kraftl. "New Directions in the Theorisation of Temporary Urbanisms: Adaptability, Activation and Trajectory." *Progress in Human Geography* 45, no. 5 (October 2021): 1237–1253. https://doi.org/10.1177/0309132520985321.

Andres, Lauren, Paul Moawad, Peter Kraftl, Stuart Denoon-Stevens, Leandro Marais, Abraham Matamanda, Luciana Bizzotto, and Leandro Giatti. *International Overview of the Impact of COVID-19 on Education, Food and Play/Leisure and Related Adaptations—PANEX-Youth WP2 Full Report.* London: University College London, 2023.

Andres, Lauren, and John Round. "The Role of 'Persistent Resilience' Within Everyday Life and Polity: Households Coping with Marginality Within the 'Big Society.'" *Environment and Planning A* 47 (2015): 676–690. https://doi.org/10.1068/a46299.

Andres, Lauren, and Amy Zhang, eds. *Transforming Cities Through Temporary Urbanism—a Comparative Overview.* Dordrecht: Springer, 2020.

Arup. *Meanwhile Use London: A Research Report for the Greater London Authority.* London: Arup, 2020, https://www.london.gov.uk/sites/default/files/meanwhile_use_for_london_final.pdf.

Arup. *Ten Ideas for Local Authorities to Help Re-build Economies After COVID-19.* PDF. London: Arup, 2021. https://www.arup.com/perspectives/publications/research/section/10-ideas-for-local-authorities-to-help-rebuild-economies-after-covid-19.

Bakare, Hakeem, Stuart Denoon Stevens, and Lorena Melgaço. "Informality and Temporary Urbanism as Defiance: Tales of the Everyday Life and Livelihoods in Sub-Saharan Africa." In *Transforming Cities Through Temporary Urbanism—A Comparative Overview*, ed. Lauren Andres and Amy Zhang, 61–72. Dordrecht: Springer, 2020.

Balibar, Françoise, Philippe Büttgen, and Barbara Cassin. "Moment, Momentum, Instant." In *Dictionary of Untranslatables: A Philosophical Lexicon*, ed. Barbara Cassin, 683–689. Princeton, NJ: Princeton University Press, 2013).

286 • BIBLIOGRAPHY

Beekmans, Jeroen, and Joop de Boer. *Pop-Up City: City-Making in a Fluid World*. London: Laurence King, 2014.

Benevolo, Leonardo. *The European City*. Oxford: Blackwell, 1993.

Berkes, Fikret, and Dyanna Jolly. "Adapting to Climate Change: Social–Ecological Resilience in a Canadian Western Arctic Community." *Conservation Ecology* 5, no. 2 (2001): 18, http://www.consecol.org/vol5/iss2/art18/.

Birch, K., and C. Ward. "Assetization and the 'New Asset Geographies'." *Dialogues in Human Geography* 14, no. 1 (2024), https://doi.org/10.1177/20438206221130807.

Bishop, Peter. "From the Subversive to the Serious." *Counterpoint* 235, no. 3 (April 2015): 136–141, https://doi.org/10.1002/ad.1913.

Bishop, Peter. "Urban Design in the Fragmented City." In *Contemporary Urban Design Thinking: The Australian Approach*, ed. Rob Roggema, 71–93. Dordrecht: Springer, 2019.

Bishop, Peter, and Lesley Williams. *The Temporary City*. London: Routledge, 2012.

Blumner, Nicole. *Planning for the Unplanned: Tools and Techniques for Interim Use in Germany and the United States, Occasional Papers*. Berlin: Deutsches Institut für Urbanistik, 2006, https://difu.de/en/publications/2006/planning-for-the-unplanned-tools-and-techniques-for-interim-use-in-germany-and-the-united-states.

Bragaglia, Francesca, and Cristiana Rossignolo. "Temporary Urbanism as a New Policy Strategy: A Contemporary Panacea or a Trojan Horse?" *International Planning Studies* 26, no. 4 (2021): 370–386, https://doi.org/10.1080/13563475.2021.1882963.

Brenner, Neil. "Debating Planetary Urbanisation: Towards an Engaged Pluralism." *Environment and Planning D: Society and Space* 36, no. 3 (February 2018): 570–590, https://doi.org/10.1177/0263775818757510.

Brenner, Neil. *New Urban Spaces: Urban Theory and the Scale Question*. Oxford: Oxford University Press, 2019.

Brueckner, Jan K., Claus Rabe, and Harris Selod. "Backyarding: Theory and Evidence for South Africa." *Regional Science and Urban Economics* 79 (November 2019), https://doi.org/10.1016/j.regsciurbeco.2019.103486.

Brun, Cathrine, Anita H. Fàbos, and Oroub El-Abed. "Displaced Citizens and Abject Living: The Categorical Discomfort with Subjects out of Place." *Norsk Geografisk Tidsskrift—Norwegian Journal of Geography* 71, no. 4 (2017): 220–232, https://doi.org/10.1080/00291951.2017.1369458.

BIBLIOGRAPHY • 287

Bryson, John R. "Obsolescence and the Process of Creative Reconstruction." *Urban Studies* 34, no. 9 (August 1997): 1439–1458, https://www.jstor.org/stable/43083989.

Bryson, John R. "Ordinary Cities, Extraordinary Geographies: Parallax Dimensions, Interpolations and the Scale Question." In *Ordinary Cities, Extraordinary Geographies: People, Place and Space,* ed. John R. Bryson, Ronald V. Kalafsky, and Vida Vanchan, 1–22. Cheltenham: Edward Elgar, 2021.

Bryson, John R., Lauren Andres, Aksel Ersoy, and Louise Reardon. *Living with Pandemics: Places, People, Policy and Rapid Mitigation and Adaptation to Covid-19.* Cheltenham: Edward Elgar, 2021.

Carmona, Matthew. "Re-theorising Contemporary Public Space: A New Narrative and a New Normative." *Journal of Urbanism: International Research on Placemaking and Urban Sustainability* 8, no. 4 (2015): 373–405, https://doi.org/10.1080/17549175.2014.909518.

Carvalho, Luís, and Mário Vale. "Biotech by Bricolage? Agency, Institutions and New Path Development in Peripheral Regions." *Cambridge Journal of Regions, Economy and Society* 11, no. 2 (July 2018): 275–295, https://doi.org/10.1093/cjres/rsy009.

Cataldi, Giancarlo. "Saverio Muratori: il Debito e l'Eredità." In *Saverio Muratori Architetto (Modena 1910–Roma 1973): A Cento Anni Dalla Nascita: atti del Convegno Itinerante,* ed. Giancarlo Cataldi, 132–135. Florence, Italy: Aión, 2013.

Centre for Cities. *Cities Outlook 2021.* London: Centre for Cities, 2021.

Cherry, Gordon E. *Cities and Plans: Shaping of Urban Britain in the Nineteenth and Twentieth Centuries.* London: Edward Arnold, 1988.

Chinis, Ioannis, Georgia Pozoukidou, and Theodora Istoriou. "Renegotiating Spatial Planning Practices: The Role of Collective Initiatives and Informal Networks." *European Planning Studies* (2021), https://doi.org/10.1080/09654313.2021.1903400.

Christophers, Brett. "The Limits to Financialization." *Dialogues in Human Geography* 5, no. 2 (July 2015): 183–200, https://doi.org/10.1177/2043820615588153.

Coaffee, Jon, David Murakami Wood, and Peter Rogers. *The Everyday Resilience of the City: How Cities Respond to Terrorism and Disaster.* London: Palgrave Macmillian, 2008.

Colomb, Claire. "Pushing the Urban Frontier: Temporary Uses of Space, City Marketing, and the Creative City Discourse in 2000s Berlin." *Journal of Urban Affairs* 34, no. 2 (May 2012): 131–152, https://doi.org/10.1111/j.1467-9906.2012.00607.x.

Colomb, Claire. "The Trajectory of Berlin's 'Interim Spaces': Tensions and Conflicts in the Mobilisation of 'Temporary Uses' of Urban Space in Local Economic Development." In *Transience and Permanence in Urban Development*, ed. John. Henneberry, 131–149. Chichester, UK: Wiley, 2017.

Commission of the European Communities (CEC). *The EU Compendium of Spatial Planning Systems and Policies.* Luxembourg: CEC, 1997.

Crump, Liz. "Reimagining Urban Planning: From Institution to Innovation—A Comparative Exploration of Temporary Urbanism and the Future of City-Making." In *Transforming Cities Through Temporary Urbanism—A Comparative Overview*, ed. Lauren Andres and Amy Zhang, 107–126. Dordrecht: Springer, 2020.

Currid, Elizabeth. "Bohemia as Subculture: Bohemia as Industry Art, Culture, and Economic Development." *Journal of Planning Literature* 23, no. 4 (May 2009): 368–382, https://doi.org/10.1177/0885412209335727.

Daniels, Alex. "São Paulo in Poverty: Improving Life in the Slums." *Buzz*, January 21, 2021, https://buzz.bournemouth.ac.uk/2021/01/nearly-20-of -residents-in-sao-paulo-live-in-poverty/.

David, Mike. *Planet of Slums.* London: Verso, 2006.

Davoudi, Simin. "Resilience, Uncertainty, and Adaptive Planning." *Journal of the Western Balkan Network on Territorial Governance* (2019): 120–128, https://doi.org/10.32034/CP-TGWBAR-I01-10.

Davoudi, Simin, Elizabeth Brooks, and Abid Mehmood. "Evolutionary Resilience and Strategies for Climate Adaptation." *Planning Practice & Research* 28, no. 3 (April 2013): 307–332, https://doi.org/10.1080/02697459 .2013.787695.

Deas, Iain, Michael Martin, and Stephen Hincks. "Temporary Urban Uses in Response to COVID-19: Bolstering Resilience via Short-Term Experimental Solutions." *Town Planning Review* 92, no. 1 (January 2021): 81–89, https://doi.org/10.3828/tpr.2020.45.

De Certeau, Michel. "Actions Culturelles et Stratégie Politique: Sortir du Cercle." *La Revue Nouvelle* (April 1974): 351–360.

De Certeau, Michel. *The Practice of Everyday Life.* Trans. Steven Rendall. Berkeley: University of California Press, 1984.

De Certeau, Michel. "Walking in the City." In *The Cultural Studies Reader*, ed. Simon During, 126–133. London: Routledge, 1993.

Denoon-Stevens, Stuart Paul, and Katrina du Toit. "The Job–Food–Health Nexus in South African Townships and the Impact of COVID-19."

In *Living with Pandemics: Places, People, Policy and Rapid Mitigation and Adaptation to Covid-19*, ed. John R. Bryson, Lauren Andres, Aksel Ersoy, and Louise Reardon, 69–78. Northampton, MA: Edward Elgar, 2021.

Deridder, Jean Paul. *Stadt Der Kinder, Berlin, City of Transience, Bilingual Edition*. Berlin: Hatje Cantz, 2008.

De Satgé, Richard, and Vanessa Watson, *Urban Planning in the Global South: Conflicting Rationalities in Contested Urban Space*. Cham: Springer, 2018.

De Vos, Jonas. "The Effect of COVID-19 and Subsequent Social Distancing on Travel Behavior." *Transportation Research Interdisciplinary Perspectives* 5 (May 2020), https://doi.org/10.1016/j.trip.2020.100121.

Douglas, Gordon. *The Help-Yourself City: Legitimacy and Inequality in DIY Urbanism*. New York: Oxford University Press, 2019.

Duby, George. *Histoire de la France Urbaine: La Ville Médiévale*. Paris: Le Seuil, 1980.

Fernandez, R., and R. Hendrikse. "Offshore Finance." In *The Routledge International Handbook of Financialization*, ed. Philip Mader, Daniel Mertens, and Natascha van der Zwan, 224–237. London: Routledge, 2020.

Ferreri, Mara. *The Permanence of Temporary Urbanism: Normalising Precarity in Austerity London*. Amsterdam: Amsterdam University Press, 2021.

Ferreri, Mara, and Alexander Vasudevan. "Vacancy at the Edges of the Precarious City." *Geoforum* 101 (May 2019): 165–173, https://doi.org/10.1016/j.geoforum.2019.03.009.

Fields, D. "Constructing a New Asset Class: Property-Led Financial Accumulation After the Crisis." *Economic Geography* 94, no. 2 (2018): 118–140.

Fields, Desiree. "Unwilling Subjects of Financialization." *International Journal of Urban and Regional Research*, 41, no. 4 (September 2017): 588–603, https://doi.org/10.1111/1468-2427.12519.

Finn, Donovan. "DIY Urbanism: Implications for Cities." *Journal of Urbanism* 7, no. 4 (March 2014): 381–398, https://doi.org/10.1080/17549175.2014.891149.

Firth, Caislin L., Barbara Baquero, Rachel Berney, Katherine D. Hoerster, Stephen J. Mooney, and Meghan Winters. "Not Quite a Block Party: COVID-19 Street Reallocation Programs in Seattle, WA and Vancouver, BC." *SSM—Population Health* 14 (June 2021), https://doi.org/10.1016/j.ssmph.2021.100769.

Florida, Richard. *Cities and the Creative Class*. New York: Routledge, 2005.

Florida, Richard, Andrés Rodríguez-Pose, and Michael Storper. "Cities in a Post-COVID World." *Urban Studies* 60, no. 8 (2023): 1509–1531, https://doi.org/10.1177/00420980211018072.

Frediani, Alexandre Apsan, and Camila Cociña. "'Participation as Planning': Strategies from the South to Challenge the Limits of Planning." *Built Environment* 45, no. 2 (Summer 2019), https://doi.org/10.2148/benv.45.2.143.

French, Matthew, Diego Ramirez-Lovering, Sheela S. Sinharoy, Amelia Turagabeci, Ihsan Latif, Karin Leder, and Rebekah Brown. "Informal Settlements in a COVID-19 World: Moving Beyond Upgrading and Envisioning Revitalisation." *Cities & Health* 5, no. 1 (2021), https://doi.org/10.1080/23748834.2020.1812331.

Friedrichs, Christopher R. *The Early Modern City, 1450–1750.* London: Routledge, 1995.

García, Marisol. "The Usefulness of Temporary Use: Narratives from Santiago's Contemporary Urban Practices." In *Transforming Cities Through Temporary Urbanism—A Comparative Overview,* ed. Lauren Andres and Amy Zhang, 127-140. Dordrecht: Springer, 2020.

Gifford, Jonny. "Remote Working: Unprecedented Increase and a Developing Research Agenda." *Human Resource Development International* 25, no. 2 (2022): 105–113, https://doi.org/10.1080/13678868.2022.2049108.

Govender, Thashlin, Jo M. Barnes, and Clarissa H. Pieper. "The Impact of Densification by Means of Informal Shacks in the Backyards of Low-Cost Houses on the Environment and Service Delivery in Cape Town, South Africa." *Environmental Health Insights* 5 (May 2011): 23–52. https://doi.org/10.4137/ehi.s7112.

Groupe LO Holding. *L'avenir du Flon.* Lausanne: Groupe LO Holding, 1998.

Growth, Jacqueline, and Eric Corijn. "Reclaiming Urbanity: Indeterminate Spaces, Informal Actors and Urban Agenda Setting." *Urban Studies* 42, no. 3 (March 2005): 503–526, https://www.jstor.org/stable/43198269.

Hall, Peter. *Cities of Tomorrow: An Intellectual History of Urban Planning and Design in the Twentieth Century.* Oxford: Blackwell, 1988.

Hall, Peter. *Good Cities, Better Lives. How Europe Discovered the Last Art of Urbanism.* London: Routledge, 2014.

Hankivsky, Olena, and Anuj Kapilashrami. *Beyond Sex and Gender Analysis: An Intersectional View of the COVID-19 Pandemic Outbreak and Response.* London: Queen Mary University of London, 2020. https://www.qmul

BIBLIOGRAPHY • 291

.ac.uk/gpi/media/global-policy-institute/Policy-brief-COVID-19-and -intersectionality.pdf.

Harris, Ella. "Navigating Pop-Up Geographies: Urban Space–Times of Flexibility, Interstitiality and Immersion." *Geography Compass* 9, no. 11 (November 2015): 592–603, https://doi.org/10.1111/gec3.12248.

Harris, Ella. *Rebranding Precarity. Pop-up Culture as the Seductive New Normal.* London: Bloomsbury, 2020.

Harrison, Phil, Alison Todes, and Vanessa Watson, *Planning and Transformation: Learning from the Post-Apartheid Experience.* London: Routledge, 2007.

Harvey, David. *Rebel Cities: From the Right to the City to the Urban Revolution.* London: Verso, 2012.

Harvey, David. "The Right to the City." *International Journal of Urban and Regional Research* 27, no. 4 (December 2003): 939–941, https://doi.org /10.1111/j.0309-1317.2003.00492.x.

Harvey, David. "The Right to the City." *New Left Review* 53 (September– October 2008): 23–40.

Harvey, David. *Social Justice and the City.* Athens: University of Georgia Press, 1973.

Healey, Patsey. "Building Institutional Capacity Through Collaborative Approaches to Urban Planning." *Environmental Planning A* 30, no. 9 (September 1998): 1531–1546, https://doi.org/10.1068/a301531.

Healey, Patsy. *Collaborative Planning: Shaping Places in Fragmented Societies.* London: Red Globe Press London, 1997.

Henneberry, John. ed. *Transience and Permanence in Urban Development.* Chichester: Wiley, 2017.

Hill, Adrian V. *Foundries of the Future: A Guide to 21st Century Cities of Making.* Deflt: TU Delft Open, 2020.

Holm, Andrej, and Armin Kuhn. "Squatting and Urban Renewal: The Interaction of Squatter Movements and Strategies of Urban Restructuring in Berlin." *International Journal of Urban and Regional Research* 35, no. 3 (December 2011): 644–658, https://doi.org/10.1111/j.1468-2427.2010.001009.x.

Honey-Rosés, Jordi, Isabelle Anguelovski, Vincent K. Chireh, Carolyn Daher, Cecil Konijnendijk van den Bosch, Jill S. Litt, Vrushti Mawani, Michael K. McCallh, Arturo Orellana, and Emilia Oscilowicz, "The Impact of COVID-19 on Public Space: An Early Review of the Emerging

Questions—Design, Perceptions and Inequities." *Cities & Health* 5, no. 1 (2021): 263–279, https://doi.org/10.1080/23748834.2020.1780074.

Horner, Rory. "Towards a New Paradigm of Global Development? Beyond the Limits of International Development." *Progress in Human Geography* 44, no. 3 (June 2020): 415–436, https://doi.org/10.1177/0309132519836158.

Hou, Jeffrey, ed. *Insurgent Public Space: Guerrilla Urbanism and the Remaking of Contemporary Cities.* London: Routledge, 2010.

Hubbard, Philip, Jon Reades, and Hendrik Walter. "Housing: Shrinking Homes, COVID-19 and the Challenge of Homeworking." *Town Planning Review* 92, no. 1 (2021): 3–10, https://doi.org/10.3828/tpr.2020.46.

Iveson, Kurt. "Cities Within the City: Do-It-Yourself Urbanism and the Right to the City." *International Journal of Urban and Regional Research* 37, no. 3 (April 2013): 941–956, https://doi.org/10.1111/1468-2427.12053.

Jacobs, Jane. *The Death and Life of Great American Cities.* New York: Random House, 1961.

Jensen, C., and N. McKerrow. "Child Health Services During a COVID-19 Outbreak in KwaZulu-Natal Province, South Africa." *South African Medical Journal* 111, no. 2 (2021): 114–119.

Jones, Paul. "Too Many Left Behind: The Failing of COVID-19 Prevention Measures in Informal Settlements and Slums." *The Conversation*, May 4, 2020, https://theconversation.com/too-many-left-behind-the-failing-of-covid-19-prevention-measures-in-informal-settlements-and-slums-137288.

Jones, Phil, Lauren Andres, Stuart Denoon-Stevens, and Lorena Melgaco Silva Marques. "Planning Out Abjection? The Role of the Planning Profession in Post-Apartheid South Africa." *Planning Theory* 21, no. 1, https://doi.org/10.1177/14730952211012429.

Jones, Rhys, Mark Goodwin, Martin Jones, and Glenn Simpson. "Devolution, State Personnel, and the Production of New Territories of Governance in the United Kingdom." *Environment and Planning A: Economy and Space* 36, no. 1 (2004): 89–109, https://doi.org/10.1068/a3685.

Jordheim, Helge. "Conceptual History Between Chronos and Kairos: The Case of 'Empire.'" *Redescriptions* 11, no. 1 (2007): 115–145, https://doi.org/10.7227/R.11.1.8.

Kamalipour, Hesam, and Nastaran Peimani. "Informal Urbanism in the State of Uncertainty: Forms of Informality and Urban Health Emergencies." *Urban Design International* 26 (2021): 122–134, https://doi.org/10.1057/s41289-020-00145-3.

BIBLIOGRAPHY • 293

Karachalis, Nicholas. "Temporary Use as a Participatory Placemaking Tool to Support Cultural Initiatives and Its Connection to City Marketing Strategies—The Case of Athens." *Sustainability* 13, no. 4 (February 2021), https://doi.org/10.3390/su13041652.

Kelbaugh, Douglas. "Three Paradigms: New Urbanism, Everyday Urbanism, Post Urbanism—An Excerpt from *The Essential COMMON PLACE.*" *Bulletin of Science, Technology & Society* 20, no. 4 (August 2000): 285–289, https://doi.org/10.1177/027046760002000406.

Kelbaugh, Douglas. "Toward an Integrated Paradigm: Further Thoughts on the Three Urbanisms." *Places* 19, no. 2 (2007).

Kong, Lilly. "Culture, Economy, Policy: Trends and Developments." *Geoforum* 31, no. 4 (November 2000): 385–390, https://doi.org/10.1016/S0016-7185(00)00004-X.

Kontokosta, Constantine E., Lance Freeman, and Yuan Lai. "Up-and-Coming or Down-and-Out? Social Media Popularity as an Indicator of Neighborhood Change." *Journal of Planning Education and Research. Journal of Planning Education and Research* (March 23, 2012), https://doi.org/10.1177/0739456X21998445.

Kraftl, Peter. "Architectural Movements, Utopian Moments: (In)coherent Renderings of the Hundertwasser: Haus, Vienna." *Geografiska Annaler: Series B, Human Geography* 92, no. 4 (December 2010): 327–345, https://www.jstor.org/stable/40981002.

Kraftl, Peter. "Liveability and Urban Architectures: Mol(ecul)ar Biopower and the 'Becoming Lively' of Sustainable Communities." *Environment and Planning D: Society and Space* 32, no. 2 (January 2014): 274–292, https://doi.org/10.1068/d210.

Kullman, Kim. "Politics of Dissensus in Geographies of Architecture: Testing Equality at Ed Roberts Campus, Berkeley." *Transactions of the Institute of British Geographers* 44, no. 2 (December 2019): 284–298, https://doi.org/10.1111/tran.12276.

Landry, Charles. *The Creative City: A Toolkit for Urban Innovators.* London: Earthscan, 2000.

Landry, Charles, and Franco Bianchini. *The Creative City, A Toolkit for Urban Innovators.* London: Demos, 1995.

Lefebvre, Henri. *The Production of Space.* Oxford: Blackwell, 1991.

Lefebvre, Henri. *Rhythmanalysis: Space, Time and Everyday Life.* London: Continuum, 2004.

294 • BIBLIOGRAPHY

Lefebvre, Henri, and Catherine Régulier. "The Rythmanalytical Project." *Rethinking Marxism* 11, no. 1 (Spring 1995): 1–13.

Lehtovuori, Panu, and Sampo Ruoppila, "Temporary Uses Producing Difference in Contemporary Urbanism." In *Transience and Permanence in Urban Development*, ed. John. Henneberry, 47–63. Chichester: Wiley, 2017.

Lemanski, Charlotte. "Augmented Informality: South Africa's Backyard Dwellings as a By-Product of Formal Housing Policies." *Habitat International* 33, no. 4 (October 2009): 472–484, https://doi.org/10.1016/j.habitatint.2009.03.002.

Lerup, Lars. *Building the Unfinished: Architecture and Human Action.* Thousand Oaks, CA: Sage, 1977.

Leyshon, A., and N. Thrift. "The Capitalization of Almost Everything: The Future of Finance and Capitalism." *Theory, Culture and Society* 24, nos. 7–8 (2007): 97–115.

Lichfield, Nathaniel, and Partners. *COVID-19 Implications for Law and Policy in England.* London: Nathaniel Lichfield & Partners, 2020. https://lichfields.uk/business-as-un-usual/changes-to-law-policy/guidance-on-planning-policy-and-law-england/#:~:text=From%20the%20obeginning%20of%20lockdown,will%20have%20faced%20implementing%20permissions.

Lloyd, Richard. *Neo-Bohemia: Art and Commerce in the Post-Industrial City.* London: Routledge, 2005.

Local Government Association (LGA). *Creating Resilient and Revitalised High Streets in the 'New Normal.'* London: LGA, 2022.

Löfgren, Lars. "Complexity of Systems." In *Systems and Control Encyclopedia: Theory, Technology, Applications*, ed. Madan G. Singh, 704–709. Oxford: Pergamon Press, 1987.

London School of Economics and Political Science (LSE); Gerald Eve, LLP; and Arup. *The Economic Future of the Central Activity Zone (CAZ) Phase 2 Final Report: Scenario Development, Model Findings and Policy Recommendations. Report to the Greater London Authority* (GLA). London: LSE, 2021.

Lussault, Michel. "Temps et récit des politiques urbaines." In *Le quotidien urbain: Essais sur les temps des villes*, ed. Thierry Pacquot, 145–166. Paris: La découverte, 2001.

Lydon, Mike, and Anthony Garcia. *Tactical Urbanism: Short-Term Action for Long-Term Change.* Washington, DC: Island Press, 2015.

BIBLIOGRAPHY • 295

Lydon, Mike, and Anthony Garcia. *Tactical Urbanism 1: Short-Term Action, Long-Term Change.* Miami: Next Generation of New Urbanists, 2011.

Lydon, Mike, and Anthony Garcia. *Tactical Urbanism 2: Short-Term Action, Long-Term Change.* Miami: Next Generation of New Urbanists, 2012.

Lynn-Ee Ho, Elaine, and Avril Maddrell. "Intolerable Intersectional Burdens: A Covid-19 Research Agenda for Social and Cultural Geographies." *Social & Cultural Geography* 22, no. 1 (2021): 1–10, https://doi.org/10.1080/14649365.2020.1837215.

Mackenzie, Donald. "An Equation and Its Worlds: Bricolage, Exemplars, Disunity and Performativity." *Social Studies of Science* 33, no. 6 (December 2003): 831–868, https://doi.org/10.1177/0306312703336002.

MacKinnon, Danny, Stuart Dawley, Andy Pike, and Andrew Cumbers. "Rethinking Path Creation: A Geographical Political Economy Approach." *Economic Geography* 95, no. 2 (January 2019): 113–135, https://doi.org/10.1080/00130095.2018.1498294.

Madanipour, Ali. *Cities in Time: Temporary Urbanism and the Future of the City.* London: Bloomsbury, 2017.

Madanipour, Ali. "Urban Design and Dilemmas of Space." *Environment and Planning D: Society and Space* 14, no. 3 (June 1996): 331–355, https://doi.org/10.1068/d140331.

Madni, Azad M., and Scott Jackson. "Towards a Conceptual Framework for Resilience Engineering." *IEEE Systems Journal* 3, no. 2 (2009): 181–191, https://doi.org/10.1109/JSYST.2009.2017397.

Manyena, Siambabala Bernard. "The Concept of Resilience Revisited." *Disasters* 30, no. 4 (December 2006): 433–450, https://doi.org/10.1111/j.0361-3666.2006.00331.x.

Markusen, Ann, and David King. *The Artistic Dividend: The Arts' Hidden Contributions to Regional Development: Project on Regional and Industrial Economics.* Minneapolis: University of Minnesota, 2003.

Martin, Ron. "Regional Economic Resilience, Hysteresis and Recessionary Shocks." *Journal of Economic Geography* 12, no. 1 (January 2012): 1–32, https://doi.org/10.1093/jeg/lbr019.

Martin, Ron, and Peter Sunley. "Path Dependence and Regional Economic Evolution." *Journal of Economic Geography* 6, no. 4 (July 2006): 395–337, https://doi.org/10.1093/jeg/lbl012.

Masboungi, Ariella. "Du bon usage de la chronotopie." In *Le quotidien urbain: Essais sur les temps des villes,* ed. Thierry Pacquot, 167–179. Paris: La découverte, 2001.

Massey, Doreen. *For Space*. London: Sage, 2005.

Matamanda, Abraham R., Mischka Dunn, and Verna Nel. "Broken Bridges over Troubled Waters: COVID-19 and the Urban Poor Residing in Dinaweng Informal Settlement, Bloemfontein, South Africa." *South African Geographical Journal* 104, no. 3 (2022): 309–327, https://doi.org/10.1080/03736245.2022.2028669.

Maxwell, Simon. "Comparisons, Convergence and Connections: Development Studies in North and South." *IDS Bulletin* 29, no. 1 (January 1998): 20–31, https://doi.org/10.1111/j.1759-5436.1998.mp29001003.x.

McFarlane, Colin. "Assemblage and Critical Urbanism." *City* 15, no. 2 (June 2011): 204–224, https://doi.org/10.1080/13604813.2011.568715.

McFarlane, Colin. *Fragments of the City. Making and Remaking Urban Worlds*. Berkeley: University of California Press, 2021.

McFarlane, Colin. "Fragment Urbanism: Politics at the Margins of the City." *Environment and Planning D: Society and Space* 36, no. 6 (May 2018): 1007–1025, https://doi.org/10.1177/0263775818777749.

Mendieta, Eduardo. "The Production of Urban Space in the Age of Transnational Mega-urbes." *City* 12, no. 2 (August 2008): 148–153, https://doi.org/10.1080/13604810802259320.

Miraftab, Faranak. "Insurgent Planning: Situating Radical Planning in the Global South." *Planning Theory* 8, no. 1 (February 2009): 32–50, https://doi.org/10.1177/1473095208099297.

Moawad, Paul. *Deconstructing the Lebanese-Syrian Borderscape Through Modalities of "Waiting" and Spatio-Temporality: An Investigative Study on Informal Tented Settlements in Lebanon Along the Borderline*. London: University College London, 2022.

Moawad, Paul. "Temporary Forms of Urbanism in Contested Urban Spaces in Lebanon: The Case of Dbayeh Camp." In *Transforming Cities Through Temporary Urbanism: A Comparative Overview*, ed. Lauren Andres and Amy Zhang, 73–88. Dordrecht: Springer, 2020.

Moawad, Paul, and Lauren Andres. "Refugees in Abject Spaces, Protracted "Waiting" and Spatialities of Abjection During the COVID-19 Pandemic." *Social and Cultural Geography* 24, nos. 3–4 (2023), https://doi.org/10.1080/14649365.2022.2121980.

Moawad, Paul, and Lauren Andres. "Tackling COVID-19 in Informal Tented Settlements (Lebanon): An Assessment of Preparedness and Response Plans and Their Impact on the Health Vulnerabilities of Syrian Refugees."

Journal of Migration and Health 1–2 (2020), https://doi.org/10.1016/j.jmh.2020.100011.

Montero, Sergio. "Worlding Bogotá's Ciclovía: From Urban Experiment to International 'Best Practice.'" *Latin American Perspectives* 44, no. 2 (2017): 111–131, https://doi.org/10.1177/0094582X16668310.

Moreno, Carlos, Zaheer Allam, Didier Chabaud, Catherine Gall, and Florent Pratlong. "Introducing the '15-Minute City': Sustainability, Resilience and Place Identity in Future Post-Pandemic Cities." *Smart Cities* 4, no. 1 (January 2021): 93–111, https://doi.org/10.3390/smartcities4010006.

Moreno, Louis. "The Urban Process Under Financialised Capitalism." *City* 18, no. 3 (June 2014): 244–268, https://doi.org/10.1080/13604813.2014.927099.

Mould, Olly. "Tactical Urbanism: The New Vernacular of the Creative City." *Geography Compass* 8, no. 8 (August 2014): 529–539, https://doi.org/10.1111/gec3.12146.

Munanga, Kabengele. "Desenvolvimento, Construção da Democracia e da Nacionalidade nos países Africanos: Desafio para o Milênio." *Cadernos CERU* 27, no. 2 (2016): 45–56, https://doi.org/10.11606/issn.2595-2536.v27i2p45-56.

Nadin, Vincent, and Dominic Stead. "European Spatial Planning Systems, Social Models and Learning." *disP* 172, no. 1 (November 2012): 35–47, https://doi.org/10.1080/02513625.2008.10557001.

Newman, Peter, Timothy Beatley, and Heather Boyer, *Resilient Cities: Overcoming Fossil Fuel Dependence*. Dordrecht: Springer, 2017.

Njoh, Ambe J. "Urban Planning as a Tool of Power and Social Control in Colonial Africa." *Planning Perspectives* 24, no. 3 (June 2009): 301–317, https://doi.org/10.1080/02665430902933960.

Nowotny, Helga. *The Cunning of Uncertainty*. Cambridge: Polity Press, 2016.

Nowotny, Helga. "The Increase of Complexity and Its Reduction: Emergent Interfaces Between the Natural Sciences, Humanities and Social Sciences." *Theory, Culture & Society* 22, no. 5 (October 2005): 15–31, https://doi.org/10.1177/0263276405057189.

Nowotny, Helga. "The Radical Openness of Science and Innovation." *EMBO Reports* 16, no. 12 (December 2015): 1601–1604, https://doi.org/10.15252/embr.201541546.

O'Callaghan, Cian, and Philip Lawton. "Temporary Solutions? Vacant Space Policy and Strategies for Re-Use in Dublin." *Irish Geography* 48, no. 1 (February 2015): 69–87, http://nbn-resolving.de/urn:irg:ie:0000-igj.v48i1.5260.

O'Connor, Justin, and Kate Shaw. "What Next for the Creative City?" *City, Culture and Society* 5, no. 3 (September 2014): 165–170, https://doi.org/10.1016/j.ccs.2014.05.010.

Oswalt, Philipp, Klaus Overmeyer, and Philipp Misselwitz, *The Power of Temporary.* Berlin: DOM Publishers, 2017.

Parnell, Susan. "Creating Racial Privilege: The Origins of South African Public Health and Town Planning Legislation." *Journal of Southern African Studies* 19, no. 3 (1993): 471–488, https://doi.org/10.1080/03057079308708370.

Peat, David. *From Certainty to Uncertainty. The Story of Science and Ideas in the Twentieth Century.* Washington, DC: Joseph Henry Press, 2002.

Peck, Jamie, and Nik Theodore. "Mobilizing Policy: Models, Methods, and Mutations." *Geoforum* 41, no. 2 (March 2010): 169–174, https://doi.org/10.1016/j.geoforum.2010.01.002.

Peraldi, Michel, and Michel Samson. *Gouverner Marseille: Enquête sur les mondes politiques Marseillais.* Paris: La Découverte, 2005.

Perec, Georges. *Species of Spaces and Other Places.* London: Penguin, 1999 [1973].

Pickerill, Jenny, and Paul Chatterton. "Notes Towards Autonomous Geographies: Creation, Resistance and Self-Management as Survival Tactics." *Progress in Human Geography* 30, no. 6 (December 2006): 1–17, https://doi.org/10.1177/0309132506071516.

Pike, Andy, Stuart Dawley, and John Tomaney. "Resilience, Adaptation and Adaptability." *Cambridge Journal of Regions, Economy and Society* 3, no.1 (March 2010): 59–70.

Pinard, Juliette. "Developing 'Transient Urbanism' as a New Urban and Real Estate Strategy: The Case of the French National Railway Company (SNCF)." In *Transforming Cities Through Temporary Urbanism—A Comparative Overview*, ed. Lauren Andres and Amy Zhang, 141–154. Dordrecht, Springer, 2020.

Pinard, Juliette. *L'urbanisme transitoire, entre renouvellement des modalités de fabrique de la ville et évolution de ses acteurs: Une immersion ethnographique au sein de SNCF Immobilier.* Paris: Université Paris Est, 2021.

Pine, Joseph, and James H. Gilmore. *The Experience Economy.* Boston: Harvard Business Press, 2011.

Pineo, Helen. *Healthy Urbanism: Designing and Planning Equitable, Sustainable and Inclusive Places.* London: Palgrave Macmillan, 2022.

BIBLIOGRAPHY • 299

Pinol, Jean-Luc. *Histoire de l'Europe Urbaine, T1: de l'antiquité au 18ème siècle.* Paris: Seuil, 2003.

Pinol, Jean-Luc. *Histoire de l'Europe urbaine, T2: de l'ancien régime à nos jours.* Paris: Seuil, 2003.

Raco, Mike, and Sonia Freire Trigo. "Urban Governance: Re-Thinking Top-Down and Bottom-Up Power Relations in the Wake of Neo-Liberalisation." In *Handbook of Urban Geography*, ed. Tim Schwanen and Ronald van Kempen, 383–395. Northampton, MA: Edward Elgar, 2019.

Reades, Jonathan, and Martin Crookston. *Why Face-to-Face Still Matters. The Persistent Power of Cities in the Post-Pandemic Era.* Bristol: Bristol University Press, 2021.

Reimer, Mario, Panagiotis Getimis, and Hans Blotevogel. *Spatial Planning Systems and Practices in Europe: A Comparative Perspective on Continuity and Changes.* London: Routledge, 2014.

Richardson, Katherine, Will Steffen, Wolfgang Lucht, Jørgen Bendtsen, Sarah E. Cornell, Jonathan F. Donges, Markus Drüke et al. "Earth Beyond Six of Nine Planetary Boundaries." *Science Advances* 9, no. 37 (September 13, 2023), https://doi.org/10.1126/sciadv.adh2458.

Robinson, Jennifer. "Global and World Cities: A View from off the Map." *International. Journal of Urban and Regional Research* 26, no. 3 (September 2002): 531–554, https://doi.org/10.1111/1468-2427.00397.

Rodrigues, Lucelia, Joanna Carla Soares Gonçalves, Renata Tubelo, Nicole Porter, Parham A. Mirzaei, Peter Kraftl, Lauren Andres, Ranny Michalski, Roberta Kronika Mülfarth, et al. "Exploring Urban Regeneration Through Temporary Uses in Central São Paulo, Brazil." In *Transforming Cities Through Temporary Urbanism: A Comparative Overview*, ed. Lauren Andres and Amy Zhang, 199–214. Dordrecht: Springer, 2020.

Rodrigues Malta, Rachel. *Refaire la Ville au Temps Présent.* Grenoble: Université Pierre Mendes France, 2005.

Roncayolo, Marcel, and Thierry Pacquot, eds. *Villes et civilisation urbaine XVIIIe—XXe siècle.* Paris: Larousse, 1992.

Rooij, Remon, Kristel Aalbers, Birgit Hausleitner, Caroline Newton, and Roberto Rocco. "Education for the Resilient City: Teaching and Learning Urban Design and Planning in COVID-19 Times." *Proceedings of the Institution of Civil Engineers—Urban Design and Planning* 173, no. 4 (August 2020): 119–124, https://doi.org/10.1680/jurdp.20.00052

Rossi, Aldo. *L'Architettura Della Città*, 4th ed. Torino: CittàStudi, 2006 [1966].

Round, John, Colin C. Williams, and Peter Rodgers. "Everyday Tactics and Spaces of Power: The Role of Informal Economies in Post-Soviet Ukraine." *Social & Cultural Geography* 9, no. 2 (May 2008): 171–185, https://doi.org/10.1080/14649360701856110.

Rydin, Yvonne, Ana Bleahu, Michael Davies, Julio D. Dávila, Sharon Friel, Giovanni De Grandis, Nora Groce, et al. "Shaping Cities for Health: Complexity and the Planning of Urban Environments in the 21st Century." *The Lancet* 379, no. 9831 (May 2012): 2079–2108, https://doi.org/10.1016/S0140-6736(12)60435-8.

Sartorio, Francesca, Patricia Aelbrecht, Hesam Kamalipour, and Andrea Frank. "Towards an Antifragile Urban Form: A Research Agenda for Advancing Resilience in the Built Environment." *Urban Design International* 26 (2021): 135–158, https://doi.org/10.1057/s41289-021-00157-7.

Sawyer, Malcom. "What Is Financialization?" *International Journal of Political Economy: A Journal of Translations* 42, no. 4 (December 2014): 5–18, https://doi.org/10.2753/IJP0891-1916420401

Selden, Thomas M., and Terceira A Berdahl. "COVID-19 and Racial/Ethnic Disparities, in Health Risk, Employment, and Household Composition." *Health Affairs* 39, no. 9 (September 2020): 1624–1632, https://doi.org/10.1377/hlthaff.2020.00897.

Sendra, Pablo, and Richard Sennett. *Designing Disorder: Experiments and Disruptions in the City*. London: Verso, 2020.

Sennett, Richard. "The Open City." *Urban Age* (November 2006), https://urbanage.lsecities.net/essays/the-open-city.

Sennett, Richard. *The Uses of Disorder: Personal Identity and City Life*. New Haven, CT: Yale University Press, 1970.

Simone, AbdouMaliq. "The Surfacing of Urban Life." *City* 15, nos. 3–4 (2011): 355–364, https://doi.org/10.1080/13604813.2011.595108.

Skinner, Caroline, and Vanessa Watson. "Planning and Informal Food Traders Under COVID-19: The South African Case." *Town Planning Review* 92, no. 3 (January 2021), https://doi.org/10.3828/tpr.2020.38.

Stevens, Quentin, and Kim Dovey. *Temporary and Tactical Urbanism: (Re)Assembling Urban Space*. London Routledge, 2022.

Storper, Michael, and Anthony J. Venables. "Buzz: Face-to-Face Contact and the Urban Economy." *Journal of Economic Geography* 4, no. 4 (August 2004): 351–370, https://doi.org/10.1093/jnlecg/lbh027.

Street Plan Collective, The. *Tactical Urbanist's Guide to Materials.* Miami: Street Plan, 2016.

Tardiveau, Armelle, and Daniel Mallo. "Unpacking and Challenging Habitus: An Approach to Temporary Urbanism as a Socially Engaged Practice." *Journal of Urban Design* 19, no. 4 (June 2014): 456–472, https://doi .org/10.1080/13574809.2014.923743.

Taylor, Michael, and Rina Chandran. "Asia's Street Food Hawkers Struggle During Coronavirus Lockdowns." *Reuters,* March 25, 2020, https://www .reuters.com/article/health-coronavirus-asia-idUSL4N2BH2ZA.

Temel, Robert, and Florian Haydn, eds. *Temporary Urban Spaces: Concepts for the Use of City Spaces.* Basel: Birkhauser, 2006.

Temenos, Cristina, and Eugene McCann. "The Local Politics of Policy Mobility: Learning, Persuasion, and the Production of a Municipal Sustainability Fix." *Environment and Planning A* 44, no. 6 (2012): 1389–1406, https://doi.org/10.1068/a44314.

Thornton, Patricia H., *The Institutional Logics Perspective: A New Approach to Culture, Structure and Process.* Oxford: Oxford University Press, 2012.

Thrift, Nigel. "Afterwords." *Environment and Planning D: Society and Space* 18, no. 2 (April 2000): 213–255, https://doi.org/10.1068/d214t.

Tipene, Luke. "Openings of Uncertainty: Critiques of Modernity in the Drawings of Lars Lerup and Gunnar Asplund." *Journal of Architecture* 25, no. 6 (October 2020): 759–786, https://doi.org/10.1080/13602365.2020 .1806337.

Tonkiss, Fran. "Austerity Urbanism and the Makeshift City." *City* 17, no. 3 (June 2013): 312–324, https://doi.org/10.1080/13604813.2013.795332.

Turner, John F. C. *Housing by People: Towards Autonomy in Building Environments.* London: Marion Boyars, 1976.

Turner, John F. C. "Issues in Self-Help and Self-Managed Housing." In *Self-Help Housing: A Critique,* ed. Peter M. Ward, 99–114. London: Mansell, 1982).

Urban Catalyst. *Strategies for Temporary Uses: Potential for Development of Urban Residual Areas in European Metropolises.* Berlin: Studio Urban Catalyst, 2003.

Urban Pioneers. *Temporary Use and Urban Development in Berlin.* Berlin: Jovis, 2007.

Urban Unlimited. *The Shadow City, Freezones in Brussels and Rotterdam.* Rotterdam: Urban Unlimited, 2004.

Vale, Lawrence J., and Thomas J. Campanella, eds. *The Resilient City: How Modern Cities Recover from Disaster.* New York: Oxford University Press, 2005.

Van Der Beuken, Frank, Luuk Boelens, Robert Broesi, Gijsn Broos, Eric Corijn, Filiep Decorte, Stefan De Corte, Frank D'hondt, Bernadette Janssen, Bram Ladage, Wies Sanders, and Jan Van Teeffelen. *The Shadow City, Freezones in Brussels and Rotterdam. Report made with the support from the Netherlands Architecture Fund and the Municipalitye (dS+V) of Rotterdam.* Rotterdam: Urban Unlimited, 2004, 2004.

Vasudevan, Alex. *The Autonomous City: A History of Urban Squatting.* London: Verso, 2017.

Vasudevan, Alex. "The Makeshift City: Towards a Global Geography of Squatting." *Progress in Human Geography* 39, no. 3 (June 2015): 338–359, https://doi.org/10.1177/0309132514531471.

Victor, Hestia. "'There Is Life in This Place': 'DIY Formalisation,' Buoyant Life and Citizenship in Marikana Informal Settlement, Potchefstroom, South Africa." *Anthropology Southern Africa* 42, no. 4 (December 2019): 302–315, https://doi.org/10.1080/23323256.2019.1639522.

Vivant, Elsa. *Le rôle des pratiques culturelles "off" dans les dynamiques urbaines.* Paris: Université Paris 8-Vincennes Saint Denis, 2006.

Ward, C., and E. Swyngedouw. "Neoliberalisation from the Ground Up: Insurgent Capital, Regional Struggle, and the Assetisation of Land." *Antipode* 50, no. 4 (2018): 1077–1097.

Ward, Stephen. *Planning and Urban Change.* London: Sage, 2004.

Warnaby, Gary, and Dominic Medway. "Productive Possibilities? Valorising Urban Space Through Pop-up?" *Qualitative Market Research: An International Journal* 25, no. 5 (2022): 557–569 https://doi.org/10.1108/QMR-12-2021-0145.

Watson, Vanessa. "Seeing from the South: Refocusing Urban Planning on the Globe's Central Urban Issues." *Urban Studies* 46, no. 11 (2009): 2259–2275, https://www.jstor.org/stable/43198476.

Webster, Chris. "How High Can We Go? Urban Density, Infectious Versus Chronic Disease, and the Adaptive Resilience of Cities." *Town Planning Review* 92, no. 1 (2021): 123–130.

Welsh, Marc. "Resilience and Responsibility: Governing Uncertainty in a Complex World." *The Geographical Journal* 180, no. 1 (March 2014): 15–26, https://doi.org/10.1111/geoj.12012.

BIBLIOGRAPHY • 303

Wenham, C., J. Smith, and R. Morgan. "COVID-19: The Gendered Impacts of the Outbreak." *The Lancet* 395 (10227): 846–848.

Wertheim-Heck, Sigrid. "The Impact of the COVID-19 Lockdown on the Diets of Hanoi's Urban Poor." *International Institute for Environment and Development* (blog), April 8, 2020, https://www.iied.org/impact-covid-19-lockdown-diets-hanois-urban-poor.

Wesener, Andreas. "Temporary Urbanism and Urban Sustainability After a Natural Disaster: Transitional Community-Initiated Open Spaces in Christchurch, New Zealand." *Journal of Urbanism: International Research on Placemaking and Urban Sustainability* 8, no. 4 (July 2015): 406–422, https://doi.org/10.1080/17549175.2015.1061040.

Williams, Jo. *Circular Cities. A Revolution in Urban Sustainability.* London: Routledge, 2021.

World Economic Forum. *A Framework for the Future of Real Estate.* Geneva: World Economic Forum, 2021. https://www.weforum.org/publications/a-framework-for-the-future-of-real-estate/.

Yousif, Mukhlid, Heather Hong, Susan Malfeld, Sheilagh Smit, Lillian Makhathini, Tshepo Motsamai, Dipolelo Tselana, et al. "Measles Incidence in South Africa: A Six-Year Review, 2015–2020." *BMC Public Health*, 22, no. 1647 (August 2022): 1647, https://doi.org/10.1186/s12889-022-14069-w.

Ziehl, Michael, Sarah Osswald, Oliver Hasemann, and Daniel Schnier. *Second Hand Spaces: Recycling Sites Undergoing Urban Transformation.* Berlin: JOVIS Verlag, 2012.

Zukin, Sharon. *The Cultures of Cities.* Oxford: Blackwell: 1995.

Zukin, Sharon. *Loft Living: Culture and Capital in Urban Change.* London: Radius, 1988.

INDEX

abjection, 3, 18, 106; explicit processes of, 169; and pandemic, 159; as reactive adaptations, 168–172

activation, 60–71, 87; asset-based, 64–65, 69, 74, 82, 84; defined, 63; physical, 63; social, 64; weak planning as setting for, 71–76

adaptable adjustments, 172–187

adaptable cities: adaptability and radical/tactical knowledge, 206–215; agenda for future scholarship, 230–239; agility with permanence as form of preparedness, 230–232; arguments for, 12–15; breaking boundaries to tackle crises, 235–239; characteristic of, 16; comfort zones, 235–239; future of, 223–239; knowledge shaping/ delivering, 201–206; latency/ creative stasis *vs.* impatience/ predictions, 233–235; paradoxes of adaptability/temporariness, 230–239; permanence, 235–239; postpandemic, 152–199; production of, 53–60; professionalization of adaptable/ temporary urbanism, 215–221; rhythms of, 53–60; skills and delivery of, 200–222; time, 53–60

adaptable urbanism, 50, 229; and place-shaping, 75; professionalization of, 215–221; and Syrian ITSs, 108; and weak planning, 52, 71–72

adaptable urban making, 12, 17, 19, 29, 51, 63, 153, 190, 192, 196, 200, 202, 219

adaptation/adaptability, 6, 60–71, 89–90; arguments for, 12–15; assetization through, 131–142; and cities, 4–5; in contemporary context, 41–50; and "cool" artificial city, 120–151; and COVID-19 pandemic, 4; creative urban making, 23–28; disorder, 31–33; and everyday resilience, 90–100; and evolution of cities, 36–41;

306 • INDEX

adaptation/adaptability (*continued*) extraction through, 131–142; key paradoxes of, 230–239; market-driven approaches to, 196–197; and permanent impermanence, 100–109; post-covid, 187–198; and radical/tactical knowledge, 206–215; reaction, 28–31; and spaces-in-waiting, 110–117; (in)stability, 34–35; and strategies, 77–86; and tactics, 77–86; and temporariness, 90–100; tool for community mobilization, 113; urban, 36–41; value creation through, 131–142

agility, 162–168; with permanence as form of preparedness, 230–232

artificial beautification, 143

asset-based activation, 64, 65, 69, 74, 82, 84

assetization, 133, 134, 150; and housing associations, 141–142; socio-economic impacts of, 133; through temporary uses and adaptability, 131–142

autonomous urbanism, 46

backyard dwellings, 208

Berlin, Germany, 43–45, 64, 71, 73, 75, 122, 127–128, 147–148, 189

Big Shift programme, 190

Bishop, Peter, 2, 7, 37, 46

bottom-up temporary urbanism, 42–46, 58

boundaries, 235–239

bricolage, 48, 66, 236; engineering, 105; power of, 225; processes of, 233

Building the Unfinished (Lerup), 5

caging, 32

calculated informality, 135

Chronos, 54–55, 57

cities. *See also* adaptable cities: and adaptability, 4–5; adaptable, 223–239; cognitive-cultural capitalism in, 197; defined, 1; evolution and adaptability, 36–41; and industrialization, 39–40; role of, 3

Cities in Time: Temporary Urbanism and the Future of the City (Madanipour), 30

city bureaucracy, 162

cognitive-cultural capitalism, 197

comfort zones, 235–239

community enhancement, 123

community-first approach to adaptable adjustments, 172–187

community groups, 227

competitiveness, urban, 123

complexity: uncertainties and, 227–230; urban making and, 227–230

consumerism, 126, 142

Continuing Professional Development (CPD), 221

"cool" artificial city, 120–151

Corbusier, Le, 32

cost-of-living crisis, 10–11

COVID-19 pandemic, 3, 18, 151, 152, 190, 226; and adaptable cities, 4; cost-of-living crisis, 10–11; hybrid temporary transformations, 49; policy, 280–281n16; and postpandemic adaptable city, 152–199; relief packages, 195; and temporary urbanisms, 9

creative brownfields, 122
creative city-economy, 122
creative destruction, 127, 133
creative spaces, 127
creative urban making, 23–28, 32, 35
crisis, 172–187; breaking boundaries
    to tackle, 235–239
cultural institutions, 220

de Certeau, Michel, 54, 77–80, 94
defensive strategies, 77
deindustrialization, 41
Department for Communities and
    Local Government (DCLG), 114
deregulation, 162–168
designing disorder, 5
detrimental responses,
    postpandemic adaptable city,
    162–172
Development Trusts Association, 216
differential spaces, 54, 72, 74
disorder: caging, 32; and cities
    adaptability, 31–33
do-it-yourself (DIY): interventions,
    162; tactics, 147; urbanism, 57–58,
    104–105; urbanists, 210; wiring
    systems, 208
Douglas, Gordon, 8, 54, 57, 110–111,
    147, 162, 210–211

École du Projet Urbain, 26
Emergency Active Travel Fund
    (EATF), 165
encampment as reactive adaptations,
    168–172
England: DIY urban making in, 147;
    Local Government Association

(LGA), 195; Network Rail in,
    141, 216
Espace, 80
ethnic minorities, 199
eurhythmia, 143
Euroméditerranée, 67, 69
Europe, 8, 36, 39, 41, 63, 165, 211,
    214; bottom-up forms of
    temporary urbanisms, 46;
    counterculture movements, 43;
    occupations of empty spaces, 43
European Union Compendium of
    Spatial Planning Systems and
    Policies, 26
evolutionary resilience, 93
exception, 172–187
experience economy, 122
experiential cities, 122, 135
Experimental Traffic Regulation
    Orders (ETROs), 165
extraction: through adaptability,
    131–142; through temporary uses,
    131–142
extraordinary responses, postpandemic
    adaptable city, 162–172

Ferreri, Mara, 8, 50, 122, 126
financial intermediaries, 134
financialization, 131–132, 134, 150
France: transient urbanism, 27;
    urbanism in, 26
freezones, 46
Frigos, 67

global capitalist space, 203
globalization, 43, 132, 135, 228
Greater London area, 217

Greater London Authority (GLA), 122–123, 217
Greater London Council, 42
Green Project in Shepherd Bush, London, 175

Hall, Peter, 36
Harris, Ella, 135, 146
Harvey, David, 54, 56–57, 128, 132, 134–135, 210
Help-Yourself City: DYI Urbanism and Urban Design (Douglas), 8
Henneberry, John, 65
Hope for Communities project (Kibeira, Kenya), 104
humanity, 236–237
hybrid adaptability, 194
hybrid temporary urbanisms, 48–50, 194

Ile de Nantes, 139, 140
inclusive adaptable narrative, 142–150
industrialization, 39–40
informality/informal placemaking, 101; constructive forms of, 110; and do-it-yourself (DIY) solutions, 104–105; and persistent resilience, 102–103
informal tented settlements (ITSs), 106–108, 170, 206–207
infra-ordinary activities/ encounters, 155
interim spaces, 127
international nongovernmental organization (INGOs), 169–170, 200–201, 207, 225, 227

Jacobs, Jane, 27
Jennings Street Open Street, The, 186–187

Kairos, 54–55
knowledge: and delivery of adaptable city, 200–222; radical, 206–215; shaping/delivering adaptable city, 201–206; and skills, 200–222; tactical, 206–215
knowledge fragments, 201–203, 206–213, 222
Kraftl, Peter, 7, 34

La Friche de la Belle de Mai in Marseilles, France, 61–62, 66–67, 69–71, 80, 87, 122, 147, 204, 212, 219, 278n39
Lambeth Council, 47, 113, 129
latency/creative stasis *vs.* impatience/predictions, 233–235
Lavedan, Pierre, 36
Lefebvre, Henri, 54–55, 57, 72, 89, 128, 134, 143, 203
legacy of post-covid adaptability, 187–198
Lehtovuori, Panu, 58, 77–78
Le marché international des professionnels de l'immobilier (MIPIM), 221
Lerup, Lars, 5, 34
Lewisham Council, 117
Lextrait, Fabrice, 212, 213
lieu proper, 79–80
lieux propres, 79, 81, 84–85

INDEX • 309

London, 42, 128; Central Activities Zone (CAZ), 197; Greater London Authority, 122–123, 217; Greater London Council, 42; London ExCeL, 165; London Legacy Development Corporation, 122; Pop Brixton, 47, 130; temporary gardening initiatives, 112; Transport for London (TFL), 189
London borough of Lambeth, 129, 190–191
London City Resilience Strategy, 217
Looking After Our Town Centres report, 114
Loughborough Farm, 112–113

Madanipour, Ali, 7, 30, 48, 100, 102
market-driven approaches to adaptability, 196–197
McFarlane, Colin, 201–202
Meanwhile Space Inc., 216
Meanwhile Use Lease Contract, 115
Meatpacking District in New York City, 125–126, 147
Mendieta, Eduardo, 54
micro DIY temporary transformations, 111
Miraftab, Faranak, 101
Moawad, Paul, 8, 106, 207

neoliberal development, 132
neoliberal experiential city, 121–131
neoliberalism, 142, 222
neoliberal postmodern society, 143
neoliberal temporary urbanisms, 128
neoliberal urban development, 127

Network Rail, 141, 216
New Art Territories (NTA), 67
"new urban 'spirit' of capitalism," 135
New York City (NYC), 49, 100, 162, 166; Meatpacking District in, 125–126; Open Streets Program, 179, 181, 218–219; outdoor dining during COVID-19, 167; Plaza Program, 179
nonadaptable city: extraordinary *vs.* ordinary, 154–156; and pandemic-led emergency responses, 154–156
noncommunicable disease (NCD), 158
nongovernmental organizations (NGOs), 170, 201, 207, 225, 227
North America, 8, 27, 30, 46, 63, 124, 147, 165, 167, 215, 217
Nouveaux territoires de l'art (NTAs, New Territory of Arts), 214, 220
Nowotny, Helga, 229, 231, 235, 238

obsolescence, 134
offensive strategies, 77
Open Streets Program in New York City, 179, 181, 218–219

pandemic-led emergency responses, 154–156
participatory citizenship, 64
path creation, 65–66
Peat, David, 229, 234
Perec, Georges, 155
permanence, 235–239; agility with as form of preparedness, 230–232

Permanence of Temporary Urbanism: Normalising Precarity in Austerity London, The (Ferreri), 8
permanent impermanence: and adaptability, 100–109; land uses, 103; South African cities, 103–104
persistent resilience, 93–95. *See also* resilience; and adaptability, 101; and informality, 102–103
physical activation, 16, 52, 63, 68
Pinard, Juliette, 67
Pineo, Helen, 158
PLACE/Ladywell project, 117
placemaking, 74, 76, 78–79, 87; informal, 101; urban, 8–9, 25
place-shaping, 74–75
Plateau Urbain, 221
pocket parks, 124. *See also* temporary gardens
Pop Brixton, London, 47
pop-up cycling initiatives, 190
pop-up malls, 136
post-covid adaptability, 187–198
postmodern cities, 135
postpandemic adaptable city, 152–199; abjection as reactive adaptations, 168–172; agility and deregulation, 162–168; detrimental responses, 162–172; encampment as reactive adaptations, 168–172; extraordinary responses, 162–172; reactive responses, 162–172; rigidity and health emergencies, 156–161
pre-shock condition, 92
private entrepreneurship, 127

production of space, 16, 53–56, 65, 77, 135, 203
professionalization: of adaptable urbanism, 215–221; of temporary urbanism, 215–221
protoindustrialization, 39
"protracted waiting," 207
public assets, 127, 142, 144

radical knowledge, 206–215
radical Left and *Autonomen* movements, 127
reaction: and adaptability, 28–31; cities' flexibility and inflexibility, 28–31; postpandemic adaptable city, 162–172
rebranding, 121–123, 150; progressive creative, 86; and transient urbanism, 140
re-equilibrium, 91–92
resilience: and adaptability, 90–100; defined, 91; evolutionary, 93; persistent, 93–95; and spaces-in-waiting, 110–117; and temporariness, 90–100
rhythmanalysis approach, 56–58
rhythms, 60–71; of change (novelty), 59; of life, 59
rigidity and health emergencies, 156–161
Rote Fabrik, Zurich, 43–44

SAMOA, 139–140
Sendra, Pablo, 32–33
Sennett, Richard, 32–33
SNCF Immobilier, 219–221

INDEX • 311

social activation, 64
Société d'exploitation industrielle des tabacs et des allumettes (SEITA), 68, 212, 213
Société nationale des chemins de fer français (SNCF), 67, 139, 141, 219–221
socioeconomic inequalities, 225
South African townships, 159–160
space(s): creative, 127; differential, 54, 72, 74; global capitalist, 203; interim, 127; production of, 16, 53–56, 65, 77, 135, 203
spaces-in-waiting: and everyday adaptability, 110–117; and resilience, 110–117
spatial expansion, 63
speculative value extraction, 133
spontaneous interventions, 30
(in)stability, and adaptability, 34–35
Stevens, Quentin, 8
Story of Science and Ideas in the Twentieth Century (Peat), 234
strategies. *See also* tactics: and adaptability, 77–86; defensive, 77; offensive, 77; urban transformations, 188
Système friche théâtre (SFT), 68, 80, 213

tactical knowledge, 206–215
tactical urbanism, 30, 44, 110, 181, 192, 210, 217–219
tactics. *See also* strategies: and adaptability, 77–86; defined, 78; and flexibility, 78

Teatro de Contêiner Mungunzá, Luz district of São Paulo, 96–98, 195
temporariness: and adaptability, 90–100; and everyday resilience, 90–100; key paradoxes of, 230–239
Temporary and Tactical Urbanism: (Re)Assembling Urban Space (Stevens and Dovey), 8
temporary autonomous zones (TAZs), 46
temporary cities: production of, 53–60; rhythms of, 53–60; time, 53–60
Temporary City, The (Bishop and Williams), 2
temporary dividend, 124
temporary gardens, 124. *See also* pocket parks
Temporary Open Restaurants Program, 176, 180
temporary shops (pop-up shops), 45
temporary urbanisms, 27, 52–53, 76, 79, 114, 142–150, 229; agenda for future scholarship, 230–239; arguments for, 12–15; as concept, 6–9; and COVID-19 pandemic, 9; as field of research, 6–9; future of, 223–239; inclusive adaptable narrative, 142–150; paradoxes of adaptability/temporariness, 230–239; and place-shaping, 75; professionalization of, 215–221; and Syrian ITSs, 108; top-down initiatives, 17; types of, 42–50; and weak planning, 52, 71–72

312 • INDEX

temporary uses: assetization through, 131–142; extraction through, 131–142; in neoliberal experiential city, 121–131; value creation through, 131–142
time-limited exclusivity, 136
top-down temporary urbanism, 46–48
transience, 7, 220; and management of land assets, 220; as mode of urban (re)development, 220
transient urbanism, 27, 139–140, 219, 221
Transport for London (TFL), 189

uncertainties: and complexity, 227–230; and urban making, 227–230
unfinishedness, 5
United Kingdom: land-use planning, 26–27; town and county planning, 26
United States: land-use planning, 26–27; micro DIY temporary transformations in, 111; pocket parks in, 124; postpandemic office districts in, 197; tactical urbanism in, 44
UN Sustainable Development Goals (SDGs), 3
urban adaptability, 36–41
urban competitiveness, 123
urban design, 1, 8, 25–26, 31, 39; DIY, 110, 124; human-scale, 217; knowledge, 216
urban dysfunctions, 31, 33, 110, 148, 210
urban fragments, 11
urbanism: adaptable (*See* adaptable urbanism); autonomous, 46; bottom-up temporary, 42–46,

58; do-it-yourself (DIY), 57–58, 104–105; in France, 26; hybrid temporary, 48–50, 194; tactical, 30, 44, 110, 181, 192, 210, 217–219; temporary (*See* temporary urbanisms); transient, 27, 139–140, 219, 231
urbanisme, 26
urban making, 2–3, 5–6, 10, 12, 50, 228; adaptable, 17, 19, 29; agile processes of, 21; and complexity, 227–230; creative, 23–28, 32, 35; and uncertainties, 227–230
urban planning, 1–2, 6, 23–26; instrumental tools of, 77; prepandemic models of, 164
urban transformations, 17, 22–23, 31, 34, 40, 47; innovative model of, 212; strategies, 188

value creation, 56; through adaptability, 131–142; through temporary uses, 131–142
Vanderbilt Avenue Open Street, Prospect Heights, Brooklyn, New York, 181–184, 186
Venice Architectural Biennale, 30–31

water, sanitation, and hygiene (WASH) conditions, 18, 152–153
weak planning, 52–53, 86–87; characterization, 73; as setting for activation, 71–76
Williams, Lesley, 2, 7, 37, 46
World Health Organization (WHO), 169
World War I, 112

www.ingramcontent.com/pod-product-compliance
Ingram Content Group UK Ltd.
Pitfield, Milton Keynes, MK11 3LW, UK
UKHW041949130225
455076UK00004B/90